Normativity and Control

Do we control what we believe? Are we responsible for what we believe? These two questions are connected: the kind of responsibility we have for our beliefs depends on the form of control that we have over them. For a number of years David Owens has investigated what form of control we must have over something in order to be held to the norms governing that thing, and has argued that belief, intention and action each require a different type of control. The forms of freedom appropriate to each of them vary, and so do the presuppositions of responsibility associated with each of them. Issues in the moral psychology of belief cast light on some of the traditional problems of epistemology and in particular on the problems of scepticism and testimony.

In this series of ten essays Owens explores various different forms of control we might have over belief and the different forms of responsibility they generate. He brings into the picture notable recent work in epistemology: on assurance theories of testimony, on 'pragmatic encroachment', on the aim of belief and on the value of knowledge. He also considers topics in related fields such as the philosophy of mind (e.g. the problem of self-knowledge and theories of the first person) and the philosophy of action (e.g. the guise of the good and the role of the will in free agency). Finally, Owens suggests a non-standard reading of the sceptical tradition in early modern philosophy as we find it in Descartes and Hume.

David Owens is Professor of Philosophy at King's College London. He is the author of *Shaping the Normative Landscape* (Oxford 2012), *Reason Without Freedom* (Routledge 2000), and *Causes and Coincidences* (Cambridge 1992).

Normativity and Control

David Owens

OXFORD
UNIVERSITY PRESS

OXFORD
UNIVERSITY PRESS

Great Clarendon Street, Oxford, OX2 6DP,
United Kingdom

Oxford University Press is a department of the University of Oxford.
It furthers the University's objective of excellence in research, scholarship,
and education by publishing worldwide. Oxford is a registered trade mark of
Oxford University Press in the UK and in certain other countries

© David Owens 2017

The moral rights of the author have been asserted

First Edition published in 2017
First published in paperback 2019

All rights reserved. No part of this publication may be reproduced, stored in
a retrieval system, or transmitted, in any form or by any means, without the
prior permission in writing of Oxford University Press, or as expressly permitted
by law, by licence or under terms agreed with the appropriate reprographics
rights organization. Enquiries concerning reproduction outside the scope of the
above should be sent to the Rights Department, Oxford University Press, at the
address above

You must not circulate this work in any other form
and you must impose this same condition on any acquirer

Published in the United States of America by Oxford University Press
198 Madison Avenue, New York, NY 10016, United States of America

British Library Cataloguing in Publication Data
Data available

Library of Congress Cataloging in Publication Data
Data available

ISBN 978-0-19-871323-4 (Hbk.)
ISBN 978-0-19-885169-1 (Pbk.)

Links to third party websites are provided by Oxford in good faith and
for information only. Oxford disclaims any responsibility for the materials
contained in any third party website referenced in this work.

For Sam

Preface

This book collects ten essays on matters I first discussed in *Reason without Freedom* (2000). Eight of the essays are previously published and appear with only minor alterations, one is published here for the first time ('Human Testimony'), and one is a heavily revised version of a previously published essay ('Value and Epistemic Normativity'). The essays are arranged thematically rather than chronologically. In order to ensure that each essay remains self-standing, I have not attempted to eliminate areas of overlap between them. There is also a substantial introduction, the purpose of which is to restate the general view of normativity, control, and responsibility sketched in *Reason without Freedom*, as developed or modified in the essays collected here.

'Epistemic Akrasia' first appeared in *The Monist* Vol. 85 No. 3 (July 2002): 381–97; 'Does Belief Have an Aim?' in *Philosophical Studies* Vol. 115 No. 3 (August 2003): 275–97; 'Deliberation and the First Person' in *Self Knowledge* Ed. A. Hatzimoysis (Oxford: Oxford University Press 2011): 261–77; 'Value and Epistemic Normativity' in *Teorema* Vol. 32 No. 3 (2013): 335–58; 'Scepticisms: Descartes and Hume' in *Proceedings of the Aristotelian Society Supplementary Volume* LXXIV (July 2000): 119–42; 'Descartes's Use of Doubt' in *A Companion to Descartes*, Eds J. Broughton and J. Carriero (Oxford: Blackwell 2007): 164–78; 'Freedom and Practical Judgement' in *Mental Action*, Eds Lucy O'Brien and Matthew Soteriou (Oxford: Oxford University Press 2009): 122–37; 'Habitual Agency' in *Philosophical Explorations*, Volume 20 (2017), special issue on *The Normative Significance of Intentions*, Eds Ulrike Heuer and Matthew Smith; and 'Testimony and Assertion' in *Philosophical Studies* Vol. 130 No. 1 (July 2006): 105–29.

While writing these essays I was sustained by the love and friendship of Sam Ishii-Gonzales.

Contents

Introduction	1

Part I. Normativity: Epistemic and Practical

1. Epistemic *Akrasia*	37
2. Does Belief Have an Aim?	51
3. Deliberation and the First Person	69
4. Value and Epistemic Normativity	87

Part II. Scepticism

5. Scepticisms: Descartes and Hume	113
6. Descartes' Use of Doubt	132

Part III. Practical Freedom

7. Freedom and Practical Judgement	151
8. Habitual Agency	169

Part IV. Testimony

9. Testimony and Assertion	193
10. Human Testimony	211

Bibliography	239
Index	245

Introduction

I.1 Problems of Epistemic Normativity

Sometimes we are guided by rules and norms. Guidance involves two further ideas. Firstly, phenomena that are guided by norms are intelligible in a special way. The planets conform to the laws of gravitation, but they do not obey them, nor could they. We can obey the laws of the road or the rules of statistical inference and this gives our behaviour a special form of *intelligibility*. In being sensitive to these and other norms, our mental and bodily movements are meaningful as those of the planets are not. Secondly, when we fail to obey these rules we are vulnerable to a special form of assessment that I'll call *criticism*. Such criticism is not mere evaluation. A fruit can be ranked, graded, or classified by reference to some standard, but no one expects the fruit to be guided by this standard of evaluation. The fruit's failure is not meaningful and the fruit is not subject to criticism for falling short.

Here we have a package of notions—guidance, intelligibility, and criticism—all bound up with normativity. Some writers wonder whether we can really make sense of the idea that human thought and behaviour is in this way guided by norms (e.g. Boghossian 2014). Often, but not always, this worry rests on a restrictive metaphysics, a conception of what kind of thing reality contains, a conception that threatens to exclude normativity altogether. Call this worry, however motivated, the *general* problem of normativity. *Special* problems of normativity are different: they rest on doubts about whether our package of notions should be applied as widely as they usually are and in particular whether they should be applied to all those aspects of our lives that we routinely characterize as (more or less) rational.

Special problems of normativity arise when we take certain phenomena (specifically action or intention) as paradigm cases of norm-governed phenomena, cases in which notions of guidance, intelligibility, and criticism have clear and unproblematic application. Normativity is then understood by reference to forms of guidance, intelligibility, and criticism that figure in the paradigm case and the question becomes whether their features are shared by other states assessed as rational or irrational, by belief, desire, emotion, and so forth. We guide or control our actions in distinctive ways and, as a result, the above-mentioned forms of explanation and criticism seem appropriate, but action-like guidance or control doesn't obviously extend to belief, desire, and emotion. That has led some to doubt whether the latter are both intelligible and subject to criticism as they appear.[1]

I shall be assuming that there are norms characteristic of belief, that there is such a thing as epistemic normativity, but I shall not be putting forward any positive conception of exactly how belief is guided by reason.[2] A positive conception of how epistemic norms guide our mental lives is not required in order to establish a contrast between belief and agency. Nor is it needed for us to appreciate the twofold significance of that contrast, first as the source of the specifically epistemological problematic to be outlined in the rest of this section and second as explaining differences in how we relate to belief and to action, e.g. in the forms of accountability we think appropriate to each of them (Section I.5).

I proceed by formulating a conception of practical freedom (in Section I.2), one clear enough for us to be able to see that it has no application to belief (as Sections I.3 and I.4 will show). That will get our problematic going. We distinguish three special problems of epistemic normativity: the problem of *control*, the problem of *scepticism*, and the problem of *testimony*. These issues are connected in that the problems of scepticism and testimony depend upon the problem of control. In Section I.6, I introduce a fourth, namely the *problem of authority*, and suggest a way of thinking about normativity which both solves the problem of authority and addresses the problem of control. It does the latter by making room for the idea that different forms of normativity (e.g. epistemic and practical) involve different forms of control.

Now let's introduce the problem of control. Suppose I am confronted by alternative courses of action. Here, a rational agent has a capacity for *reflective control*, a capacity with two aspects:

---

[1] For example, see the medieval discussion about whether faith could be a virtue given that we don't seem able to choose what to believe (Aquinas 2010 Part II–II, Questions 1–5). Aquinas entertained no doubts about normativity as such.

[2] (Korsgaard 2009), (Boyle 2011), (Moran 2012), (Burge 2013: 389–92), and (Soteriou 2013: Chapter 11) in various ways look to the idea that thinking, judging, and believing and so forth are activities, are things we do, in order to elucidate the relevant notion of rational guidance. For this move to be helpful, our grasp of the notion of activity must be firmer than, or at least somewhat independent of, our understanding of the notion of rational guidance. For an opposing view see (Strawson 2003).

First a subject can make a judgement about what they ought to do; second their judgement about what they ought to do can directly determine what they actually do (or at least intend to do) i.e. they can act (or plan) on that judgement.[3]

This conception of reflective control and specifically (I shall argue) its second aspect underlies each of the above problems.[4]

Two ideas are crucial to the above formulation. First, it employs the notion of a capacity, of there being things one *can* do whether or not one actually does them. Trees, spiders, and humans all do some things whilst failing to do others and we routinely distinguish the things they failed to do but could have done from other things they couldn't have done at all. Some writers have attempted to explain this distinction in terms of the truth (or falsehood) of various conditionals, statements about what the tree or the spider would do in certain specified circumstances. I simply appeal to commonsensical thoughts such as 'Jane can now lift a 100 pound weight but not a ton' which may or may not equate to claims about what Jane would do under certain specified conditions. The metaphysical questions raised by capacities are very general (even more so than the general problem of normativity) and I leave them on one side.

The second notion implicit in my conception of reflective control is that of direct determination. To fix ideas I'll contrast it with other forms of determination. You may have great influence over what I do in that your judgements about what I ought to do usually determine what I actually do but this cannot happen without my endorsement or acquiescence. My own judgements can directly determine what I do in a sense that your judgements never could. That doesn't mean that I'll always do or even try to do what I judge that I ought to do but it does mean that I *can* act on my own judgement. Now consider our emotional lives. I feel angry, afraid, joyful, etc. I can make judgements about whether I ought to feel angry, joyful, afraid, and so forth but it is quite unclear that these judgements can (in the above sense) directly determine what I feel, whether I am angry, etc. Of course I can act on these judgements in that, if I judge that I ought not to be angry, I might distract myself or even visit the therapist. But those are the very things I might do were I looking to make someone else's emotions

---

[3] For the terminology of reflective control see (Owens 2000: Chapter 1). In Chapter 7 I use 'choice' to refer to an exercise of reflective control, but in Chapter 8 I employ a broader notion of choice, one not tied to normative judgement in that way.

[4] In Chapter 8: Section 8.4 I argue that practical control often involves judgements about the value of the habits manifested in an act rather than about the value of any individual action. Here I ignore this complication.

conform to my views about how they ought to feel. It is quite unclear that my judgements about how I ought to feel can determine what I actually do feel in any more direct fashion. (I'll say more about this in Section I.2.)

Are beliefs like actions or like emotions? On this question writers divide. They agree that we can make judgements about what we ourselves ought and ought not to believe and they agree that these judgements sometimes influence what we actually believe, but it remains a question whether this influence involves the sort of direct determination to be found in the case of action. Some, myself included, see a similarity between becoming convinced that John stole my bike and becoming angry that John stole my bike.[5] Our beliefs and our anger may be more or less reasonable, but simply being a rational subject does not give us the sort of control over our beliefs or over our anger that we have over what we do. If we are inclined to do the wrong thing, we can set ourselves right simply by reminding ourselves of what we ought to do, whilst it is much less clear that we can set our beliefs and feelings right so immediately.

More will be said both in elucidation and in support of the above claims, but we should now have enough of a handle on the problem of control to see a connection with the other problems mentioned earlier. That of scepticism takes many forms. Some scepticisms apply to both theoretical and practical reason, but a central strand of sceptical argumentation is directed specifically at the norms of belief formation, and that strand is my present concern. According to the Cartesian sceptic, we can reasonably form a belief only where we have conclusive evidence for the truth of that belief, i.e. evidence which guarantees its truth. In Descartes' view, the mere likelihood or probability that a certain course of action is best suffices to make it the reasonable choice, but reasonable belief requires certainty. Since almost all of our beliefs are in fact based on inconclusive evidence, this requirement would undermine most of our convictions.

What is the connection between this demand for certainty and the problem of control? It might seem as if the Cartesian sceptic doesn't query our ability to be guided by authoritative epistemic norms but merely insists that the relevant norms require certainty. So interpreted scepticism needs motivating: at least on a superficial view, it looks as if we feel fully entitled to form beliefs on the basis of inconclusive evidence, and fallibilist epistemic norms would endorse many or most of our actual beliefs. On the reading defended in this book, sceptical argumentation is meant to show that our beliefs could not be subject to fallibilist norms because judgements about inconclusive evidence cannot directly determine belief. The norms for belief formation are infallibilist because we cannot control our

---

[5] In Chapter 4 I argue that the point of belief is to enable emotions like anger.

beliefs by reference to fallibilist norms. By contrast, no such worry applies to the norms governing what we ought to do: as Descartes insists, there are valid norms telling us how to behave under uncertainty, and we can guide our action by reference to these norms. The sceptical argumentation that threatens to undermine theoretical reason has no application to practical reason. Scepticism occupies Chapter 4 of *Reason without Freedom* and is taken up again in Chapters 5 and 6 of this volume.

Then there is the problem of testimony. We frequently acquire beliefs by taking someone's word for it, by believing what they tell us. Indeed, it seems likely that the vast majority of our beliefs about the world beyond our immediate environment are acquired in this way and the sheer extent of our trust in other people outruns any non-testimonial evidence we might have for their truthfulness or reliability. When we take someone's word for it, we seem to be deferring to their judgement about whether this is a reasonable thing to believe, a judgement they make in the light of reasons available to them but often not to us. How can it be reasonable for me to believe that p if I have no way of assessing how reasonable it is to believe that p?

I first considered the problem of testimony in Part 3 of *Reason without Freedom*; Chapters 9 and 10 elaborate that treatment. I argue that taking someone else's word for it involves *inheriting* their belief on the matter, together with whatever justification they have for it. On this model, I inherit a justified belief even though I am myself quite unaware of how it is to be justified. Now, according to the conception of guidance as reflective control, my beliefs are under proper normative discipline only if I am in a position both to form a view about whether the assertion is supported by sufficient reason and to govern my own belief by reference to that view. The inheritance model of testimony excludes the exercise of that sort of control, for the inheritance of belief is not under my control in this way. Once again, this is a point of contrast between belief and action, for I can always settle whether I follow another's practical advice by making a judgement about whether I ought to.

We've now introduced the various special problems of epistemic normativity. For more detailed discussion of the problems of scepticism and testimony, readers must refer to the chapters that follow. In this Introduction I shall elaborate the problem of control. In Section I.2 I'll put forward a positive conception of reflective control, of the kind of control that rational agents have over their own actions (and their intentions). In Sections I.3 and I.4 I'll argue that we lack this sort of control over our own beliefs and emotions and that the possession of such control is no part of our ideal of a rational believer, etc. In Section I.5, I'll draw out the implications of this asymmetry of control for accountability, and in Section I.6 I'll contend that we've done enough to resolve the special problems of epistemic normativity.

I.2 Practical Freedom and Reflective Control

This section argues that some parts of the rational mind are free in a way that others are not, though all are subject to rational criticism. Here I establish the contrast between action and feeling, arguing that we can control both what we do and also what we intend (or plan) to do in a way that we can't control what we feel. I'll bring out the asymmetry by focusing on failures of self-control.

I.2.1 Reflection and Self-Control

There is a medical procedure that I've decided that I ought to undergo but I've yet to actually arrange because I fear the procedure even though, as I know, there are few grounds for thinking that it will be either risky or painful. Eventually, I judge that I ought to delay no longer but I continue to prevaricate. This is an instance of what philosophers call *akrasia*, a case in which we fail to do what we judge that we ought to do. It is also an example of one's experiencing a fear which one knows to be irrational. I judge both the omission and the fear to be irrational and though this combination of attitudes is awkward, it is not in any way paradoxical. The mere fact that I take a dim view of both my omission and my fear throws no doubt on the psychological reality of either the omission, the fear, or my negative assessment of them. Furthermore, it throws no doubt on the idea that these acts and attitudes are all *mine*, are to be ascribed or imputed to me.[6] I can become aware of them in the standard first-personal fashion (i.e. without observing my own behaviour and without consulting either psychologists or brain scanners) and I accept criticism for my present failure both to act and to feel as I ought, just as I would in a case where I had first endorsed the actions and feelings in question and later came to think worse of them.

These similarities notwithstanding, there is surely an important difference between the omission and the fear. I am expected to have rational fears and will be criticized for feeling otherwise, but I am not expected to be able to control my fears *simply* by making judgements about whether they are reasonable. Here, my fear is unreasonable, and this makes me vulnerable to criticism for the way

---

[6] Moran appears to deny this (e.g. Moran 2001: 127–8). Elsewhere I argue that Moran does not get the relevant phenomena into focus because he elides some crucial distinctions (Owens 2003); see also (Finkelstein 2003: 158–68). Clear-eyed *akrasia* is a familiar and non-pathological phenomenon, and I shall ask whether there is anything like it in the case of belief. See also Chapter 1, Section 1.3.

that I feel, but the fact that I am aware of the problem, that I explicitly judge my fears to be irrational, does not add any *extra* grounds for criticism, for my ability to make such higher-order normative judgements does not (in itself) give me any further leverage over my fears. When the fear persists and no therapeutic strategies are available, I may conclude that I have done all I can. That observation does not deflect criticism of my fear, but it does excuse my resignation, my inactivity in the face of it.

By contrast, I am not criticized solely for the irrationality of my failure to arrange the medical procedure. The fact that I am fully aware of my practical irrationality and yet continue to prevaricate provides *further* grounds for criticism: here I am guilty of a failure of self-control. And that further criticism is apt even when there is nothing more I could do to overcome my fear of the arrangement other than reminding myself that I ought to make it. Resignation has no place here, for I am expected to be able to control what I do simply by making judgements about what I ought to do.[7] An agent has the capacity to determine what they do by making a practical judgement, a judgement about what they ought to do. This is a capacity they have simply in virtue of being a rational agent, i.e. an agent whose actions can be assessed as more or less rational and who can understand and appreciate those assessments as assessment of their own doings. Given the relevant physical capacities, an action of my own is an event of a kind whose occurrence I can control simply by assessing its rationality.[8]

The intended asymmetry between action and feeling will not be grasped unless three important qualifications are noted. First, perhaps someone *might* have the capacity to determine what they feel simply by making judgements about what they ought to feel and without doing anything further to influence their own emotions. I shall not argue that such a thing is impossible. What I deny is that this is a capacity they have simply in virtue of the fact that they are rational subjects of emotion, for there are people who aptly appraise their own emotions as rational or irrational but who lack this capacity. Feelings are not amenable to reflective control simply in virtue of being felt by someone with the requisite conceptual sophistication. Reflective control of feeling is a further capacity, one that a rational being with an emotional life might not (and, in my view, generally does not) possess. By contrast, possession of a capacity for reflective control of one's

---

[7] At least where future action is in question, this exercise of practical control might go via the formation of an intention, but the ability to form such intentions simply by judging that one ought to is itself part of what it is to be a rational agent.
[8] We may assume that I have the physical capacity both to get to the hospital and to stay away from it.

own actions is part and parcel of being a rational agent, an agent whose actions are subject to reason.

We can now provide the promised further elucidation of the notion of 'direct determination' introduced in Section I.1. The capacity to directly determine what I do is not just a capacity that I exercise without doing anything apart from making judgements about what I ought to do: it is a capacity to determine what I myself do that I possess simply in virtue of being a rational agent, simply in virtue of having the capacity to make such practical judgements. Even if I had the capacity to determine what *you* do simply by making judgements about what you ought to do, that would not give me reflective control over what you do (in the relevant sense) because this is not a capacity I possess simply in virtue of being a rational agent.

Now to the second qualification. I've said that if an agent fails to do what they judge they ought to do, then they are vulnerable to a specific form of criticism over and above the criticism that they did the wrong thing, namely that they failed to exercise the special capacity for practical self-control just described, a failure known as *akrasia*, but I don't think that an agent should always be subject to criticism simply for being *akratic*. That depends on the quality of the agent's judgement and on why they act against their judgement.

Suppose the agent makes a poor judgement about what they ought to do and then fails to act on that judgement: a Jehovah's Witness judges that they ought not to have a blood transfusion, but their desire to live overcomes them and they akratically agree to the treatment. Here the reasons on which they act (the desire to live, etc.) are much sounder, as we may suppose, than any supporting their practical judgement. The Jehovah's Witness does indeed suffer from a failure of self-control, from a failure to conform their action to their judgement about what they ought to do. Nevertheless, they did the right thing, and what's more, they were moved to do it by their awareness of a good and sufficient reason for doing it (whether or not they thought of it as such). Here we might criticize their judgement, we might even call it irrational, but we would not say that what they *did* was irrational just because it failed to conform to their irrational judgement.[9]

Distinguish two claims: (i) that all agents have, simply in virtue of their rationality, a capacity to make their actions conform to their practical judgement; and (ii) that every failure to exercise this capacity constitutes a failure of rationality or gives grounds for rational criticism.[10] (ii) does not follow from (i) and nor

---

[9] The case is different if the agent ends up doing the right thing by accident and not because of their awareness of what is in fact a good and sufficient reason for doing it.

[10] My discussion of these issues in Chapter 7 of *Reason without Freedom* was hampered by a failure to make this distinction.

do I endorse it. True, when the agent fails to act on a sound practical judgement, they are to be criticized not only for failing to do what they ought to do but also for failing to exercise this agential capacity for self-control. Still, this capacity should be exercised only to implement sound practical judgements, and the mere fact that I judge that I ought to do something gives me no reason to do it.[11]

Now to our final qualification. I characterized *akrasia* as a failure to do as you judge that you ought to do. It may now be objected that essentially the same failure of self-control is present when the temptation to do the wrong thing intervenes at an earlier stage, causing you to make a faulty judgement about what you ought to do (or even to ignore the matter altogether by declining to attend to what you ought to do). Suppose fear of pain causes me to judge that I ought not to have the procedure. Doesn't that show a lack of self-control quite on a level with making the judgement but not acting upon it ((Watson 2004a: 43–4), (McIntyre 2006: 286–8))?

The objector is quite right that *akrasia* need not involve a failure to do what you judge you ought to do, for one can fail to exercise one's capacity for reflective control at an earlier stage and in a way that exhibits essentially the same flaw. The making of a practical judgement *is itself under the control of practical judgement* (Chapter 7: Section 7.4). When I'm tempted either to ignore some of the evidence or else overlook the matter altogether, I can get myself to make a judgement about what I ought to do on the basis of all the evidence before me precisely by judging that I ought to make such a judgement. But—a point crucial for my argument about belief—such a judgement must be distinguished from a *belief* or *conviction* about what I ought to do, for (as we shall see) the agent's beliefs or convictions are not under the control of their judgements.

I've now stated the intellectualist conception of practical freedom on which the contrast between action and emotion (or belief) turns. That conception employs the notion of reflective control, i.e. the idea that, simply in virtue of being rational agents, we can control our own actions by making judgements about what we ought to do. In the remainder of this section, I'll first distinguish my intellectualist conception of practical freedom from another more voluntaristic conception and then respond to some potential objections.

---

[11] See the worries about 'bootstrapping' in (Kolodny 2005: 512). Because the judgement that I ought to A is not itself a reason to A, one might deny that the movement from the judgement to the decision and/or action is a form of *reasoning*, but the capacity to make that move may still be a rational capacity, i.e. a capacity an agent has simply in virtue of being rational (Raz 2011: 88).

I.2.2 Reflective Control and the Will

In formulating this asymmetry of control between action and emotion, I have said nothing about the grounds on which judgements about what one ought to do or what one ought to feel are made; I have said nothing about the difference between reasons to act and reasons to feel. Many think that these reasons differ in the following respect: one settles whether one ought to arrange a medical procedure by asking whether arranging the medical procedure would be desirable, but one can't settle whether one ought to fear the procedure simply by asking whether fearing it would be desirable, for the rationality of the fear depends on the undesirability (and probability) of the fear's object, namely the procedure.

Furthermore, many suppose that this asymmetry of rationality is linked to a further asymmetry of control between action and emotion. An agent of normal capacities can show up for the medical procedure 'at will', can show up simply because they form the intention to show up, but it is fairly obvious that they cannot determine in a similar fashion whether to fear the medical procedure: merely intending not to fear the procedure will not calm the normal agent. Action but not fear is *subject to the will* (Owens 2000: Chapter 5). We might offer to explain this new asymmetry of control as follows: *action is subject to the will because the rationality of the action is a function of the (apparent) desirability of performing it, i.e. of ensuring that it occurs.* That is why you can raise your arm simply because you are paid to do so. By contrast, the rationality of fear is not a function of the (apparent) desirability of the fear's being felt, for even though it may be highly desirable for us to fear something, that fear may still be quite irrational. This is why we cannot fear simply because we are well paid to do so; why we cannot fear 'at will'.

Let's suppose that the above asymmetry of rationality does indeed generate the above asymmetry of control by settling which phenomena are subject to our will. Still, it does nothing to explain the asymmetry of control that interests me. When characterizing reflective control, I made no mention of the will.[12] This is because, in my view, intentions are subject to our power of reflective control without being subject to our will in the above sense. Since intention formation is a paradigm case of the exercise of practical freedom, the extent of our practical freedom cannot turn on what is subject to the will. Let me explain.

---

[12] In this respect my conception of reflective control differs both from Moran's conception of choice (Moran 2012: Section 5) and from Hieronymi's conception of voluntariness (Hieronymi 2008).

I need to decide now in order to plan my day around the visit to the hospital, and so the question before me is not simply whether to have the procedure tomorrow (say) but rather whether I ought to decide now to have the procedure tomorrow. Here I'm considering whether to form a future-directed intention to visit the hospital tomorrow and I'm able to control the formation of such intentions much as I can control the performance of subsequent actions. A rational agent can determine what they intend to do tomorrow simply by making judgements about what they should intend to do. Like actions and unlike feelings, intentions are under reflective control, but in another respect, intentions are like feelings and unlike actions. I cannot settle whether I should intend to go tomorrow simply by asking myself whether it is desirable that I intend to go and regardless of whether it is desirable that I actually go. Like feelings, the rationality of intention depends at least in part on the desirability of something other than the intention itself, namely that of the action intended. The mere fact that intending to go would be highly desirable (e.g. to win a prize for so intending) does not establish that it would be reasonable for me to intend to go and so I cannot intend 'at will'. On that point, intentions are out of the same box as emotions like anger. Thus, we can't explain the asymmetry of control between my actions and my intentions on the one hand and my feelings on the other by reference to how their rationality is determined.[13]

I.2.3 Objections

I've argued that we can reflectively control both what we do and what we intend to do in a way we can't control what we feel. Reflective control over agency is a feature that distinguishes rational agents like ourselves from higher animals who deliberate, who are moved by the pros and cons but who lack reflective control. Many higher animals surely act in the light of the costs and benefits of various courses of action, but they can do so whilst being quite unable to think of these considerations as reasons for action or of an action as one they *ought* to perform (or of an intention as one they *ought* to form).[14] Reflective control as I have characterized it involves the deployment of normative concepts and their application to broadly psychological phenomena like intention and action. So

---

[13] See (Owens 2000: Chapter 5). It might be argued that intention can be factored into two elements: first an act of intention formation which is indeed subject to the will, and second the intention formed which is no more under our control than our feelings. But I doubt that we can decide to decide simply in response to (say) a prize for so deciding unless there is a sensible decision to be taken. See (Pink 1996: 200–6).

[14] (Korsgaard 2009: 30–2) and (Burge 2013: 398). It may be that higher animals can see food *as* tasty or a shelter *as* warm and so have primitive evaluative concepts, but it does not follow that they make judgements about what they ought to do.

long as the agent's focus is on the painless, riskless, and life-saving qualities of a medical procedure, they need be employing none of this cognitive apparatus: practical deliberation need involve no practical judgement.

These remarks may raise the worry that my characterization of self-control is over-intellectual and that we have been looking for our capacity to control our emotions (and actions) in the wrong place. In the above example, I tried to exert control over my fear by assessing its rationality, i.e. by deploying a psychological concept 'fear' and a normative concept 'irrational'. Isn't that just too fancy? Suppose I instead refocus my attention on the fact that the medical procedure involves no risk or pain, i.e. on the facts in virtue of which it is irrational for me to fear it. Call this (first order) *deliberation* (Chapter 3: Section 3.1). Isn't deliberation a way of controlling this emotion and a way for me to control my own emotions in particular?[15] Of course, there can be no guarantee that I'll succeed in quieting even my own fear by such deliberation, but equally, there is no guarantee that I'll have the procedure simply because I judge that I ought to have it.

Deliberative control is indeed frequently available in the case of both action and feeling. I can often refocus my attention on the features of the medical procedure that tell for or against it and such deliberation may well have the effect of dampening my fear. Nevertheless the contrast between action and feeling remains. With action, I have the *further* capacity to control what I do by acting on my judgement of what I ought to do, a capacity that may be present even where I don't have the opportunity to deliberate, i.e. to focus my attention on the underlying considerations. Suppose the issue is complex and I took a view about what ought to be done about it some time ago. I have probably forgotten at least some or even most of the considerations bearing on my medical procedure. Still, I'm confident I ought to go ahead and I can act on that judgement without performing any further act of reviewing the relevant considerations. Alternatively, suppose I haven't forgotten, but the matter is urgent and there is no time for review. Again I can act on my ought-judgement without revisiting the underlying considerations, and this may be expected of me. No similar expectation applies to my fears.

Some writers doubt that the capacity for reflective control can play an independent role in the psychology of a rational agent. For example, Scanlon tells us that 'from the point of view of the deliberating agent' the requirement to do what you judge that you ought to do is 'self-effacing'. Where someone feels reluctant to do what they judge that they ought to do, Scanlon doubts that they can master

---

[15] Should my father share my irrational fears, I can't expect to reassure *him* just by focusing my own attention on the benign character of the procedure.

themselves by reflecting that they would otherwise be irrational; rather, they must revert to the details of the case for doing the thing in question.[16] And such judgemental self-effacement may seem called for by the fact (noted earlier) that your judging that you ought to do something gives you no reason to do it.

I agree that the mere fact that you judge that you ought to do A gives you no reason to do A over and above whatever reasons count in favour of A-ing, but practical judgement may still be a source of motivation available to someone *qua* rational agent, one that can be tapped without focusing one's attention on the facts which count in favour of A-ing. People do sometimes get themselves to do what they judge that they ought to do by reminding themselves that doing otherwise would demonstrate a lack of self-control. Yet Scanlon is surely right that such thoughts will often seem rather too abstract or pallid and you are better off focusing on the specific character of the threat to your continence.

Consider the phenomenon of executive virtue.[17] Modifying our example once more, suppose the medical procedure I fear will, though risk-free, be rather painful. Here it is perfectly reasonable for me to fear the pain and so to feel inclined to avoid the procedure. It takes a certain amount of courage to go through with it. I might be able to overcome the fear (i.e. arrange for the procedure in the teeth of my fear) simply by focusing my attention on the benefits of the procedure. But should this fail, I have another resource. Having made the judgement that I ought to have the procedure, I can invoke the idea of courage and thereby tap into a further source of rational motivation. I can get myself to have the procedure by thinking, 'Let cowardice not get the better of me'.

Note what is going on here. I regard my fear as perfectly reasonable and am seeking to 'control my fear' only in the sense that I aim to ensure that it does not prevent me from having the procedure. I exercise this form of self-control by balancing the considerations highlighted by my fear (the pain) against those that count in favour of the procedure and then judging that I ought to have the procedure.[18] Having made that normative judgement, I might prod myself into action by castigating my hesitation as 'unreasonable'. Should this fail, I can instead reach for a more specific thought, one invoking an ideal of continence

---

[16] (Scanlon 2003: 20) and (Kolodny 2005: 547).

[17] (Watson 2004a: 39–41) and (Kolodny 2005: 546–7 and 553–4).

[18] The exercise of executive virtue involves making a judgement about the eligibility of the act in question and this is (like intention formation) something one can do simply in virtue of being a rational agent. Thus, as a tool of self-management, it is fundamentally different from those devices of self-manipulation which people employ, e.g. to get themselves to give up smoking. The availability of nicotine pills, societies of non-smokers, occasions for public humiliation, and so forth is not guaranteed simply by the fact that the smoker is a rational agent. Hence, it is misleading to treat the exercise of reflective control as just another form of self-manipulation (Hieronymi 2014).

specifically concerned with how we respond to fear.[19] This is also an exercise of the capacity for reflective control.

What I've said of courage and fear applies to the whole range of executive virtue. Each such virtue is, like courage, there to counteract some specific threat to continence. I can resist the temptation to grab a third slice of cake by deploying the ideal of temperance and recalling the shame of gluttony. Bringing to mind the hothead or the sleaze ensures that I don't lash out in anger or turn around in the street and stare at an attractive stranger. All this can work without making me feel any the less angry or lustful. Executive virtue shores up our capacity for self-control through the application of concrete ideals of courage, temperance, etc., ideals directed at specific passions and temptations rather than by invoking a generic notion of rational agency.

Three points of clarification. First, courage, as I understand it, facilitates *rational* agency: it is simply foolhardy to get yourself to run stupid risks by telling yourself not to be a coward. Second, courageous behaviour is often spontaneous and involves no practical judgement. Still, the ideal of courage may be invoked when the outcome is in doubt and you are trying to get yourself to do what you think you ought to do. Third, where courage facilitates the implementation of practical judgement, that implementation may also involve your forming certain future directed intentions (e.g. planning to go to the hospital), and being resolute in the execution of those intentions may also involve a display of courage, but courage does not always require such resolve: you are equally courageous when you face down a present danger without forming any such future directed intention.

It is worth contrasting executive virtue with non-executive virtues like kindness, generosity, and gratitude. The kind person is sensitive to the needs and feelings of others and is moved simply by an awareness of these needs and feelings. The notion of kindness may be employed by others to describe the kind person, but it plays no essential role in that person's thinking about what to do. One who needs to ask themselves what the kind person would do in order to get themselves to behave kindly is deficient in kindness. The same applies to generosity and gratitude—if you have to invoke the image of the ingrate in order to get yourself to send a thank-you note then you are deficient in gratitude. Executive virtue is different. True, someone can courageously undergo a painful medical procedure simply because they grasp its benefits and without thinking of what they are doing as courageous, but things might fall out differently. Perhaps

---

[19] People are often courageous without being temperate and so forth: there is no unity of executive virtue.

the inclination to procrastinate is hard to resist, though the agent clearly sees it for what it is. Here an extra motivational resource is available. The agent can appeal to an ideal of self-control: doing what you know you must, your (reasonable) fears notwithstanding. And to have the procedure because you wish to live up to this ideal, because you don't want to be a coward, is a paradigm instance of courage.[20] Here, practical judgement is not self-effacing.

I.3 Epistemic *Akrasia*?

In the case of action, the form of self-control that interests me was illustrated by the *akratic* who fails to exercise that control. In this section, I inquire whether we have a similar form of control over belief by asking whether there could be anything analogous to *akrasia* in the case of belief. But let's begin with the nature of belief itself.

There are various conceptions of belief. On some (rational) belief formation involves no more than a passive registration of the amount of evidence in favour of the proposition to be believed. For example, on the Bayesian conception of belief, to believe that p to a certain degree is to be in state which both registers the fact that there is a certain amount of evidence in favour of the truth of p and disposes you to behave as if p is true (to the relevant extent). The Bayesian omits a crucial element of the ordinary conception of belief formation, namely the idea that one who forms the belief that p *makes their mind up* about whether p is true by becoming convinced of p's truth. On this ordinary conception, *akratically* forming a belief that p would involve making up one's mind that p is true whilst judging that there is insufficient evidence to settle the matter in p's favour. In the Bayesian picture it can't be quite like that since there is (normally) no room for 'making up one's mind that p'. A good Bayesian will have reciprocal degrees of belief in both p and not-p, degrees proportional to the evidence for them and, as the evidence comes in, their degree of belief in p and in not-p will shift accordingly. Unless absolute certainty is available, the Bayesian has no use for the idea that at some point we might settle the matter for or against p (Chapter 4: Section 4.1).

I've said that the believer makes up their mind about whether p and does so even in the absence of absolute certainty. What does that involve? Someone who believes that p is convinced that p is true. To make up your mind that p is to

---

[20] For some nice illustrations of this point, see (Miller 2000: 84–8). Williams assimilates generosity to courage in this respect, wrongly inferring that (unlike justice) they both exclude thought of the virtue (Williams 1985: 10–11).

become convinced of p's truth and to be convinced of the truth of p is also to be convinced of the falsity of not-p, it is to have your mind made up (more or less firmly) in p's favour.[21] Making one's mind up in p's favour sounds more like a deed than the mere passive registration of evidence for and against p; it sounds as if we are doing something on the basis of that evidence, that we are taking a (more or less firm) decision in p's favour.[22] But what sort of action could constitute becoming convinced of the truth of p? Belief might be conceived of as a private conscious endorsement of the proposition to be believed, as a persisting inner assertion of p (where inner insincerity is ruled out). Now I don't deny that our beliefs may find expression in conscious mental acts, but such an act is guaranteed to reflect my belief only if my now believing that p is largely or wholly constituted by its occurrence. Surely belief is a richer psychological phenomenon than that. Belief involves, amongst other things, my now being disposed to infer related propositions, to revise the belief in question in response to certain forms of evidence, to feel and act in various ways which make sense given the truth of p. Why expect that our private assertions about p (or any other occurrent mental states) will always reflect this underlying psychological reality? The possibility of a mismatch cannot be assumed away (Chapter 9: Section 9.1).

This private assertion of p has a different subject matter from the judgement that I take to be involved in epistemic *akrasia*, namely a higher-order normative judgement about how well supported a belief in p is or would be. Still, once these two things are in play, it is natural to suppose that they must cohere with one another. What sense would it make to inwardly assert a proposition that you think the evidence does not support?[23] Such a mental occurrence could only be an intrusive thought, symptomatic of a divided mind. By equating belief with private assertion we make it hard to see how someone could self-ascribe a belief that they themselves think to be irrational (i.e. insufficiently supported by the evidence). Epistemic *akrasia*, so construed, would be a pathological phenomenon.[24]

---

[21] Conviction is itself a matter of degree, but there remains a line between being convinced of the truth of a proposition and having an open mind about it. The strength of your conviction is a measure of how hard it is to get you back across that line and into a state of agnosticism (Owens 2000: 142–5).

[22] This connotation is emphasized by (Moran 2001: Chapters 2 and 3) and (Boyle 2011).

[23] The claim here follows from the stronger claim that there is 'no-gap' between thinking there to be sufficient evidence to demonstrate the truth of p and actually believing that p or else between believing the evidence for p to be insufficient and failing to believe that p (Raz 2011: 38). Raz says that there is no gap 'in reasoning' between these attitudes, but the surrounding text makes it clear that he would also endorse the above claim except in pathological cases. See also (Adler 2002).

[24] That epistemic *akrasia* would have to be pathological in this way is suggested by both (Burge 2013: 83–5 and 393) and (Raz 2011: 92–3). Raz's views on this point are striking, since he agrees that

Suppose instead that belief is not a (perhaps persistent) mental occurrence but a richly dispositional state. Can't I judge that a belief of mine so understood is poorly supported by the evidence that I currently possess? That seems to be how it is with emotions. I fear flying and the reason I fear flying is that flying seems dangerous to me: the chance that the plane will fall out of the sky strikes me as significant. Here, I know that I fear flying, why I fear it, and how the fear shapes my activity (e.g. that it prevents me boarding a plane) and I know of these things in the usual way: I have 'first-person access' to them. My fear is not unintelligible: aircraft do crash. Since the fear makes some sense to me, I have no problem seeing it as mine. Nevertheless I regard my fear as insufficiently supported by the evidence as a whole, I think my fear irrational, and I make this further judgement without concluding that the fear is any the less my fear (a fear for which I may be criticized, or can criticize myself) than the various other emotions I feel and hold in higher esteem.[25]

Fear involves the suspicion, rather than the belief that flying is dangerous (Chapter 4: Section 4.4). Still, the flying example establishes that one's suspicions can break free of one's views about whether they are justified by the available evidence, and the sceptic about epistemic *akrasia* needs to say why belief should be any different, why there should be any more difficulty in my judging one of my beliefs to be irrational, at least where the belief has *some* basis in indications of its own truth.[26] Furthermore, there are many examples of recalcitrant emotions that do (as will be argued) involve belief (Chapter 4: Section 4.4). I can't be angry at John for stealing my bike unless I believe that John stole my bike. I can also judge that the evidence no longer establishes that he stole my bike without ceasing to be angry at him for this, and all that was said of the fear of flying is equally true of this irrational anger.

So far we have seen no reason to rule out the possibility of epistemic *akrasia*, but *akrasia* involves two separable elements, both of which are required to constitute an *akratic* belief (Chapter 1). First, there is a certain combination of psychological states, namely the belief that p and the judgement that the evidence in p's favour does not suffice to justify belief in it. I've suggested

---

belief is a multitrack psychological disposition and acknowledges that states similar to beliefs in this regard (i.e. emotions) commonly break free of our normative judgements (Raz 2011: 48).

[25] The example comes from (Shah and Velleman 2005: 507), but a similar one is mentioned in passing by (Moran 2001: 63). For discussion of related matters, see (Moran 2012: Section 3), (Boyle 2011: 9–11), and (Soteriou 2013: 354–6).

[26] Moore's paradox is sometimes taken to provide such a reason (Moran 2001: 69–77), as is the fact that someone who decides that p is false must cease to regard apparent evidence for p as providing any reason to believe it (Raz 2011: 42). For a critique of both lines of thought, see Chapter 1.

that this combination is perfectly possible. Second, we need the idea that simply in virtue of being a rational believer, I have the capacity to control my beliefs by making judgements about what I ought to believe. On this point, the sheer psychological complexity of belief tells neither way. Intentions and emotions both share belief's multifaceted dispositional character whilst differing from each other in this regard: we can choose our intentions in a way we can't choose our emotions. The possibility of epistemic *akrasia* turns on whether we can in this way choose our beliefs.

This issue must be carefully distinguished from the question as to whether one can 'believe at will'. Events are subject to the will when we can bring them about simply because we determine that their occurrence would be desirable. Now most writers agree that we do not have the capacity to form ungrounded beliefs simply because we judge that it would be highly desirable to have those beliefs, their baselessness notwithstanding. For example, I can't decide to believe that my boss is good at his job in order to secure a promotion. If I want to get myself to believe this, I must implement various strategies of self-manipulation in an effort to induce the relevant belief: merely judging that it would be desirable to so believe will not do the trick. As we noted in the last section, much the same is true of intention. I can't form an intention to do something patently silly simply because I have been offered a large reward just for forming the intention to perform the silly action. Some self-manipulation is needed if I am to acquire this prize-winning intention. None of these observations settles the question of whether we have reflective control over belief. Our lack of any capacity to believe at will leaves it open whether the capacity to determine what we believe by making judgements about what we ought to believe is a capacity we possess simply in virtue of being a rational believer. We can't intend at will, but we clearly can choose when to form future-directed intentions and which such intentions to form. Someone who judges that they ought to form a certain intention and then fails to do so is failing to exercise a capacity that they possess simply in virtue of being a rational agent. Epistemic *akrasia* would have to involve a failure to exercise an analogous capacity for epistemic self-control.

When discussing practical *akrasia* I argued that someone who fails to do what they correctly judge that they ought to do is to be criticized not just for performing an irrational action but also for a certain lapse of self-control, for failing to ensure that their actions conform to their practical judgement. Is something similar true in the case of belief? We do criticize people for having irrational beliefs, beliefs ill-supported by the available evidence. Do we also think that such people can control their own beliefs by first deploying normative notions like 'sufficient evidence' to assess their conviction and then ensure that their convictions conform to this assessment? Where awareness of evidence alone does not produce or eliminate conviction, do we think higher-order normative judgement can do the trick?

I.4 Belief and Reflective Control

I maintain that a rational believer may lack the capacity to determine what they believe simply by making a judgement about what they ought to believe. I'll lay out a two-step argument for this conclusion and spend the rest of the present section defending each step.

Here is the argument:

(a) The rationality of the belief that p is determined not just by the strength of the evidence for and against p but also by the desirability of forming a belief about whether p.

(b) One cannot determine whether one forms a belief about whether p on the available evidence by making the judgement that it would be desirable to form a belief about whether p on the available evidence.[27]

Therefore: We cannot determine whether we form the belief that p by making a judgement about whether such a belief would be reasonable, i.e. we lack reflective control over our beliefs.

Both (a) and (b) are disputable, but before defending them I should note that, in my view, there is no parallel argument for intention. The analogue of (a) is indeed perfectly true: the rationality of now intending to A is a function *both* of the case for A-ing when the time comes *and* of the desirability of deciding now rather than later whether to A. But the analogue of (b) is false: a rational agent *can* determine whether to decide now on their future A-ing simply by making the judgement that they ought to decide now, on the information currently available about the merits of A-ing, whether they shall A. Hence, we have reflective control of our intentions.

I.4.1 Evidentialism

Let's begin with (a). In the case of both belief and (future-directed) intention there are two logically distinct questions. The first question is whether you ought to settle the matter now by forming either a belief or an intention rather than keeping an open mind. If you ought to make up your mind, the second question

---

[27] 'On the available evidence' here falls within the scope of 'the judgement': one is making a judgement about whether it is desirable to form a belief on the basis of the available evidence.

arises: what ought you to believe or what ought you to do? Settling the latter question involves directing one's attention exclusively to the objects of the belief/intention—to the merits of the proposition to be believed and of the action to be intended—but it is hard to see how one might settle the former question simply by focusing on the objects of these attitudes alone.

Aren't our two questions to be considered simultaneously rather than consecutively? Isn't the issue of whether one ought now to have a view about whether p to be decided in the light of the balance of available evidence for and against p? We can indeed merge the two questions by asking ourselves whether the evidence in p's favour is sufficient to justify belief in p, but that doesn't show that the balance of evidence alone can settle both questions. We need to determine what constitutes sufficient evidence for p, how much of a preponderance of evidence in p's favour is required for p to be what I ought now to believe, and that question can never be resolved simply by noting indications of the truth or falsity of p.

So what does determine whether it is reasonable to form a view about p on the evidence before us? Broadly speaking, this turns on how much it matters that I have a view about p and given that I do have a view, how much it matters whether I'm right or wrong. If it matters a great deal that I be right in what I think, the relevant evidential threshold will be high: there must be a great deal of evidence in p's favour. If, on the other hand, it wouldn't matter hugely should I be wrong about this, the evidential threshold for reasonable belief will be rather lower.

To address these further non-evidential issues, we must focus on the role played by belief both in the psychology of individuals and in human social life. It is widely agreed that the point of belief is to represent how things are, a fact that helps to explain the evidential constraints on belief formation. For example, it can never be reasonable to believe that p if the amount of evidence in p's favour is no greater than the amount of evidence against p. But there is more to belief than representation. Suspicion shares its representational function, and consequently it is unreasonable to suspect that p is true where the amount of evidence in p's favour is no greater than the amount of evidence against p, yet suspicions differ from beliefs—belief has a stronger and more pervasive influence on both action and emotion than suspicion—and so it is more important to be right in what we believe than in what we suspect.

These observations are enough to establish the truth of (a). To say more might be to labour the point since many writers now agree that the amount of evidence required to justify belief is determined by the importance of the issue at stake. But amongst these writers there is a widespread tendency to equate that with the *practical* importance of the issue and to regard belief primarily as a motivator of action.[28] In fact, our curiosity, our felt need to know, is not solely a function of practical concerns: we feel curious whenever our emotions are engaged and we need beliefs that are fairly constant over time and largely shared with those around us (at least on topics which matter to us) to orient our passions and affections.

This bears on the content of our epistemic norms. Were the level of evidence needed to justify belief a function purely of the practical significance of the issue in question, that level would vary greatly from person to person and from time to time. Suppose I'm the one who gets to decide whether someone is to be punished for a certain crime. If the practical import of this issue sets the threshold of epistemic sufficiency, the amount of evidence I require to become convinced of their guilt will be greater before the decision than afterwards and greater (at least at that moment) for me than for others. I doubt standards of epistemic sufficiency are so sensitive to parochial and ephemeral practical concerns and, if they were, that would call into question the idea that knowledge might be transmitted by means of testimony between individuals whose practical interests in the matter are quite various ((Chapter 7: Section 7.3) and (Hinchman 2014: 4–10)).

Variations in the significance of a given issue *do* affect the standard of evidential sufficiency, but the standard in question will be a social standard and one fairly stable over time. For example, suppose I overhear that a tenth planet has been discovered in the solar system. As a mere amateur, I might be perfectly entitled to take the person's word for it whilst you, a professional astronomer, would not. The issue matters more to you and your community in all sorts of ways, and were you to accept testimony on the matter, it would have to come (directly or indirectly) from another professional astronomer. Here the standard of evidence sufficient to justify belief is set in part by social convention, a convention itself underwritten by the importance of that issue to the relevant community. As a result, the convention applying to me differs from that which applies to you.[29]

The temptation to reject (a) and adopt evidentialism (namely the view that rational belief should be based on evidential considerations alone) rests largely

---

[28] Here, I have in mind the doctrine of 'pragmatic encroachment' (Fantl and McGrath 2009). The local practical significance of an issue may indeed determine whether it is reasonable for you to act on a given belief, but that is a different issue. See Chapters 4: Section 4.4 and 7: Section 7.3.

[29] I used the astronomy example in (Owens 2000: 26) There I styled non-evidential considerations relevant to the justification of belief 'pragmatic considerations'; here I stick with 'non-evidential'. For discussion of the way social considerations might fix the evidential standard, see (Craig 1990) and (Grimm 2015), though both writers focus exclusively on practical considerations.

on a fact about doxastic deliberation, that when we consider whether or not Oscar Pistorius murdered his girlfriend what comes to mind is just evidence for and against the proposition that O.P. is a murderer. Considerations bearing on the desirability of having a belief on the matter (as opposed to a mere suspicion or no view at all) seem not to occur to us. We form a belief (or indeed a suspicion) by forming a view about the world rather than by forming a view about the merits of believing (or suspecting). True enough, but do these facts about doxastic deliberation really support the idea that evidence alone constitutes reason for belief?

So long as I'm inquiring into whether O.P. murdered his girlfriend, I'm focused on what he says, on what other people say, on various forms of physical evidence, and on how likely this all makes it that he murdered her. The topic here is the (probabilistic) connections between phenomena in the world. I need not conceive of these phenomena *as* reasons for belief, nor need I ask myself whether a belief would be justified in the light of them. Such deliberations can and do lead me to become convinced on the point without my even addressing these normative issues. So why suppose we can arrive at a full inventory of reasons for belief (i.e. of the factors relevant to the *normative* issues) by asking what sorts of considerations arise in the course of inquiry?

Of course I *could* start thinking in normative terms about the matter. For example, I could judge that physical evidence provides sufficient grounds for concluding that O.P. murdered his girlfriend, given what is at stake here. But now I am facing the question of sufficiency and now I am in the business of contemplating such non-evidential factors as the importance of having a view and of being right in the view that I form. We generally engage in such 'normative ascent' in the course of assessing, from a third-personal standpoint, the rationality of our own beliefs or, more likely, the beliefs of others: 'given how much it mattered, we ought to have kept an open mind about it', etc. One does not make these normative assessments in the course of considering what is the case because (as the evidentialist insists) reflection on such non-evidential considerations won't convince us on a point of fact.[30]

---

[30] This will be missed unless we keep firmly in view the distinction between first-order deliberation or inquiry on the one hand and higher-order normative judgement on the other (Owens 2000: 11–12 and 82–7). Some authors move freely between the claim that we can determine what we believe by deliberation or inquiry and the very different claim that we can determine what we believe by making judgements about what we ought to believe (Moran 2001: 134–51), (Boyle 2011: 7–8). Others argue that inquiry necessarily involves a higher-order consciousness of what we are trying to do, one that facilitates normative assessments (Soteriou 2013: 351–5). The latter may be true of practical deliberation, but I doubt that it is true of theoretical deliberation (Chapter 3: Section 3.3).

I.4.2 The Impotence of Reflection

That brings us to (b). Perhaps there are creatures who can determine what they believe by forming a view about what it would be reasonable for them to believe, by focusing on the whole range of considerations, both evidential and non-evidential, relevant to the latter question. But most of us cannot, we cannot become convinced on a point of fact by reflecting (however rightly) that it is about time we made up our minds on the matter. This inability provides us with no grounds for self-criticism: having such an ability is no part of being a rational believer.

On this point, the contrast with future-directed intention is stark. Recall my need for medical treatment. I have a series of pressing engagements in the next few days and so, if I'm to have the treatment next week, I need to decide this now so that I can plan my week around it. Here, two sorts of consideration support my deciding now to have the treatment next week. First, there is the medical case for having the treatment within the next week; that concerns the desirability of the action to be decided upon. Second, there is the case for making the decision now about exactly when to have the treatment; that concerns the desirability of making up my mind today (rather than tomorrow) to have the treatment. Suppose I'm reluctant to have the treatment and am finding it difficult to make up my mind to have it, to form a timely plan on the matter. As a rational agent I can remind myself not just of the benefits of the treatment but also of the need to decide *now* exactly when I'm to have the treatment, i.e. of the desirability of taking that decision as well as the desirability of the action decided upon. Here, by reflecting on the point of making this and other decisions, on the role that intentions should play in my life, I can resolve the matter by making up my mind. I have no such power over belief.

We've now traced the absence of reflective control over belief to our inability to regulate our beliefs by reflecting on non-evidential considerations, considerations nevertheless relevant to the rationality of belief. In the rest of this section, we shall consider objections. Some are inclined to accept (b) whilst rejecting (a). They treat the fact that we are unmoved by reflection on non-evidential considerations as grounds for doubting that they do indeed constitute reasons for belief, but I'll start with those who accept (a) whilst rejecting (b), who insist that we can in fact regulate our beliefs by reflection on non-evidential considerations.

In making the case for (b) I focused on belief formation, on whether reflection on non-evidential considerations could help convince us of the truth of some proposition. There is another possible form of influence to consider. Might such reflections at least undermine our belief in a proposition of which we were are currently convinced (or else prevent us forming a belief on the evidence before us)? Suppose I come to realize that a lot more hangs on whether John borrowed Jim's bike without permission than I previously appreciated: the consequences were more serious than I thought and John's standing now turns on this. Mightn't I reflect that we all need more evidence on the point and without it any conviction that he stole the bike is no longer reasonable, and mightn't such reflection serve to undermine that conviction in a case where I was otherwise reluctant to abandon it (or prevent me from forming it where I was otherwise so inclined)? Here, I supposedly open my mind on the matter simply by judging that I can't reasonably hold a view on the basis of the evidence currently available to me but need to investigate further (McHugh 2011: 259–60).

Were the objector right that reflection can veto belief even though it can't determine which belief we adopt, such an asymmetry would still be enough to distinguish belief from intention in respect of the type of control we enjoy over them. Still, I think any asymmetry here may be explained without conceding a reflective veto. Having realized that a factual issue is more important than previously thought, there is something else you can do, namely remind yourself of the other considerations in play, i.e. the evidence for and against the proposition in question. You can do this whether or not you have already opened your mind on the matter precisely in an effort to get yourself to open your mind on it. By contrast, where the problem is rather that we can't come to believe something that we think we ought to believe on the basis of evidence already reviewed, it is unclear what shift of attention might help. If reflection on the probative force of the evidence has not convinced us, why should first-order deliberation help? That is why we might feel better placed to veto an ill-supported belief than to impose a well-supported belief upon ourselves.

I'm not denying that non-evidential considerations can and will motivate the formation of belief in a rational person. If non-evidential considerations could not somehow guide the formation of belief, there would be no case for insisting that they constitute reasons for belief, i.e. considerations that render belief intelligible and can form the basis for rational criticism of belief. As noted at the outset, I am not offering any positive conception of epistemic guidance. My point is negative: we can't control our beliefs by assessing the normative significance of these non-evidential considerations. Non-evidential considerations guide belief in a way that does not require my judging them to be reasons for belief.[31]

---

[31] For discussion of this point, see (Owens 2000: 13–15) and (Boghossian 2014).

Could it instead be denied that these non-evidential considerations constitute reasons for belief?[32] I'll conclude the section by sketching a line of thought that accepts (b) whilst rejecting (a), one that takes off from a familiar distinction between premises and rules of inference. As is well known, not everything relevant to reasoning can be treated as a premise in reasoning (Carroll 1895). To move from premise to conclusion, we must rely on some rule of inference of the form 'if p infer q', a rule that is not incorporated into our premises. True we *can* add 'if p then q' to our premises, but that takes us no further forward. In order to conclude that q from this more complex set of premises, we must rely on a more complex rule of inference which incorporates 'if p then q' as a premise alongside p and tells us to infer q from their combination.

Let's now suppose that our reasons for a given belief are laid out as premises in a chain of reasoning. Perhaps a certain amount of reconstruction is required to arrive at the elements of this chain, but let's not worry about that. The crucial claim is that only those considerations serving as premises in our reasoning, those that are in the foreground of our reasoning, count as reasons for belief. The rules of inference we employ are indeed required for the reasoning to go through, but so long as they play this role they cannot serve as reasons for belief. It is by remaining in the background that these rules facilitate rational belief formation. Now, among the rules of inference employed in theoretical reasoning are rules telling us when a certain quantity of evidence for p suffices to justify belief in p. We need some such rule in order to move from premises describing our evidence for p to the conclusion that p is true, and the rule will facilitate this movement of thought only so long as it remains in the background. Converting this rule into a premise takes us no further forward: we must fall back on some further rule that tells us when to conclude that p from these premises. The thought that evidence mentioned in our premises is sufficient to justify belief in the conclusion can do its inferential job only so long as it remains in the background, only so long as it does not serve as a reason for belief. From all this one might conclude that it is no surprise that we cannot decide whether to believe by reflecting on non-evidential considerations. The role of such considerations is to support the rule of inference that authorizes us to draw a certain conclusion from certain premises. If these considerations are to do the job of facilitating rational belief formation by supporting that inference, they cannot serve as premises in our reasoning and so, the objection goes, cannot be amongst

---

[32] (Raz 2011: 37) maintains that such non-evidential considerations help to determine the rationality of belief without themselves being reasons for belief.

our reasons for belief. They must remain in the background, just like the rule that they support.

This line of thought fails to explain why we cannot decide whether to believe by reflecting on non-evidential considerations. Consider practical reasoning. Here too we need a rule of inference to move from premises concerning the relevant features of the various options to a conclusion about which option we ought to take. The rule will specify when the premises about the relative desirability of the options provide sufficient support for a practical conclusion about which option we ought to take. Now suppose that such a rule cannot be amongst the premises of our practical inference for the very reasons just rehearsed. Were the above line of thought sound, we would be unable to decide what to do by reflecting that we have enough information about the various options to make a decision about what to do, given the importance of the issue, the need for a decision, and so forth. It would follow that these considerations could not serve as premises in our practical reasoning and so could not be amongst our reasons for choice. Yet, as already noted, we clearly can get ourselves to take a decision by making a judgement about the desirability of, say, deciding now rather than later and so there are no grounds for doubting that these considerations are amongst our reasons for taking the decision. Thus, the distinction between premises and rules of inference cannot explain the asymmetry between theoretical and practical reasoning outlined in this section.

I.5 Forms of Accountability and Control

If I'm right, we do not control what we believe (and feel) as we control our intentions and actions. Why does it matter whether and how we control belief, intention, and action? What hangs on this? One answer is that we are held responsible only for things that we control, but this response is too simple. Different forms or degrees of control underwrite different forms or degrees of responsibility. In this section, I'll describe one way in which our lack of reflective control over belief affects our responsibility for belief, but I want to begin by highlighting another respect in which our responsibility for belief remains unaffected.

Until now, I have spoken of people being subject to 'rational criticism' for their beliefs. Criticism comes in many forms and it is often thought that certain forms are appropriate only where the object of the criticism had the ability to avoid that criticism by making better choices. In particular, it is widely believed that we are rightly *blamed* only where we could have avoided becoming worthy of blame. Given that we are often unable to control what we believe, either by will or by judgement, this view would seem to imply that criticism of our (irrational) beliefs cannot take the form of blame.

Immunizing irrational belief against blame in this way would undermine everyday conceptions of epistemic responsibility. Consider the terms in which Freud expresses his hostility to religious faith:

'Well then, if even obdurate sceptics admit that the assertions of religion cannot be refuted by reason, why should I not believe in them, since they have so much on their side—tradition, the agreement of mankind, and all the consolations they offer.' Why not, indeed? Just as no one can be forced to believe, no one can be forced to disbelieve. But do not let us be satisfied with deceiving ourselves that arguments like these take us along the road of correct thinking. If ever there was a case of lame excuse we have it here. Ignorance is ignorance; no right to believe anything can be derived from it. In other matters no sensible person will behave so irresponsibly or rest content with such feeble grounds for his opinions and for the line he takes. (Freud 1961: 41)

Note the terms of the criticism. Freud is not displeased or disappointed by religious belief, as one might be sad that people are not better mathematicians. Nor is he embarrassed by religious belief. Nor is he feeling ashamed on the believer's behalf. His critical reaction is more pointed than that. Freud is *indignant* at the wishfulness of the religious, at the mere fact of their having these beliefs, at their simple failure to 'think correctly'.[33] And to justify this reaction, he feels no need to ascribe harmful effects to these illusions. Indeed, the illusion is admitted to be consoling.

Those who deny that we can be blamed simply for the irrationality of our beliefs might insist that such criticism is in place only where there is something the believer could have done to ensure that they obeyed the rules of correct thinking, some book they could have read, some class they could have attended. Freud does not inquire whether such means of self-improvement are available to the religious believer, and I would maintain that irrational beliefs (like emotions) are blameworthy even where we have no capacity to either control our beliefs directly or to affect our beliefs by performing various belief-influencing actions (Owens 2000: 117–20).

We should give up on the idea that blameworthiness presupposes reflective control, but this may leave us wondering about the significance of this power: why worry about whether beliefs are under reflective control unless this bears on our responsibility for belief? To see how our lack of reflective control over belief affects our accountability for belief we need to distinguish two different forms of responsibility: *attributive* and *substantive* (Scanlon 1998: Chapter 6). When a

---

[33] Since Aquinas thought faith a virtue and unbelief a sin, he would endorse Freud's view that we are accountable for our religious beliefs, though of course not his hostility to religious faith.

state or an action is attributed to me, I am held responsible for it in the sense that I am subject to either praise or blame in virtue of being in that state or of performing that action. By contrast, one is responsible for a state or action in the substantive sense when that state or action potentially changes what one is obliged to do. I'll conclude this section by arguing that, whilst, as we just saw, attributive responsibility does not presuppose reflective control, substantive responsibility often does.

I'll argue for two claims. First, the extent of one's substantive responsibility for an action often turns on whether one performed it intentionally. To bear certain forms of substantive responsibility, it isn't enough that one *could* have intended to perform it, that the act *could* have been done at will; one must actually have decided to perform it, one must have knowingly performed an act with that character. Secondly, intention has this significance because our intentions (and so the character of the acts that we knowingly perform) are under our reflective control. I shall not argue that all forms of substantive responsibility require this measure of control, merely that some do.

As to the first point, consider two examples. One acquires a promissory obligation to perform a given act only where one undertook this obligation intentionally. Someone who negligently leads another to expect them to perform some act may well have to warn them or compensate them if they fail to perform, but the further obligation to actually fulfill this expectation (usually) exists only where the agent chose to undertake the relevant obligation. A second example: the amount of compensation owing for some harmful act very often depends on whether that harm was inflicted intentionally. Some torts like negligence are not committed intentionally, but there are others like battery and defamation that are always intentional and the nature of the legal remedy depends on this.[34]

The obvious explanation for these facts is that it is appropriate to subject the agent to the extra penalty or else have them bear the burden of performance because they chose to do what they did and their choices are under their reflective control. In determining whether it is fair to make someone bear these costs and burdens, a crucial consideration is whether they had an adequate opportunity to avoid bearing them. Those who did not will often have good grounds for objecting to such costs, but where they had the power to choose whether to run the risk of incurring them and had a reasonable opportunity to exercise that power, without undue constraint, with other eligible alternatives and so forth,

---

[34] (Scanlon 1998: 260). I take it that there are non-legal duties to compensate that work in this way. We might also have considered the role of choice in rendering one liable to punishment, but the criminal law raises more controversial issues.

their complaints on this score will be harder to sustain.[35] The point here cannot be that our choices are themselves subject to the will for (as we saw in Section I.2) the will is not subject to the will. Rather, our choices are under our reflective control, and it is that which generates substantive responsibility both for our choices and for the actions chosen.

There is an alternative explanation of what is going on here. Acts like making a promise or committing a battery are subject to the will, i.e. the agent is able to perform them simply because they regard them as desirable or avoid them because they are undesirable. Since the agent's performance depends on their view of the costs and burdens associated with performance, it is often appropriate to attach such costs and burdens to performance as a way of incentivizing the right choice. This would be quite inappropriate were the agent unable to take such considerations into account. For example, agents can't generally determine what they believe or feel by attending to penalties (or incentives) associated with these beliefs or feelings. Perhaps that is why we don't impose costs and burdens on people simply because of their beliefs or feelings, however unreasonable they may be.

Can we explain the above difference in forms of accountability by reference to the scope of the will, rendering reflective control explanatorily redundant? This will-based account assumes that the point of our negative reactions to such things as torts and breaches of promise is to act as forms of deterrence. Whilst the idea that remedies in tort are disincentives has *some* plausibility, it is much less persuasive when applied either to non-legal duties to compensate or to promissory morality. The conscientious promisor does not keep their promise because they fear they will be blamed for non-performance and the point of blaming breach is not to incentivize performance (Owens 2012: 70–3). And even in the more favourable case of civil wrongs there is the following difficulty: we need to explain why actual decision-making is crucial to certain torts. For example, where an agent is penalized for negligence it might well be assumed that the degree of care they took was subject to their will, but it is certainly not assumed that they actually decided to be careless. By contrast, the actual decision they took is crucial to torts like battery, and this fact makes sense only if we think of the taking of the decision itself as something the agent controls even though (as argued above) decisions themselves are not subject to our will. I conclude that, in these cases, the form of the substantive responsibility turns on the capacity for reflective control.

---

[35] See (Hart 2008: Chapter 2), (Scanlon 1998: 267–94), and (Scanlon 2008: 179–204). See also (Watson 2004a: Chapter 9).

Returning finally to substantive responsibility for belief, I have argued that we have no reflective control over belief. I have also argued that belief is not subject to the will. The various forms of substantive responsibility just described depend on whether the matter in question is under at least one of these two kinds of control. In so far as belief is under neither, we would not expect people to be held substantively responsible for their beliefs in these ways. Attributive responsibility for belief is a different matter. The above reasoning about the need for extra control where penalties and burdens will be imposed does not apply to the avoidance of blame since blame is not a penalty. No doubt it is frequently unpleasant to be the object of blame, and blame can surely damage one's interests in other ways, but such damage is usually the result of the expression of blame rather than of blame itself. Furthermore, even where unexpressed blame causes damage (e.g. by spoiling a beautiful friendship), the point of blame is not to impose such a cost on the culprit. Rather, to blame someone is to make an emotionally charged assessment of what they have done, felt, or thought. Any costs imposed by such an assessment are incidental to blame and irrelevant to its intrinsic appropriateness (Owens 2012: Chapter 1).[36]

So when is blame apt or deserved or fair? The main factor here is the significance of the object of blame—the bad thought, feeling, choice, or action. Arguably, an *action* may often be devoid of any special significance *qua* action unless the agent had a real choice about whether to commit the deed for which they are blamed, but things are otherwise in the case of thoughts and feelings. Disapproval of a bad attitude is frequently apt even though its subject had no direct control over their attitude and so no opportunity of that sort to avoid whatever costs your disapproval imposes on them. Whilst our substantive responsibility for thoughts and feelings turns on whether we have reflective control over our thoughts and feelings, their blameworthiness does not.

---

[36] I've argued that various attitudes are potentially blameworthy whether or not they are subject to reflective control, but perhaps the severity of the blame remains a function, at least in part, of whether those attitudes were so controlled. Can't poor choice determine the degree or extent of our attributive as it does of our substantive responsibilities? Aren't we more blamed where we actually choose to ignore a reminder of the danger than in a case where we ought to have known of the danger but did not deliberately remain in ignorance? The point is debatable, but I'm inclined to think that where choice affects responsibility in cases like this, it does so by introducing a new object of responsibility in addition to one's negligent attitude rather than by making us more blameworthy for that attitude. To choose to ignore a warning is to make a blameworthy choice, a choice that is not made by the negligent character who never notices the warning.

I.6 The Problems of Authority and Control

We do not control our beliefs (and emotions) as we control our actions (and intentions). Nevertheless, there is such a thing as epistemic normativity: we are criticized for what we believe (and feel) as well as for what we do. This is a happy situation only if we should be content with the idea that states subject to different norms are also under different forms of control, that the relevant form of guidance might vary along with the norms that should be guiding us. This concluding section supports that contention and the resolution it suggests of the problem of control and so of the special problems of epistemic normativity.

From where do the various norms that govern our lives derive their authority? These norms vary in respect of what they require of us as well as in respect of the parts of our lives to which they apply. For example, what norms of prudence require of action is rather different from what epistemic norms require of belief. Still, there is a question which might be posed of them all: why should we take them seriously, why should we worry about whether our own lives or the lives of others conform to them? This is what I call (in Chapters 2 and 4) the problem of authority. Like the general problem of normativity, it applies to norms as such, but it constitutes a further issue. Even if we have the ability to be guided by some norm or other (the general problem of normativity notwithstanding), why should we be guided by these norms in particular? Why does it make sense to follow them rather than some quite different norms and why should we offer or accept criticism for their violation? Some writers argue that certain norms are constitutive of belief and agency in that it is impossible to believe or act without being subject to the authority of those norms. In the face of this essentialist manoeuvre we should reformulate our question: what is the point of believing or acting so understood; why acquiesce in the states and processes which subject us to these norms rather than doing our best to rid ourselves of them or else bemoan the fact that we can't (Chapter 4: Section 4.1)? I answer by trying to show how being subject to the relevant norms is in our interests, is good for us. That answer secures the two connotations of normativity: if something is good for you, this makes sense of allowing yourself to be guided by it and it also explains why a failure to be guided by it should often be a matter for criticism.

I'm suggesting that the various norms mentioned so far all derive their authority from a common source, namely, human interests, but such uniformity makes room for variety in the way these norms serve our interests. This variety manifests itself in two dimensions: first, in the differing content of the norms in play, and second, in the differing ways that those norms are expected to guide our lives and in the forms of responsibility to which they give rise. An extended defence of my solution to the problem of authority must be postponed until Chapter 4. Here, I'll confine myself to highlighting two themes of the book as a whole. First, in several places I explain the content of the norms governing a type of mental state by reference to their function (i.e. to the human interests they serve) a fact which suggests that our solution to the problem of authority is along the right lines. Second, I also explain variations in the forms of control one has over different types of mental state by reference to their divergent functions, a fact which bolsters our solution to the problem of control.

As to the first point, recall my critique of evidentialism about belief, of the view that evidence alone is relevant to the rationality of belief. A state the function of which was simply to register the amount of inconclusive evidence for and against our beliefs (such as Bayesian belief) could not play the role in human life that human belief does, could not serve our interests in the relevant way. We need to make up our mind on many matters, but the relevant evidence is almost always inconclusive, and so long as this is so, evidence alone will not determine at what point we should make up our mind: non-evidential considerations are needed to set the threshold of evidence at which it is reasonable to take a view. So consideration of the interests served by belief shows that evidentialism about the content of epistemic norms must be false.

The same dependence of the relevant norms on the underlying interests can be seen in the case of states that are like belief in that they depend on evidence for their rationality but which do not share the function of belief. We can 'make up our minds' by making a practical judgement, entertaining a suspicion, or even hazarding a guess. Each of these forms of mentation plays a different role in our lives, serves a different interest, and so the norms that govern them and in particular the level of evidence required to justify them, differs accordingly.[37] Evidence can justify a guess that p without, say, entitling us to suspect that p is true, and we might be entitled to suspect that p is true without being justified in believing that p. In each case, the content of the norms governing the mental phenomena in question depends on the role those phenomena play in our lives.

Now to our second point. As we saw in the last section, different types of control underwrite different forms of responsibility. For example, there is no sense in attaching penalties to thinking or doing a certain thing unless we suppose that the thoughts or actions in question are subject to the will; are such that we can engage in them simply because of the desirable or undesirable consequences of so doing. Note how control and responsibility are connected

---

[37] For discussion of guessing, see Chapters 1: Section 1.1 and 2: Sections 2.2 and 2.3, for suspicion see Chapters 4: Sections 4.2 and 7: Section 7.1, and for practical judgement see Chapter 7: Section 7.1.

here. We are supposing that an interest is served by subjecting people to certain forms of substantive responsibility, namely, whatever interest is served by the occurrence or non-occurrence of the phenomena required or forbidden by the norm. But that interest will be served only where people have a specific form of control over whether they conform to the relevant norms. If they can't respond to the incentives *qua* incentives then there is no point in subjecting them to that form of substantive responsibility.

In the example just given, we assumed the presence of an interest in being subject to a certain norm, an interest which explains both the content of the norm in question and the form of control presupposed by subjection to that norm. In that example the interest in question was instrumental; it was an interest in the desirable effects of conformity to the relevant norm. I maintain that human beings also have normative interests, that they are interested in normative phenomena for their own sake (Owens 2012: Introduction). Being subjects of rights, obligations, of norms of rationality and appropriateness can be non-instrumentally valuable to us. If that is correct then the forms of responsibility associated with various norms share this non-instrumental value, at least so long as the relevant forms of control are available to us. And where different interests are served by different norms, different types of control are required to realize this value.

For example, Chapter 4 argues that certain forms of emotional engagement with the world are good for us, forms that involve being subject to certain norms and so being blameworthy should we violate those norms. In order to realize that value, it is not required that we be able to determine what we feel simply by making judgements about what we ought to feel. Indeed, the distinctive significance of the emotions may depend on our not being able to do this, on our feelings not being under our control in this way. The value of this form of responsibility does not presuppose reflective control.[38] Chapter 4 also argues that the function of belief is to facilitate emotional engagement with the world,

---

[38] Chapter 8: Section 8.4 suggests that sometime like what I have just claimed to be true of passive states of feeling is also true of certain forms of activity, namely those habitual actions that express virtues. The truthful person is not someone who weighs the pros and cons of truthfulness before saying the honest thing. The truthful person is someone with a habit of speaking truthfully, and being truthful out of habit excludes acting on the judgement that one ought here to be truthful and on the considerations that would support such a judgement. Indeed, there are cases in which one couldn't act on such a judgement precisely because there is nothing to be said for being truthful. If the argument of Chapter 8 is right, the distinctive value of truthfulness depends on these facts; depends on our not exercising reflective control over whether we speak truthfully on this particular occasion, though truthful speech remains a form of activity because we *can* control it by asking whether the habit of truthfulness is a virtue.

so the remarks just made about reflective control over emotion apply also to belief. The interest we have in belief does not require belief to be under our reflective control. Thus, the very interest which explains the authority of epistemic norms also explains why guidance by these norms need not take the form of reflective control. No such story applies to the norms of practical reason, nor to the intentions and actions they govern: their function is quite different, and requires the sort of control that we have over them.[39]

---

[39] Thanks to Maria Alvarez, Julien Dutant, Oliver Black, Nishi Shah, James Stazicker, and Conor McHugh for their comments on this Introduction

PART I

Normativity: Epistemic and Practical

1

Epistemic *Akrasia*

One way of discerning what sort of control we have over our mental lives is to look at cases where that control is not exercised. This is one reason why philosophers have taken an interest in the phenomenon of *akrasia*, in an agent's ability to do, freely and deliberately, something that they judge they ought not to do. *Akrasia* constitutes a failure of control but not an absence of control. The *akratic* agent is not a compulsive; an *akratic* agent has the ability to control their action, to make it conform to their judgement, but they fail to exercise that ability. They freely and deliberately give in to temptation.

In the hope of getting clearer about the sort of control we have over belief, some philosophers have gone on to ask whether there is any phenomenon analogous to *akrasia* in the epistemic realm. Epistemic *akrasia* is possible only if (a) a person's (first-order) beliefs can diverge from their higher-order judgements about what it would be reasonable for them to believe, and (b) these divergent (first-order) beliefs are freely and deliberately formed. Call (a) *the judgement condition* and (b) *the control condition*.

It has been argued that one can't possibly believe something one thinks one ought not to believe: the judgement condition cannot be satisfied. In the first half of the chapter, I shall criticize these arguments. But even if we can believe what we think we ought not to believe, it still remains an open question whether this constitutes a failure to exercise control over belief, a control which we retain even whilst we fail to exercise it. Mere judgemental disapproval of some mental phenomenon does not make that mental phenomenon *akratic* unless it is the sort of thing we are expected to exercise judgemental control over. In the second half of the chapter, I argue that it is the control condition which cannot be satisfied. So, in the end, I conclude that epistemic *akrasia* is impossible and that its impossibility casts a shadow over the whole idea of doxastic control.

1.1 The Judgement Condition: Moore's Paradox

The *akratic* does what he or she believes should not be done or fails to do what he or she believes should be done. If epistemic *akrasia* is possible, we must be capable of judging that our own beliefs are unreasonable: that we believe things we ought not to believe or that we fail to believe what we should.[1]

Some writers argue that epistemic *akrasia* is impossible because this judgement condition cannot be met:

> Imagine that your beliefs run counter to what evidence and fact require. In such a case, your beliefs will not allow those requirements to remain visible because the offending beliefs themselves give you your sense of what is and your sense of what appears to be. You are therefore denied an experience whose content is that you are believing such and such in defiance of the requirements of fact and evidence. This is why, as G.E. Moore observed, you cannot simultaneously think that while you believe that p, yet it is not the case that p. (Pettit and Smith 1996: 448)

I doubt the possibility of epistemic *akrasia* can be dismissed so quickly.

Let's start by disentangling what fact requires from what evidence requires. One can judge that one is believing either against, or regardless of, the evidence without judging that one is believing against the facts. Someone who judges:

(1) I believe Jones is innocent, but this belief is based on insufficient evidence.

isn't (yet) expressing any view about Jones's guilt or innocence. (1) is not equivalent to:

(2) I believe Jones is innocent, but he is guilty.

For instance, I might think (1) when despite having received information which undermines, in my own eyes, whatever evidence supported my belief in Jones's innocence, I find myself still convinced of his innocence. And I can have information which undercuts this evidence without having any indication as to whether Jones is, as (2) claims, guilty.

(2) is the sort of sentence which Moore found highly paradoxical: even though (2) might well be true, someone who asserts it appears to take back in the second

---

[1] In this chapter, I am concerned exclusively with judgements about what it would be reasonable for me to believe, not with judgements about which beliefs it would be reasonable for me to cause or induce in myself. For example, it might be reasonable of me or even morally required of me to cause myself to acquire a certain belief, a belief which is quite irrational because there is insufficient evidence for it. If I judge that this is so, I am judging that a certain action is required of me: namely the action of inducing an irrational belief. If, having made that judgement, I then fail to perform such an action, this is an example of practical, not epistemic *akrasia* (Owens 2000: 25, 182).

part of the sentence the very thing that they asserted in the first. Many have assumed that (2) is paradoxical because the state of mind which it is naturally taken to express is impossible. Pettit and Smith appear to equate (2) with (1) and thence infer that the state of mind expressed by (1) must be impossible also. But if the state of mind expressed by (1) is impossible, it is not for this reason.

Would Pettit and Smith fare any better if they formulated Moore's paradox in a slightly different way? Compare

(3) The evidence is sufficient to establish Jones's guilt, but I just can't believe that he is guilty.

with

(4) Jones is guilty, but I don't believe it.

Are these equivalent? I think not. (4) is paradoxical because I appear to be asserting Jones's guilt and then taking my assertion back in the same breath. There is no such incoherence in (3). In (3) I am not both committing myself on the facts of the matter and also evading this commitment; rather, I am saying that a reasonable man would adopt a certain belief but that I am not, in this instance, being reasonable. (3) does indeed report an unhappy state of mind but not an impossible one. Most of us have had occasion to utter a sentence like (3) at some point in our lives.

We can get closer to the situation which Pettit and Smith might have in mind by combining (1) and (3) with a further judgement about the balance of evidence. Say I judge that the evidence points towards Jones's guilt: the testimony of the eyewitnesses to the crime is more plausible than that of those brought in to support his alibi. (3) allows that I may nevertheless fail to believe that he is guilty, even if I also judge that the eyewitness testimony is sufficiently plausible to establish his guilt. (1) allows that I may believe Jones to be innocent, even if I also judge that his alibi is not enough to establish Jones's innocence. Combining these possibilities, I end up in the situation of believing p even though I judge that a reasonable person would believe not-p.

Some writers take this sort of situation to be definitive of epistemic *akrasia*. I suggest that we employ a broader notion of 'epistemic *akrasia*', one on which either (1) or (3) would suffice on their own for epistemic *akrasia*: epistemic *akrasia* does not require that one believe 'in the teeth of the evidence'. In fact, I do think it possible to hold a belief in the teeth of the evidence in this sense (though, as we shall see, I don't think it possible to form such a belief freely and deliberately); I just don't think the possibility of epistemic *akrasia* depends on this being so.

1.2 The Judgement Condition: Transparency

Clearly, Pettit and Smith won't establish that the judgement condition can't be met by simply equating (1) and (3) with (2) and (4). But there are other lines of thought which lead in the same direction. Moran tells us that:

> If my beliefs just are what I take to be true, then when I am asked what I believe about something I will answer this by directing my attention to the world independent of my mind. When asked whether one believes that Oswald acted alone, one normally responds by attending to facts about Oswald etc. and does not scan the interior of one's own consciousness. This feature is sometimes called the 'transparency' of one's own thinking in that, for me, a question about my belief is 'transparent' to a question which is not about me but about the world, and is answered in the same way. Thus, I can answer a question about my belief by directing my attention to what is independently the case, and not by considering evidence, behavioural or otherwise, about anyone's state of mind.
>
> (Moran 1997: 146)

Moran uses this transparency feature to account for the special epistemic authority we all appear to have in the matter of what we ourselves believe. But perhaps this transparency feature is also what Pettit and Smith have in mind when they write that one's beliefs must occlude any doubts one might have about the rationality of those very beliefs.

How might one move from the transparency of belief to the impossibility of thinking your own beliefs to be unreasonable?[2] One line of thought goes as follows: the way to form a belief on a given topic is to work out what the truth is, and the way to do that is to look for evidence sufficient to establish the truth. But exactly the same method is used to work out whether a given belief would be reasonable. So the method you use to determine what is the case must deliver the same result as the method you use to discern what it would be reasonable for you to believe. How, then, can you end up with a belief which you yourself think to be unreasonable?[3]

---

[2] Moran himself does not seek to make this move. See (Moran 2001: 60-5).

[3] Someone convinced by this line of thought need not deny that we do sometimes attribute unreasonable beliefs to ourselves whilst trying to make sense of our behavior, etc. For example, my analyst might convince me that the best way of explaining various thoughts, feelings, and actions of mine is by supposing I believe that my father was cruel to me. Here, I accept the analyst's conclusion and so am prepared to *report* that I believe my father was cruel to me. But, as Moran observes, my acceptance of the analyst's conclusion does not make me inclined to *avow* this belief. In fact, when I recall my father, it seems to me that he was not cruel at all. It is hard to know exactly how to describe such cases, but I don't think we need to resolve this matter here, for we shouldn't assume that anyone who finds their own beliefs to be unreasonable can discover what they believe only by making inferences from their own behaviour or by relying on the testimony of an expert.

We can see that there must be something wrong with this line of thought by applying it to our emotions. Take anger. Suppose I am angry with my friend because he can't fix my computer. I am angry at his apparent incompetence. This anger is unreasonable and I know it. I have insufficient expertise to determine whether his failure to fix my computer shows anything about his competence. Now, how do I discover what I think of my friend's computing skills here? I don't need to visit an analyst or make inferences from observation of my own behaviour. Rather, I simply look at (or recall) the nonsense on the screen, my friend's ineffectual tappings, etc. and am infuriated by the picture of ineptitude he presents.

This example shows that we can't move from the premise that which attitude I take is determined by my attending to (or recalling) the world, to the conclusion that it is impossible for me to regard this attitude as unreasonable. I don't scan the contents of my consciousness to assess my friend's competence; rather I glare at the pathetic figure he cuts. In so doing I discern some evidence as to his competence—after all, he hasn't fixed my computer—but I put far too much weight on this meagre data and I know it. I am angered by his failure, but I am also convinced that there isn't enough evidence to justify this anger.

To decide what I think of my friend's performance, I attend to the relevant bit of the world, but to decide what I think of the normative quality of my anger, I attend to the strength of the evidence on which it is based. These are two different procedures which, in this case, deliver different results. I can't contemplate my friend's computing skills without recalling that exasperating experience, but, equally, I can't reflect on the probative force of the experience without thinking I am putting too much weight on it.

In describing the above example, I have remained neutral on the question of whether I *believe* my friend to be incompetent. Certainly, being angry that p involves representing p to oneself as being true, which is why evidence as to p is relevant to the rationality of my anger.[4] I used the verb 'think' to encompass both belief in p and the mode of representation of p which is involved in being angry that p, whatever that mode is. But whether or not 'thinking' that p implies believing that p, we have shown the argument from transparency is not, as it stands, cogent.

The transparency feature of belief can't be used to bolster Pettit's and Smith's position. Furthermore, it is worth pointing out that the argument from transparency would make practical *akrasia* seem no less problematic than theoretical

---

[4] For further discussion of these issues, see (Greenspan 1988).

akrasia. And this is a consequence which Pettit and Smith would not welcome. As they observe:

it is all too common an experience that your evaluative commitments lead you on one path but that you go nonetheless another; the spirit is willing but the flesh is weak. Agents are aware in such an experience of what the right requires them to desire and do, at least in the light of their evaluative commitments, despite the fact that their actual desires and actions do not conform to that requirement. (Pettit and Smith 1996: 449)

Here, the agent's 'evaluative commitments' are expressed in their judgements as to what they ought to desire and do. Pettit and Smith want to allow that an agent's evaluative commitments and their actions can come apart.

How does one decide whether to holiday in France or South Africa? One looks at features of the two destinations in an effort to determine which is the more desirable. Having decided in favour of France, one forms an intention to go there and makes the necessary preparations. In forming that intention, one's gaze is directed outwards, at the world. Now suppose one is instead asked what decision one *ought* to make about one's holiday: ought one to form the intention to go to France or the intention to go to South Africa? Again the desirability of France and South Africa seem to be the only things relevant to this decision. So how, we might wonder, could one end up in the position of judging that one's holiday intentions (and the behaviour which implements them) are unreasonable?

Yet such a thing is perfectly possible. Suppose there is a slight risk of civil unrest in South Africa but you judge this risk insufficient to outweigh South Africa's many obvious advantages over France. This judgement notwithstanding, you just can't bring yourself to decide to holiday in South Africa because of a morbid fear of social disorder and the random violence it breeds. Slightly ashamed, you play safe and plan on taking the French option while maintaining until the day you leave that South Africa would have been better. In the view of Pettit, Smith, and many others, there is nothing particularly paradoxical about the confession: 'South Africa was the right option but I couldn't persuade myself to take it'.[5]

---

[5] Here, it is important to distinguish practical *akrasia* (a clash between practical judgement on the one hand and intention or action on the other) from an unreasonable failure to implement an intention (Holton 2009: Chapter 4). Both phenomena are often called 'weakness of will', but they are quite distinct, and it is the former, not the latter, which concerns us. There is indeed something rather paradoxical about the sentence 'I intend to go to South Africa but I shan't', uttered by a person who has had all too much experience of their own backsliding. In what sense can this person seem to themselves to be set on going to South Africa if it also seems to them that they won't actually go? (Moran 1997: 148–50, 156–7). I shall not pursue this interesting thought here because it does not bear on the issue before us. You may have little doubt that you will end up in France on holiday. You may be as certain that you will execute that intention as you are of carrying out various other

To sum up, we have seen no reason to think that the judgement condition for epistemic *akrasia* cannot be satisfied. Doubts about the possibility of epistemic *akrasia* should focus on the control condition.

1.3 The Control Condition: Evidential *Akrasia*

Both belief and intention can fail to correspond to our judgement of what they ought to be. Yet *akrasia* involves more than such a failure. At the outset, I said that the *akratic* agent does freely and deliberately something that they judge they ought not to do. That is why *akrasia* constitutes a failure to exercise control over one's action rather than an absence of such control. Is there an analogue of control in the case of belief? Where your beliefs diverge from your views about what you ought to believe, can this constitute a failure to exercise a power of doxastic control which you nonetheless possess?

Many philosophers think it obvious that we don't control our beliefs, that we don't form beliefs freely and deliberately, whether continently or not. According to these philosophers, control is a matter of being subject to the will: belief is not subject to the will, therefore it is not under our control. In their view, practical *akrasia* occurs when our will diverges from our practical judgement, when we intentionally act in a way which we judge not to be best. Since there can be no analogue of this for belief, there is no such thing as epistemic *akrasia*.

I agree that belief is not subject to the will, but I deny that subjection to the will is the only notion of control available to us. Elsewhere, I have argued that we control our practical decisions even though they are not subject to the will (Owens 2000: 81–2 and 104–8). And this fact is crucial to the possibility of practical *akrasia* since one can be *akratic* in forming intentions as much as in carrying them out (as when I judged that I ought to decide to holiday in South Africa and yet formed the intention to holiday in France instead). Here I shall describe another model of control which clearly does apply to both actions and intentions. We shall then consider whether it can be applied to belief in such a way as to underwrite the possibility of epistemic *akrasia*.

Actions are our paradigm of the free and deliberate, and in action we pursue desirable goals. Action is purposive. Now, at any moment it is open to agents to pursue all sorts of goals, to set themselves a variety of ends. An agent deciding on

---

intentions which you think to be perfectly reasonable. After all, the political climate in South Africa is unlikely to change in the immediate future. Nevertheless, you might still think that a different decision would have been more reasonable, precisely because you think you shouldn't be putting so much weight on that single consideration.

what to do has to make a choice as to which of these many desirable objectives they should aim for: should the agent enjoy the taste of the chocolates now or should they ensure an indigestion-free future? Both courses of action have something to be said for them and the points in their favour may be registered in judgement. To resolve the matter, the agent must form a view about which course of action is best all things considered. Yet such an 'all things considered' judgement allows that rejected alternatives may have their value: if I judge that I ought not to eat these chocolates because of the indigestion they will cause and on this occasion I heed my judgement, I may still reasonably regret missing out on the indulgence which would have preceded the indigestion (Williams 1973: 170).

This suggests a model of control on which practical judgement (rather than the will) is the instrument by which we control our agency. Specifically, we exercise control over our agency by forming a view of the merits of the proposed course of action. I can judge that, all things considered, it would be best if I didn't eat the chocolates. But I also judge that the pleasure of eating the chocolates counts in favour of eating them: indigestion notwithstanding, there remains some reason to eat the chocolates. What happens in a case of *akratic* action is that I act on the latter judgement rather than the former.[6]

On this judgement-based model of control, it is clear why the *akratic* action is performed freely and deliberately. When I don't heed my judgement and do eat the chocolates, my action is still motivated by a goal whose value is acknowledged in judgement (though outweighed, in the eyes of judgement, by another incompatible objective).[7] In this respect, my *akratically* eating the chocolates is on a par with all the other purposive activities I engage in. The fact that this action conflicts with my 'all things considered' practical judgement need not render it unfree. And much the same can be said of an *akratic* intention.

To apply all this to yield an account of epistemic *akrasia*, two things are required.

First, believing must be purposive; belief must be aimed at a goal. It has been suggested that belief is indeed purposive, for a belief is necessarily adopted with the goal of having the belief only if it is true (e.g. Velleman 2000: 244–55). This

---

[6] There are many parallels between this judgement-based model of *akrasia* and that described in (Davidson 1980: 21–42). The main difference is that, for Davidson, the essence of *akrasia* lies in the divergence between the agent's 'all things considered' practical judgement and his 'all-out' or 'unconditional' judgement about what it would be best to do. Since Davidson allows that the latter 'all out' judgement is based on a conditional judgement about the (weaker) reasons in favour of that course of action, this difference may not be significant.

[7] For the purposes of my discussion of epistemic *akrasia*, it does not matter whether this is a sufficient condition for non-compulsive, free, and deliberate action; it might be only a necessary condition.

hypothesis is meant to explain why I can't believe some absurdity merely because I have been offered $1 million, unless that $1 million provides some (apparent) evidence for the truth of the belief. For, given the purpose which is constitutive of believing, I need evidence that the proposition to be believed is true before I can adopt the belief.

For believing to fall under the judgement-based model of control, it isn't enough that believing be purposive. A second condition must be satisfied: believing must, like action, serve a variety of goals. Hurley argues that belief fails this second condition: belief has truth as its only goal and so we haven't got the plurality of goals necessary to apply the judgement-based model of *akrasia*. I think a case can be made along these lines against the possibility of what I shall call 'evidential *akrasia*', but evidential *akrasia* is only one form of epistemic *akrasia*.

In the rest of the chapter, I shall proceed as follows. First, I shall distinguish evidential from epistemic *akrasia*. Then I shall construct an argument for the impossibility of evidential *akrasia* along the lines Hurley suggests. Finally, I shall give a rather different argument of my own against the possibility of epistemic *akrasia*, one which rejects some of the assumptions of the earlier argument against evidential *akrasia*.

Evidential *akrasia* is what I earlier called 'believing in the teeth of the evidence'; it occurs when I believe that p even though I judge that there is sufficient evidence to establish the truth of not-p, that is, to make a failure to believe not-p unreasonable.[8] Hurley argues that this sort of thing is impossible because:

> in the case of what should be done there may be conflict within an agent, there may be conflicting reasons competing for authority. But in the case of what should be believed, truth alone governs and it can't be divided against itself or harbour conflicts. It makes sense to suppose that something is, ultimately, good is some respects but not in others... in a way it does not even make sense to suppose that something is, ultimately, true in some respects but not in others.   (1993: 133)

By applying the judgement-based model of *akrasia* to belief, I think we can use Hurley's observation to construct an argument against the possibility of evidential *akrasia*.

First, note that simply believing p when there is no evidence for p (which I allow to be possible) does not in itself constitute *akratic* believing. Why not? If a belief that p is caused by the desire that p be true without the presence of any

---

[8] Note that Hurley defines 'evidential *akrasia*' rather differently, so she may or may not be interested in the possibility of evidential *akrasia* in my sense. Nevertheless, her argument inspired the one I consider here.

evidence for p, why isn't that a case of *akrasia*? The answer is that beliefs which are the product of such purely wishful thinking are not formed freely and deliberately: they are not produced by a judgement that there is some reason for the belief in question. Such a judgement is possible only when there is at least some (apparent) evidence in favour of the proposition to be believed, and here there is none. So on the judgement-based model of control, the control condition cannot here be satisfied.

Is there any difficulty about *akratically* believing a proposition with at least some (apparent) evidence in its favour? I suggest that this too is impossible on the judgement-based model of control. For such a belief to be formed freely and deliberately, the agent must be in a position to judge that a certain bit of evidence provides some reason for the belief, whilst also judging that this evidence is decisively outweighed by other evidence. But no one can freely and deliberately form the belief that p when they think the evidence sufficient to establish its falsehood because no one can judge that there is *any* reason to believe p in such a situation.

Scanlon objects that outweighed evidence can still *appear* to support the proposition in question. Even if I think the evidence shows John to be untrustworthy, his charming behaviour in my presence may strike me as a reason to believe that he is trustworthy and that appearance might be sufficient to motivate the belief that he is (Scanlon 1998: 36). But this does not bear on the point at issue unless John's charming behaviour really does constitute a reason in my eyes to think him honest, my overall judgement of the evidence notwithstanding. On a judgement-based model, my belief in him is adopted freely and deliberately only if I can judge that John's charming behaviour is a good, though overridden, reason to think him trustworthy. And can I really judge this whilst also judging that there is sufficient evidence to show that he isn't really trustworthy at all?

Several authors have argued that in judging e sufficient to establish p, one must also be judging that any evidence e' which appears to favour not-p is misleading, is not a good indication of how things are and therefore provides no reason for belief (Dretske 1971: 216–17 and Harman 1980: 168–70). I agree (Owens 2000: 142–5). If one thinks the evidence establishes p, one must think that apparently countervailing evidence can be explained on the hypothesis that p and so provides no grounds for thinking not-p to be true. Should one nevertheless be swayed by the appearance of that counterveiling evidence, one is being swayed by a consideration whose probative force one can't acknowledge in judgement. Therefore, this can't happen freely and deliberately.

To appreciate the plausibility of this view, recall Jones's trial. I am weighing the testimony of the eyewitnesses to the crime against that of the eyewitnesses to Jones's alibi. So long as I am still deliberating, both sorts of evidence appear to have some probative force, even if one seems to have more force than the other. But to think the evidence sufficient to establish Jones's guilt, I must also think it sufficient to establish that the alibi witnesses are either lying, or honestly mistaken, or that their testimony, though correct, doesn't really provide an alibi.... And to establish this is to establish that their testimony gives us no reason to believe in Jones's innocence.

As Williams urged, the practical case is altogether different. When refusing the chocolates, you judge that it would be best not to eat them whilst also judging that the pleasure of eating them still tells in favour of eating them. The pleasures of eating them is a real, not merely an apparent reason: that's why regret at having forgone the chocolates may, without irrationality, be combined with the judgement that you had to forgo them. Should you flout your judgement and eat, you are being moved by something you judge to be a genuine reason; therefore, this action may be performed freely and deliberately. Practical *akrasia* is perfectly possible.

Have we finally located the crucial difference between theoretical and practical reason, the difference which rule out epistemic *akrasia* as such? I think not. We may well have shown that a subject can't judge that they have any reason to believe the opposite of what they take the evidence to establish. Given the correctness of the judgement-based model of *akrasia*, this establishes that they can't freely and deliberately form a belief in the teeth of the evidence, even though they may find themselves believing in the teeth of the evidence. And since the subject can judge that they have some reason to do the opposite of what they judge they ought to do, there is a clear disanalogy here between belief and action.

But to establish that epistemic *akrasia* as such is impossible, we must do more than rule out evidential *akrasia*. We must demonstrate that a subject can't freely and deliberately believe something on evidence which they take to be insufficient, and that they can't freely and deliberately remain agnostic when they think they ought to believe. Neither of these situations need involve basing a belief on evidence which you judge to be decisively outweighed by other evidence and therefore neither of them is ruled out by the above argumentation. Someone who finds themselves convinced of Jones's innocence when they judge the evidence insufficient to establish Jones's innocence is a good candidate for epistemic *akrasia*, whether or not they also judge that the evidence demonstrates Jones's guilt.

1.4 The Control Condition: Epistemic *Akrasia*

In Section 1.3, we operated on the assumption that believing is purposive and that the purpose of belief is to have only true beliefs. We also assumed that a belief is formed freely and deliberately when it is formed because the subject judges that they have some reason to form it. So, to believe freely and deliberately, we must believe because we judge that this belief would serve the goal constitutive of believing, that it would be true. This seems to rule out not only free and deliberate believing based on no evidence at all but also free and deliberate believing in the teeth of the evidence. Yet, even granting these assumptions, we have yet to rule out all forms of epistemic *akrasia*.

This can be shown by applying the judgement-based model of *akrasia* to a phenomenon which certainly does aim at the truth, namely guessing. *Akratic* guessing is perfectly possible, even though *akratically* guessing in the teeth of the evidence is not. If believing were like guessing, similar forms of *akratic* belief would also be possible. But in fact they are not possible. This is because belief formation is not purposive in the way that guessing is.

Guessing aims at the truth. A guesser guesses with the purpose of guessing correctly: you can't guess that p (freely and deliberately) when you think that there is evidence sufficient to establish not-p. Someone who does this is not really intending to guess correctly and so is not really guessing. You can *say* 'I guess that I am eight feet tall' simply because you have been offered some reward for saying these words, but you can't sincerely guess that you are eight feet tall simply because you judge that making the guess is desirable (Chapter 2: Section 2.2).

Yet *akratic* guessing is easy to imagine. Suppose the following quiz. In a given round I have a minute to answer as many questions as I can. I am not expected to know the answer to many of these questions straight off, so the question master gives me a series of clues which are designed to help me guess the answer. I must decide how many clues I shall listen to before making a stab at it. Clearly, at any given point, I should weigh the likelihood of getting this particular question right if I wait for another clue against the likelihood of getting it right now and moving onto the next question, or at least of getting it wrong and perhaps moving onto a more tractable question. Here, even if I never guess regardless of, or in the teeth of, the evidence, the situation is rich in *akratic* possibility.

What makes room for *akrasia* is the fact that even though, in making an individual guess, I am trying to get that particular matter right, the correctness of this particular guess is not the only goal I am pursuing. My judgements about when to guess, about how many clues I ought to wait for before hazarding an opinion, will be informed by the need to win as many points as I can. Now, it might well happen that I judge that I ought to guess now because of this wider objective, yet I refrain from guessing because of my adherence to the goal of getting this particular guess right. Conversely, it may happen that I judge that I should wait for another clue and yet the wider objective of getting other guesses right moves me to make a guess now anyway.

On the judgement-based model of *akrasia*, we can see how these *akratic* guesses can be made freely and deliberately. Even though I judge that, all things considered, I ought to wait for another clue, I also judge that there is some reason to terminate consideration of this question and move onto the next. And if I do guess before I judge that I ought to because I judge that moving onto the next question has some value, I do so freely and deliberately. *Mutatis mutandis* for the case where I wait for the next clue even though I judge that I ought not to.

In Section 1.3, we assumed that each belief must be formed with the purpose of having a true belief. But even if someone who believes must do so with the purpose of only believing what is true, their belief will still be influenced by their pursuit of goals other than the truth of that particular belief. In particular, they will be moved by the need to have true beliefs on other matters. Indeed, anyone whose *sole* purpose in forming the belief that p were to form it only if p is true would have to insist on conclusive evidence for p. But, of course, people form beliefs on the basis of inconclusive evidence all the time because they want to have a view of the world and not just of the matter before them. So mustn't believing (like guessing) be motivated by a variety of other goals which guide and constrain our pursuit of the truth?

These considerations encourage us to look for an epistemic analogue of *akratic* guessing. If we can freely and deliberately guess when we think we ought not to because there is a clash between the goal of getting this individual guess right and the wider goals which make us guess at all, why can't we freely and deliberately believe when we think we ought not to? Suppose I feel the time has come to make up my mind about whether my old friend Jones is guilty: the evidence favours his guilt and I need to resolve the matter. The need for peace of mind, to be free to think about other things, etc. might motivate me to form a view on what I judge to be insufficient evidence. And if I form this belief because I judge that I need peace of mind, why doesn't that count as freely and deliberately forming that belief, and thus as an instance of epistemic *akrasia*?

Nothing said so far about belief rules this out. But, I take it, believing differs from guessing; the possibility of *akratic* guessing does not make epistemic *akrasia* possible and that is because guessing is purposive and believing is not. In querying the purposiveness of belief, I don't mean to deny that true beliefs are correct and false beliefs incorrect. There is more to purposiveness than that. Purposiveness implies that a subject forms beliefs in pursuance of a certain goal, that they control their beliefs by aiming them at that goal.

On this teleological model of belief formation, the believer makes judgements about how likely they are to achieve various goals if that belief is formed. The truth of this particular belief will be one such goal but, as we have seen, wider goals are needed if we are ever to make up our minds given that we could always wait for more evidence to come in on this particular matter. So if belief were purposive, the rational subject would be in a position to get themselves to believe that p simply by judging whether they have sufficient evidence for the truth of p, given their wider purposes in believing. That is what made it so natural to apply the judgement-based model of *akratic* action to belief formation, once we had ascribed such a purpose to each believer.

Needless to say, this is not what happens. A rational believer does not get themselves to believe that p by judging that they have sufficient evidence for the truth of p to form a view about it, given their purposes in forming that belief. Third parties might make judgements of this sort; they might think that given the constraints on our subject's deliberations and the relative importance of the issue before them, that subject has sufficient evidence to form a view about p. But if our subject finds themselves reluctant to form a belief on the basis of such evidence, rationality alone won't guarantee that they can get themselves to form a view simply by judging that the time has come to make up their mind (Owens 2000: 32–4).

In this, believing is very different from guessing. A rational guesser can overcome a reluctance to chance their arm by judging that they have heard enough clues to make a guess given their wider goals; and in so far as they are rational, they can resist the temptation to plump for a certain answer before they have sufficient evidence by reminding themselves of the need to get it right. In sum, the guesser can exercise control over their guesses by reflecting on how best to strike a balance between the goal of truth and the other goals their guessing serves; the believer cannot.

It should now be clear why the judgement-based model of *akrasia* cannot be applied to belief. We can't control our beliefs by making judgements about how well they achieve certain goals. We simply lack that sort of control over belief. So, at least on the model of control under discussion, there is no question of forming beliefs freely and deliberately, either in accordance with our judgement about what we should believe or against those judgements. Other models of control might be suggested which allow for *akrasia* in some other way, but until they are produced, we should conclude that epistemic *akrasia* is not possible.[9]

---

[9] I thank Robert Hopkins, Richard Moran, and especially Ward Jones for their help with this chapter.

2

Does Belief Have an Aim?

Why ascribe an aim to belief? Those who ascribe an aim to belief hope to explain at least three features of belief.[1]

First, beliefs are right or wrong, correct or incorrect. Call the basis of this form of normative assessment *the standard of correctness* governing belief. Many writers think we can explain this standard of correctness by supposing that belief has a goal which it is striving towards, or a function which it is seeking to discharge. A correct belief is one which attains its goal and discharges its function.

Second, beliefs are rational or irrational, justified or unjustified. These too are normative assessments—rational belief is good belief, irrational belief is bad belief—but they are, to this extent, independent of judgements of correctness: a correct belief can be irrational and an incorrect belief can be rational. Call the basis for this second form of doxastic assessment *epistemic norms*. Many writers have thought that the standard of correctness for belief and the epistemic norms governing the acquisition of belief are connected as follows: the standard of correctness for belief sets a goal and epistemic norms are instructions about how to reach that goal.[2]

Making this connection simplifies our account of the normative assessment of belief. It also removes a worry which many people have about epistemic norms. We are familiar with instrumental or teleological norms from the case of action. The source of the authority of these norms seems clear to many philosophers: they tell anyone who happens to have a goal how they should go about pursuing that goal. By contrast, epistemic norms appear *sui generis*. Why should believers be held to these norms? Where does their authority over us

---

[1] (Velleman 2000: 244–6) gives us a list of three 'ulterior reasons' for being interested in the aim of belief which mention explananda corresponding to each of the three just described, though he does not set out to defend the claim that ascribing an aim to belief can explain all three.

[2] For example (Foley 2001) recasts all epistemic norms as teleological norms.

come from? Call this *the problem of authority*. If believing involves having an aim and these norms can be seen as instructions about how to achieve that aim, the solution is obvious.[3]

Postulating a goal for belief explains not only the authority of epistemic norms but also their motivational efficacy. And, in the eyes of many philosophers, this is essential for epistemic norms to have any authority. In calling a belief rational or irrational, justified or unjustified, we are judging not just the belief but also the believer. A person who believes irrationally is, to that extent, an irrational person: a normative assessment of someone's belief is a normative assessment of *them*. Now (many writers think) this can be so only if that person is capable of being moved by epistemic norms, only if these norms can guide their acquisition of beliefs. So we must explain what is it about believers which ensures they have this capacity, that they can indeed be moved by their recognition of the authority of these epistemic norms. Call this *the problem of doxastic control*.

Suppose all believers have a characteristic goal. Then all believers will be motivated to pursue that goal. Since epistemic norms tell us how to achieve that goal, it is no surprise that all believers have (at least some) motivation to conform their beliefs to these norms. Anyone who lacked all such motivation wouldn't count as a believer precisely because they would lack a goal that all believers necessarily have (Railton 1997: 54–9, Velleman 2000: 182–8). Problem solved. In the last section of the chapter I shall discuss the nature and limits of doxastic control, but first let us examine the account of the authority of our epistemic norms that is on offer.

2.1 Truth as the Aim of Belief

What is the goal of belief? The most common suggestion is truth. On this hypothesis, when we intend to form a belief, we are intending to form a true belief. Believing is essentially purposive, so one is not really forming a belief unless one is intending to form a belief which is true, unless one has that purpose in believing.

Since the truth of a proposition is, in general, quite independent of whether it is believed by me (or anybody else), truth is well suited to be the standard of correctness for belief. But not every action governed by a standard of correctness

---

[3] Most of those who endorse this idea hold that belief has a constitutive aim: truth. But at least one such philosopher (Papineau 1999) denies that belief has any constitutive aim. Papineau holds that our 'most significant epistemic norms' can be explained on the weaker assumption that much of the time we do happen to value true belief.

is performed with the purpose of meeting that standard. For example, false assertions are incorrect assertions, but not every assertor has the goal of making an assertion only if it is true. Liars make genuine assertions with the aim of asserting something false, with a view to violating assertion's standard of correctness. If beliefs differ in this respect, if belief is necessarily adopted with the purpose of being true, that fact accounts for belief's standard of correctness and thereby discharges the first of our explanatory obligations.

What of the epistemic norms which govern the acquisition of belief? On the present model, believing propositions is somewhat like setting out to acquire stamps but only those which are Penny Blacks. We may try to explain the norms governing Penny Black collecting activity by seeing them as instructions about how to achieve that hobby's characteristic aim. Similarly, we might hope to explain the norms governing the acquisition of belief by referring to belief's characteristic aim (Railton 1994: 75). A believer is intending to get at the truth and the way to do that is to base one's belief on evidence. That is why the epistemic norms, the norms which determine the rationality of belief, are norms of evidence.

Again, none of this applies to assertion. A liar may be perfectly reasonable in asserting that p regardless of the evidence. Just because a state or an activity is governed by a standard of correctness it does not follow that we can explain what makes it reasonable to be in that state or to engage in that activity by reference to this standard. This follows only if we further suppose that the phenomenon in question is purposive and that its purpose is to meet its own standard of correctness.

The truth-aim theory sets out to explain the fact that reasonable belief requires evidence by ascribing a purpose to belief. How exactly does this explanation work? The two key notions invoked are 'truth' and 'aim at'. The account will avoid circularity only if both notions can be defined without reference to the need for evidence. Truth is relatively unproblematic: there are some who want to define truth in epistemic terms, but, for the purposes of this chapter, I shall assume that truth is a non-epistemic notion. What of 'aim at'?

Here we seem to encounter a problem. An agent with an aim has set themselves an end and is thereby obliged to take the means to that end. Call this *the means–ends principle*. The problem is that in order to apply this principle, the agent must already have some beliefs about what constitutes a means to that end. Where do these beliefs come from and what makes them reasonable? So long as we are concerned just with the rationality of agency, we can parry this question: agents conform to the means–ends principle by adopting the means they *believe* will secure their end and that policy makes them *practically* rational.

But shouldn't a theory of epistemic normativity tell us what makes all beliefs (including beliefs about means) reasonable?[4]

Where truth is the aim in question, the means are evidence. Now, principles of instrumental rationality alone are not going to explain why it is reasonable to believe that perception or memory or inductive inference are sources of evidence, are reliable guides to the truth. A person who has no idea how to go about seeking the truth will not be helped by our reminding him of the means–ends principle. But suppose we hold, on whatever grounds, that a sensory experience as of p is a reliable indicator of p's truth. We may still ask: what has the fact that someone has a sensory experience as of p got to do with whether he ought to believe that p? The truth-aim theory of epistemic normativity sets out to answer *this* question and to answer it when it is raised about any belief (including our beliefs about evidence). The truth-aim theory tries to explain the normative force of evidential norms, not what constitutes evidence.[5] How does it do this?

We are wondering whether a given subject ought to believe that p. He is aware of a certain amount of evidence for p, but what has this got to do with whether he ought to believe p? (Perhaps he has been offered a huge prize to believe not-p: doesn't that make it more reasonable for him to believe not-p, regardless of the evidence?) The truth-aim theory offers the following reply: this subject won't count as believing p at all unless he adopts this belief with the aim of believing it only if it is true; given that he has this end, the means–ends principle (whose authority we already acknowledge) tells us that his beliefs about the evidence for and against p are relevant to the rationality of belief in p (the prize notwithstanding).

It seems the hypothesis that belief aims at the truth can (without circularity) tell us why a believer should base his beliefs on (apparent) evidence rather than just on the prospect of financial reward. Has it thereby done all we should expect an instrumental theory of epistemic normativity to do? Not quite. There is a certain vagueness in the means–ends principle. In the practical case there is usually a choice of possible means, each of which would be reasonably effective in attaining the end. Some of these means will make the attainment of the end more likely than others, but more effective means may also be more costly, or more unpleasant, or be more likely to conflict with the attainment of other ends. Clearly, there is a balance to be struck here, and it is the job of instrumental

---

[4] A similar line of thought is deployed against internalism about epistemic rationality in (Goldman 1980). For a response from an internalist who wants to defend a really strong form of instrumentalism about epistemic norms, see (Foley 1993 and 2001).

[5] Velleman allows that believers may have extremely perverse views about what counts as evidence and yet still be aiming at truth. See (Velleman 2000: 113 n.34).

rationality to strike that balance. Should similar issues arise in the epistemic realm and given that believing is, as we are supposing, purposive, we shall expect the principles of instrumental rationality to resolve these issues for us.

Similar issues do indeed arise in the epistemic realm once we ask *how much* evidence is required for rational belief.[6] Rational belief is rarely based on conclusive evidence, and once inconclusive evidence is admitted, we must ask what level of inconclusive evidence suffices for rational belief. Requiring more evidence makes the attainment of the goal of truth more likely, but it may also impose costs and burdens which a rational person would wish to avoid. We shouldn't expect precise answers here—norms of evidence are doubtless vague—but the truth-aim theory should be able to account for such facts as the following: (i) reasonable belief in p requires some evidence in p's favour; (ii) reasonable belief requires more than a little evidence in p's favour; and (iii) reasonable belief in p requires that there be more evidence in favour of p than in favour of not-p.

To bring home the importance of specifying how much evidence is required for rational belief, consider how we should respond to the discovery of an apparent contradiction in our belief system. The answer might seem clear: since belief aims at truth and contradictory beliefs cannot all be true, we must remove the contradiction by abandoning (at least) one of the contradictory beliefs. But it is not quite that simple. Firstly, not all contradictions are obvious. If the discovery of this contradiction involved a complex proof, or some contentious principles of reasoning, there will be a question of how much further confirmation of the soundness of the proof we should require before accepting that there is indeed an inconsistency. Secondly, even when the contradiction is obvious, it need not be obvious what ought to be done about it. All we now know is that there is a falsehood among the inconsistent beliefs and there might be a substantial number of important beliefs in that inconsistent set. Should we abandon them all? Should we single out some member of the set to preserve consistency, and if so, which one? Clearly, the relative strength of the evidence in favour of individual beliefs, taken together with our need to have beliefs about a range of matters (a non-evidential consideration), should determine the answer. If there is no belief with conspicuously weak support, it may be reasonable to hang onto the inconsistent set for the time being rather than dropping one of its members (Foley 1993: 162–73), (Harman 1999: 19).

---

[6] The phrase 'how much' refers to the probative force of the evidence. In what follows I shall speak indifferently of the *quality* and the *quantity* of available evidence; both phrases should be taken to denote probative force.

What is in question throughout this chapter is the rationality of belief, *not* the rationality of the activities of evidence-gathering, or of evidence-storage and retrieval, or of thinking about the value of evidence before you. I shall call these activities *inquiry*. Inquiry often precedes belief formation and is motivated by all sorts of non-evidential considerations: only if I am interested in whether OJ is guilty will I go to the trouble of reading the newspapers, thinking about the evidence reported, trying to memorize it, and so forth. This chapter focuses on the role that non-evidential considerations play *after* we have ensured (perhaps by means of inquiry) that a certain quantity of evidence on the matter is before us. Suppose the evidence favours OJ's guilt. Still, the question remains: does it favour OJ's guilt enough to make it reasonable for me to make up my mind on the matter and form the belief that OJ is guilty? I maintain that this question cannot be answered without invoking non-evidential considerations (the importance of the issue, etc.).[7] And this question is not equivalent to the question: should I go on gathering evidence or thinking about OJ's guilt? There are all sorts of reasons why I might stop inquiring into OJ's guilt without forming a belief (I got bored) or continue my inquiry despite having formed a belief (I need to convince someone else). The same points apply where the issue is whether I ought to abandon (rather than form) a belief, as in the example of discovering a contradiction.[8]

If we were out to explain the rationality of inquiry, we could simply observe that such inquiry is motivated by the desire for a true belief on a certain matter, where the satisfaction of this desire is constrained in the usual way by other demands. But, I take it, the truth-aim hypothesis is *not* put forward as part of a theory of the rationality of inquiry but rather as an account of the rationality of belief formation (and abandonment). That is a quite different task and the prospects of success are much more uncertain.

I have sketched how the truth-aim hypothesis *might* explain both belief's standard of correctness and what makes belief reasonable. In the next section, I shall assess the solution to the problem of authority we have just been offered, leaving the problem of doxastic control until later. My conclusion will be that the explanatory strategy behind it is perfectly sound: if believing were purposive, we could explain the above features of belief by reference to belief's purpose. We can see this by applying the strategy to something which does aim at the truth, which

---

[7] Several authors have noted that practical considerations help to determine how much evidence is required for rational belief, e.g. (Nozick 1993: Chapter 3) and (Wedgwood 2002: 273–8).

[8] For more on the distinction between the rationality of inquiry and the rationality of belief, see (Owens 2000: 18–20, 24–34, and 85–7).

really is purposive in just the way we supposed believing to be: *guessing*. Yet the obvious differences between believing and guessing suggest that belief does not aim at the truth in the sense required by our explanatory project.

2.2 Believing and Guessing: Rationality

Before going any further, we must formulate the truth-aim hypothesis under discussion a little more precisely:

ø-ing that p aims at the truth if and only if someone who øs that p does so with the purpose of ø-ing that p only if p is true.[9]

Three points are worth noting. First, the aim of truth is stated negatively as the purpose of avoiding error; it imposes no obligation on believers to seek out all, or even some truths. Since we are trying to find an aim which is common to all believers, negativity is a must. Second, the aim applies to beliefs taken individually; one can't pursue truth in this sense by adopting a particular belief, regardless of whether one has reason to think it true, provided its adoption is likely to lead to the adoption of many more true beliefs.[10]

Thirdly, an aim may be pursued more or less well. Someone who bases a belief on wholly inadequate evidence still counts as believing provided they are intending to get at the truth. It may be hard to draw the line between an irrational believer who is aiming at the truth, albeit ineptly, and someone who isn't really

---

[9] This is close to formulations offered by (Sosa 2001: 52), (Humberstone 1992: 73), and (Velleman 2000: 251), although it differs markedly from Velleman's in one respect: it attributes the aim in question to the subject of the belief. Velleman argues that believing is purposive even if the aim of belief is not an aim adopted by the subject of the belief (Velleman 2000: 184–8, 252–3). At least sometimes, he suggests, it is a belief-forming subsystem in the subject, rather than the subject himself, which pursues the aim of belief. If this were so, it would be hard to see why the normative standing of the belief-forming subsystem should have any implications for the normative standing of the subject. How can the norms of rational belief formation have any authority over me, how can violation of them by my beliefs make *me* irrational, unless I share the aims of the subsystem which give those norms their authority?

Velleman tells us that the subject might choose to endorse or associate himself with the doings of his belief-forming subsystem, in which case he will get egg on his face should the system misbehave (Velleman 2000: 252–3). But such endorsements are contingent and even voluntary. That's not how it is between me and my beliefs. If I have an irrational belief, I am (to that extent) irrational regardless of the endorsements I have made or withheld. In so far as I have beliefs, I am always subject to the authority of epistemic norms; that is the fact we have to explain.

[10] Railton observes that a belief does not become reasonable simply because adopting that belief would have the effect of making you acquire lots of other true beliefs, and he concludes from this that 'if belief is to be said to "aim at" truth, then this would appear not to be "aiming at" in the familiar, teleological sense in which a goal is regulative of action' (1994: 74). But all that really follows from this observation alone is that each belief must be adopted with the aim of adopting that particular belief only if it is true.

intending to get at the truth and so doesn't count as forming beliefs, whether rationally or irrationally. But there is a distinction here, as there is between a very poor shot and someone who isn't aiming at the target at all.

Guessing aims at the truth in the sense just defined. Clearly, truth is the standard of correctness for a guess and, I maintain, what explains this is the fact that a guesser intends to guess truly. The aim of a guess is to get it right: a successful guess is a true guess and a false guess is a failure as a guess. Someone who does not intend to guess truly is not really guessing.

In this respect, guessing is unlike, for instance, imagining. To imagine that I have been elected president is to imagine that it is true that I have been elected president, but imagining does not aim at truth as guessing does. The act of imagining may be a complete success in that it is extremely gratifying or deeply revealing or merely distracting: truth is not required for imaginative success. Similarly for supposition: I may suppose or hypothesize that an extension is added to my house as an aid to working out how desirable this building would be. It is no part of my purpose in supposing that p that I should suppose p only if it is true, though, of course, I suppose p to be true and do so in order to learn something (Railton 1994: 74, Velleman 2000: 112–14, 183, 250–2). But we guess with the purpose of making a guess which is true.[11]

Both believing and guessing satisfy the above definition of 'aiming at the truth'. A believer satisfies a further condition; in believing that p he actually believes that the aim of belief has been achieved, for he believes that p is true. By contrast, a guesser merely guesses that the aim of guessing has been achieved (and a Penny Black collector merely thinks it sufficiently likely that he has got a Penny Black).[12] Someone might suggest that we redefine 'aiming at truth' so as to exclude guessing etc. as follows:

ø-ing that p aims at the truth if and only if someone who øs that p does so with the purpose of ø-ing that p only if (p is true and they believe this).

But such a restriction would be no better motivated than one which excluded belief from the set of states which aim at the truth by instead requiring that the subject merely guess p to be true. Better take the generic notion of aiming at the

---

[11] Railton says that 'It is *distinctive* and constitutive of belief not only that it represents its content as true but that it takes itself to be correct only if that particular content really is true' (my italics) (Railton 1994: 74). If a psychological state of the sort I take guessing to be is even possible then Railton is wrong about this. (Williamson 2000: 244) makes an analogous observation about assertion and conjecture.

[12] (Williams 1978: 39) notes this disanalogy between seeking true beliefs and collecting pre-historic flints.

truth and see what work it can do for us in accounting for the normative character of both believing and guessing.

Guessing's standard of correctness is embodied in a purpose which any guesser must have. This should lead us to expect that guessing is governed by evidential norms. Since we guess with the purpose of guessing correctly and evidence is an indication that the guess will be correct (i.e. true), a reasonable guess should be based on the available evidence. Indeed it is so. I am asked to guess approximately how many people voted in the last U.S. presidential election and I plump for 98 per cent. That is a silly guess, given what I know about turnout at previous elections. And it remains silly even if I happen to be right. I also guess that it will rain at some point during the next two weeks within the boundaries of Manchester city centre. That is a reasonable guess, one well grounded in my extensive experience of Manchester city centre. And it remains a good guess even if it turns out to be wrong.

Can we say anything more about the quality of evidence required to make a guess reasonable? If what I said in Section 2.1 is correct, the truth-aim hypothesis shouldn't just tell us that rational guesses are somehow based on evidence; it should also give us some way of determining how much evidence is required for rational guessing. Clearly this will be a function of two factors: first the aim of making only correct guesses which any guesser must have and second the subject's other desires and purposes. Not getting it wrong may be the only purpose constitutive of guessing, but if that were the guesser's only purpose, he could achieve it simply by making no guess at all. We need to integrate error-avoidance with other aims which lead the guesser to guess and thus determine when the guesser has sufficient evidence to hazard a guess.

Let's take an example. Suppose the quiz master asks me whether the earth's population is greater than 7 billion. There is $1 million at stake. I wouldn't claim to know the answer, but no answer means no money. Obviously, I ought to make a guess. So I plump for the answer 'yes'. My guess is a sensible one, even though I have no evidence on the matter, because if I don't guess at all I am certain to lose the money. In fact, a guess would be sensible even if I had to get the population of the world to within ten million. Here, I'm pretty unlikely to be right, but, so far as my evidence goes, any guess I make is as good as any other, and I have to make some guess to win.

Alternatively, suppose that, to win, I must answer a series of questions in a short time. After being asked a question, I am given a series of clues as to the answer. Here, it might be sensible for me to wait until the evidence tips decisively in favour of a particular answer before making a guess (though at some point I will want to get this question out of the way and move onto the next). Clearly, such variations in the quality of evidence required for a reasonable guess are due to variations in the purposes/situation of different guessers.

This example suggests that we treat the rationality of guessing just as we would the rationality of any other action: guessing that p is reasonable when aiming at the truth by means of a guess that p would maximize expected utility. That requirement integrates the purpose constitutive of guessing with the subject's wider purposes in a familiar and well understood fashion. On this view of guessing, not every expected-utility-maximizing utterance of 'I guess' will count as a guess ('I guess' is not a performative).[13] For example, a subject offered a large amount of money simply to utter the words 'I guess that I am seven feet tall' won't count as guessing that he is seven feet tall unless he utters these words with the purpose of uttering them only if he is seven feet tall. Nevertheless, whether it is reasonable to do something with the truth aim and how it is reasonable to go about doing it will be determined by expected utility.

Must reasonable guesses satisfy any of the three evidential norms we formulated for belief? The quiz example establishes that neither (i) nor (ii) apply. What of (iii)? If the evidence favours p over not-p, would guessing not-p always be unreasonable? I'm not sure. Suppose I must choose between p or not-p and the evidence favours p, but I am also told that I will get a much greater reward if I correctly guess not-p than I will if I correctly guess p. Given that, would it be reasonable for me to guess not-p?[14] It might be reasonable for me to *say* 'I guess not-p'. But in saying this, am I sincerely guessing that not-p? Am I really trying to win the prize by stating the truth? Or am I simply saying whatever will maximize my expected winnings?

One line would be that one is not really aiming at the truth unless one follows the (apparent) balance of evidence, so the above statement could not be an expression of a reasonable guess. But someone else might take the view that one can be aiming at the truth in guessing that not-p provided one does not have evidence sufficient to *establish* that p (i.e. sufficient to make it unreasonable to fail to believe p). If so, 'I guess that not-p' might well express a sincere attempt to get at the truth—the only way of winning—as 'I guess that I am seven feet tall' does not. Whatever view we take on this matter, the evidential norms governing guessing clearly differ from those governing belief.

In the quiz situation, with the $1m on offer (and no clues forthcoming) I can make a perfectly reasonable guess as to the exact population of the world, but

---

[13] (Cohen 1974: 194) argues that the English word 'guess' is in fact ambiguous, having both a speech-act and a mental-act sense. He may well be right about this.
[14] I am grateful to Mark Kaplan for this example.

I am in no position to form a reasonable belief about whether there are at least 7 billion people on the evidence before me. Even less can I reasonably believe not-p rather than p because the rewards for correctly believing not-p are greater than those for correctly believing p. However great an incentive I am given for forming a view about whether p, reasonable belief requires (at least) that I have more evidence in p's favour than against it. It looks as if our epistemic norms are much more demanding when it comes to determining the means which ought to be taken in pursuing the goal of truth. Can we explain this difference between believing and guessing by way of instrumental reasoning, on the hypothesis that belief aims at the truth?[15]

Some might think that believing is unlike guessing in that the *only* purpose with which the belief that p is formed (and not just the only purpose *essential* to believing) is the purpose of believing that p only if p is true. If so, there would be no question of having to integrate the goal of getting this particular matter right with other goals. Yet this can't be correct. Were avoiding error one's only objective in forming any particular belief, one could very easily achieve that objective simply by forming no beliefs at all. Reasonable people form beliefs and they do so on the basis of much less than conclusive evidence. This practice makes sense, on the purposive model of belief, only if believers have some objective in forming beliefs other than the mere avoidance of false beliefs. Can we adapt our model of guessing rationality to the case of belief in an effort to explain how the rational believer integrates the aim of avoiding error with his other goals whilst also accommodating the obvious differences between believing and guessing?

One strategy would be to suppose that the believer attaches a higher value to avoiding error than the guesser. Since the believer's interest in the goal of truth is stronger than the guesser's, it will be more weighty relative to the agent's other goals and so more trouble will be taken to get things right. On this account, the $1 million prize must be enough to make the agent risk an erroneous guess but not a false belief. This is totally implausible. No sane person would want to avoid erroneous belief on this demographic issue more than they want a 50 per cent (or even a 0.1 per cent) chance of $1 million; yet the rational believer will still remain agnostic. Clearly, we can't determine what beliefs it would be reasonable for someone to form by weighing the believer's interest in truth against the other interests which might be served by the formation of a belief.[16]

---

[15] (Nozick 1993: 85–100) considers a quasi-instrumental model of belief rationality which makes believing look rather like guessing and he notes some difficulties for it.

[16] (Williamson 2000: 244–9) presents a different but related argument for the conclusion that we can't explain the amount of evidence required for assertion by supposing that assertion aims at the truth.

Another strategy would be to limit the sorts of goals which are relevant to the rationality of belief. So we might explain the quality of evidence required for reasonable belief by postulating a number of specifically epistemic goals—error avoidance, comprehensiveness, and, perhaps, simplicity—and assigning weights to them. For example, most believers are prepared to run a substantial risk of error in order to avoid a widespread agnosticism. These epistemic goals could then be integrated with one another by seeking to maximize the expected *epistemic* utility of one's beliefs on given evidence, thus determining what it was reasonable to believe on that evidence.[17]

I doubt whether there is any way of isolating a purely epistemic set of goals. Think of all the factors which go to determine just how curious one is, which fix just how important it is to have a (correct) view on a certain matter. They will determine how much evidence one requires to make up one's mind. It is not the sheer comprehensiveness of a belief system (however that is to be measured) which makes it worthy of belief but rather the significance of the topics it is informing you about. Clearly, practical concerns are critical here and so we are confronted once more by the difficulty of using instrumental norms to integrate these 'non-epistemic' concerns with the goal of error-avoidance.[18]

But even if we could specify some set of distinctively epistemic goals which underlay our epistemic norms, this won't help us with the broader explanatory project. By insisting that our other 'non-epistemic' goals are simply irrelevant to the rationality of belief we deepen the very crisis of normative authority which ascribing a goal to belief was meant to resolve. Why should we be held to norms which take no account of many of the things which matter most to us? And how, in any case, can we be moved by such norms?[19]

That completes my case against the truth-aim theorist's account of the rationality of belief. Someone convinced by everything said so far may still wonder whether we are asking too much of the truth-aim theory. Might that theory provide a perfectly satisfying explanation of why evidence is relevant to the rationality of belief without also telling us how much evidence is required to

---

[17] For a good discussion of the formal aspects of epistemic utility theory, see (Kaplan 1981).

[18] Would things be any easier if we ascribed the aim to a belief-forming subsystem, rather than to the believer himself? (cf. note 9) I can't see how. The system would need to be sensitive to a whole range of non-evidential considerations for it to produce reasonable beliefs, and the same problem of integration would arise.

[19] Where a subject's wider purposes would be served by having an irrational belief, it might be rational for them to induce that belief. But what they are doing here is performing an action which, though it may be a rational action, has the effect of making them irrational. And an irrational subject is someone who is violating norms which have some rational authority over them. Our problem is to explain that authority.

make a given belief reasonable? Certainly, the theory's advocates have not felt any pressure to undertake the latter task. This may be because they overlooked the fact that belief isn't the only thing which aims at the truth in their sense. But once this fact is acknowledged, can't the truth-aim theorist offer to explain the similarities between believing and guessing—their shared correctness condition and the relevance of evidence—without pretending to account for their differences? I think not.

The truth-aim theory seeks to explain both the correctness condition of belief and the role of evidence in justifying belief by ascribing a *purpose* to every believer. If this talk of purpose is to be more than an empty metaphor, the notion of purpose invoked must be one that does explanatory work for us outside the domain of epistemic norms. And, surely, it is our ordinary notion of a purpose which the truth-aim theorist means to be employing. Now, such purposes interact with each other in certain familiar ways, so if a subject really does form a belief with the purpose of forming it only if it is true, his pursuit of that goal should be constrained by his other goals and objectives in (something like) the usual fashion. That is just what happens in the case of guessing, which is why we are fully justified in treating guessing as a purposive activity. But we failed in our attempts to treat the 'purpose' allegedly shared by all believers as something which interacts with their other objectives in familiar ways. So what is left of the idea that they share a purpose? The truth-aim theorist can't evade this problem simply by declining to explain the differences between believing and guessing, since what these differences suggest is that our notion of a purpose does not apply to belief at all.

2.3 Believing and Guessing: Control

Until now I have concentrated my attention on attempts to explain the authority of our epistemic norms. But even if ascribing an aim to belief cannot help with that question, an aim might still be needed to explain certain facts about how belief is motivated, facts which can't be accounted for simply by noting either belief's standard of correctness or the content of our epistemic norms. Perhaps the truth-aim hypothesis can help to explain the nature and limits of doxastic control.

It is possible to violate, deliberately and self-consciously, many of the norms which govern our mental life. But philosophers who hold that belief aims at the truth have inferred from this that a believer can't self-consciously disregard indications of the truth (i.e. evidence) in forming a belief. Williams writes that 'If in full consciousness I could will to acquire a belief irrespective of its truth, it is unclear that before the event I could seriously think of it as a belief i.e. as something purporting to represent the truth' (1973: 148). If a believer must form a belief with the purpose of believing something true, he cannot 'in full consciousness' decide to believe that he is a foot taller than he is on the grounds that it would be very desirable for him to have this belief (as a boost to his confidence) (Velleman 2000: 118).

For Williams's line of reasoning to have any force, 'aim at truth' must mean more than 'have truth as your standard of correctness'. Assertion aims at truth in that sense and yet it would be superstitious to imagine that this somehow deprived people of the ability to make groundless assertions. What might deprive people of the ability to believe whatever they like, in full consciousness of what they are doing, is the fact that belief's standard of correctness is embodied in the very purpose of the belief-former. That restricts the grounds on which he can form a belief in a perfectly non-magical way.

To see how this works, consider the action of shooting at a goal. No one can shoot at a goal unless they do so with the purpose of hitting the goal. True, they can perform many of the bodily movements which would be involved in shooting without having that purpose, but these movements will not then constitute shooting at the goal. Now suppose someone comes along and offers me the usual $1 million if I perform the action of shooting at the goal but in a rather unusual way, by deliberately throwing my ball into the stands. I just can't comply with such a request, however much money is on offer. To comply with it I would have to cease intending to reach the goal and then I would no longer be shooting at it.[20]

Something like this is true of guessing. I don't know my height though I know what sort of height I'm likely to be. Say that someone offers to give me $1 million provided I guess that I am exactly seven feet tall. What does it matter to me whether I make this guess or not? The money is more than adequate compensation. I tell myself to go ahead and guess, but I can't do it. The explanation is obvious: to guess I must make some attempt to get at the truth and, given what I know, I could not make such an attempt by guessing that I was exactly seven feet tall.[21]

---

[20] Compare Pink's discussion of what he calls 'special-purpose agency' (Pink 1996: 248–52).

[21] Might guessing what you know to be false be impossible not because guessing aims at the truth but rather because guessing requires ignorance of the truth? As Alexander Bird pointed out, it is no easier for me to *guess* that I am more than six inches tall than it is for me to guess that I am more than seven feet tall. This is certainly the right thing to say about states like doubting or wondering. The correct explanation of why we can't doubt that, or wonder whether, p where we know p is false is that doubting or wondering requires ignorance of p's truth. Neither state aims at the truth in the sense I defined. But consider fantasizing that p. Here too, we can't fantasize that p when we know p to be true, but the reason isn't that we must be ignorant of whether p is true; on the contrary, we can

Of course, I could insincerely hazard an opinion in an effort to give the impression that I had made the required guess. Alternatively, I could take steps to make myself guess, regardless of the evidence, by means of drugs or hypnosis, etc. But I can't get myself to make this guess in the way I can get myself to make most guesses, simply by reflecting on the desirability of so doing. To make myself hazard such an absurd opinion, I need to go in for a bit of self-manipulation. I encounter no such obstacles to imagining or supposing that I am seven feet tall: I can imagine this 'at will' simply because imagining it seems desirable. So the fact that guesses aim at the truth limits our ability to guess at will.

Are there similar limits on how belief can be motivated? And can we explain these limits only by supposing that belief aims at truth in just the sense in which guessing does? Let's grant that it is indeed impossible to acquire a belief simply by reflecting on how desirable it would be to have that belief and regardless of the evidence for it. That gives us no grounds for thinking that belief is purposive unless we can also get ourselves to form beliefs, as we can get ourselves to make guesses, by reflecting on what the best way to achieve the aim of belief would be. The fact that belief aims at the truth will not explain why knowingly forming certain absurd beliefs is impossible unless our consciousness of the aim of belief can also explain how we get ourselves to form more normal beliefs.

The guesser aims to get it right. He plumps for an answer when he thinks the answer sufficiently likely to be correct, sufficiently likely given his other purposes in making the guess. If he is making the guess—aiming to get the answer right— with the further purpose of winning the quiz then all sorts of considerations, both evidential and non-evidential, will be relevant to whether his guess is reasonable. It is by reflecting on these factors before making a guess that he exercises control over his guessing. By contrast, a believer doesn't shoot at truth once he decides that it is sufficiently likely he'll get it, given his wider purposes in believing.

That is not because a believer has only one purpose: to avoid error. As already noted, this objective could be achieved easily enough by believing nothing at all, by declining to shoot at the target. Believers with limited cognitive resources wish to form a view on a large number of matters, and so the formation of a particular belief will be reasonable only if it is part of a general policy of belief

---

fantasize that p when we know p to be false. And this is because of the distinctive aim of fantasy: it aims to provide pleasure by entertaining thoughts which we don't know to be true, or something like that.

I would argue that we should look to guessing's aim in order to explain why we can't guess something we know to be true. I suggest that we can't guess something we know to be true because guessing aims at truths of which we are ignorant. And that also explains why we can't guess something we know to be false. So the orientation which guessing has towards truth in virtue of its aim is indeed essential to any account of the limits on what you can guess.

formation which is itself reasonable.[22] Such policy must be sensitive to various non-evidential considerations. As James points out, believers must strike a balance between the agonies of agnosticism and the risks of error; evidence alone cannot strike this balance for them (James 1956: 17–19).

If believing were purposive, this sensitivity to non-evidential considerations would involve integrating the goal of having this belief only if it is true with the subject's wider purposes in forming beliefs. And this is something agents do all the time. But this sensitivity to non-evidential reasons for belief is not the sort of thing which is registered efficaciously in the subject's deliberations about what he ought to believe. Our subject can't get himself to believe by reflecting that he has sufficient evidence to form a belief, given his wider purposes in forming beliefs. When we bystanders consider whether it is reasonable for our subject to form a belief on this matter, we will attend to the importance of the issue, the limited cognitive resources which he has to devote to it and so forth. But reflection on these matters will not move the believer himself to belief, as it moves him to guess (Owens 2000: Chapter 2). Guessing can be controlled by reflection on how best to achieve an aim; believing cannot.[23]

Chasing Penny Blacks is a goal-directed activity. You're out to acquire Penny Blacks: you don't want to be taken in by fakes, but nor do you want to miss out on the genuine Penny Blacks which cross your path. You must strike a balance between the risk of being duped and the risk of ending up with no Penny Blacks at all. Given that, when offered a stamp you'll run some checks and ask for some documentation, but at some point you will be satisfied, you will have sufficient evidence that it is a Penny Black and you'll buy. What we do about an individual stamp will be constrained not just by the goal of buying that stamp only if it is a Penny Black but also by the more general goal of which this is a subgoal—buying Penny Blacks as such.

From the outside, belief formation seems much the same. You are out to acquire true beliefs. You don't want to be taken in by falsehood but nor do

---

[22] Velleman maintains that 'one's acceptance of a proposition can amount to a belief without being part of any global epistemological project of accumulating true beliefs. What distinguishes believing a proposition from imagining or supposing it is a more narrow and immediate aim—the aim of getting the truth value of that particular proposition right, by regarding the proposition as true only if it really is' (Velleman 2000: 252). One can agree with Velleman that this is the sole purpose essential to the acquisition of a particular belief, the only purpose one must have to qualify as a believer in p, whilst also insisting that all beliefs must be acquired with some other purposes in mind, purposes which help to determine whether the belief in question is reasonable.

[23] Of course, I don't deny that our actions can affect our beliefs, but, as I have argued elsewhere, such indirect control over belief does not help us to understand the motivational role of epistemic norms (Owens 2000: 82–4).

you want to miss out on truths. You must strike a balance between the risk of error and the costs of agnosticism. When evidence suggests that a proposition is true, you may run some checks and wait for a bit more confirmation, but at some point you are satisfied, you have sufficient evidence that the belief is true and you'll believe. Isn't that process under your control no less than stamp collecting?

From the inside, the comparison between believing and Penny Black collecting feels much less apt. I can get myself to purchase a stamp by telling myself that I have considered the matter quite long enough and, if I am ever to purchase another stamp, I must now make a decision about whether to buy on the basis of the evidence before me. In the rational Penny Black collector, the subject's pursuit of the goal of acquiring this stamp only if it is a Penny Black is regulated by the subject's reflections on how this goal fits with his wider objectives. But I can't get myself to form a *belief* by rehearsing the same train of thought, by reflecting on some broader aims, epistemic or non-epistemic. Or, at least, my rationality alone does not guarantee that such reflections will have any influence on my beliefs.

In respect of control, guessing is much more like imagining or supposing than believing. Guessing is a mental action executed for a purpose in a way that believing is not. A guess aims at the truth; the guesser has the truth as his goal and can guide his guess towards the truth, taking into consideration his other goals and purposes. This whole process is, in a very obvious sense, an exercise of control. If what I have said about belief formation is correct, nothing like that is true of belief. Belief has a standard of correctness, but this standard of correctness does not set a goal towards which the subject can direct his beliefs by asking himself whether he is sufficiently likely to have hit it.

2.4 Conclusion

Truth may be belief's standard of correctness, but, I have argued, there is little explanatory point in describing truth as the *aim* or the *goal* of belief. Those who employ these locutions mean them to do real explanatory work: 'To say that belief aims at the truth is not simply to re-express the norm stipulating that a belief must be true in order to be correct; rather, it is to point out a fact about belief that generates this norm for its correctness' (Velleman 2000: 16–17). Belief's aim is meant to underwrite that norm, to explain not just belief's standard of correctness but also what makes our beliefs reasonable or unreasonable and how we go about controlling our beliefs. I have argued that the truth-aim hypothesis cannot fulfil its early promise: it accounts for neither the authority nor the motivational efficacy of our evidential norms. I suspect that ascribing the truth aim to belief is indeed just 'to re-express the norm stipulating that a belief must be true in order to be correct'.

In considering whether belief has an aim, I have examined only the most common view: the truth-aim hypothesis. Are there alternatives? To have a hope of explaining the norms of correctness and rationality governing belief, the aim in question must entail truth, and I can think of only one truth-entailing aim other than truth itself, namely knowledge. Some authors (including myself in Owens 2000: 35) have recently proposed that belief aims at knowledge. Since a guesser aims at truth and not knowledge, this might explain why reasonable belief requires more evidence than a reasonable guess: the goal of a belief is simply more demanding than that of a guess. Do the arguments of this chapter work only against the truth-aim hypothesis?

I have no more objection to the idea that knowledge sets the standard of correctness for belief than I have to the view that truth sets this standard, but neither hypothesis can do much explanatory work. Plausible accounts of what it is to know that p insist that the possession of evidence for p, or at least the absence of evidence against p, is a necessary condition for knowledge of p; this is because it is a necessary condition for reasonable belief in p and one can't know that p unless one reasonably believes p. This raises the question: what level of positive evidence is required for reasonable belief in p, or else what level of countervailing evidence is required to undermine reasonable belief in p? It is hard to see how this question can be answered, rather than begged, simply by ascribing a knowledge-aim to belief.[24]

What of the two problems which we hoped to solve by attributing an aim to belief? Are these to fester unsolved? We might instead query the assumptions which generated those problems. Is the authority of instrumental norms really any more secure than that of non-instrumental norms? Can obedience to norms be understood only on the model of an agent pursuing some goal which he finds valuable? Why not allow that different mental states—beliefs, desires, emotions, intentions, etc.—are governed by different norms, only some of which take a teleological form? Perhaps the authority and motivational efficacy of these norms looks problematic only once we try to force them into the mould of the teleological norms which govern action.[25]

---

[24] For further discussion of the truth aim and the knowledge aim see (Williams 1978: 38–45), (Williamson 2000: 208), and (Wedgwood 2002: 289–91).

[25] Many thanks to Jonathan Adler, Alexander Bird, Paul Horwich, Barry Loewer, Peter Milne, Mark Kaplan, and, especially, Paul Noordhof for comments on earlier drafts of this chapter.

3

Deliberation and the First Person

Having renounced his inherited convictions in the *First Meditation* and thereby taken control of his cognition, Descartes sets himself the task of working out what to believe and (more in the *Discourse* than the *Meditations*) what to do. In Descartes' view, there is a form of thinking by which each of us can determine both when we are convinced and how we are to act. The availability of this form of cognitive self-control is what makes Descartes a rational being, directly responsible for what he believes or decides to do.

A crucial feature of this form of cognitive self-control is that it involves the subject thinking of themselves *as* employing that very form of self-control. For Descartes, the meditator must conceive of himself as the agent of his own meditation. In the *Second Meditation*, Descartes famously describes himself as a thing that 'doubts, understands, conceives, affirms, denies, wills, refuses' (1984: 19), a piece of knowledge which does not merely survive the sceptical reflections of the *First Meditation* but is actually presupposed by them. For Descartes, rational self-control involves first-personal thought.

Is there a form of thinking which satisfies Descartes' specification, which involves conceiving of yourself as its agent and is a method by which you can directly control your own beliefs and decisions? Plain reasoning is not a strong candidate, for much of the reasoning by which we arrive at beliefs and decisions is tacit, automatic, or even unconscious and doesn't involve thinking of oneself in any particular way. But other more sophisticated forms of thought might fit the bill. I shall examine three: *deliberation*, *reflective maintenance*, and *reflective reasoning*. Let us start with deliberation.

3.1 What is Deliberation?

As I shall use the term, *deliberation* is a conscious, intentional activity whose aim is to resolve a certain question. I'll take these features in order.

First, deliberation is *conscious*, that is, it occupies the deliberator's attention (Peacocke 1998: 65–7). I assume there is a resource, conscious attention, which we employ in various ways: we can listen carefully to the person now addressing us, attempt to recall their name, try to visualize them naked. These activities compete for our attention and may well interfere with one another. Deliberation is another such activity: in wondering what we ought to say to them, or in asking ourselves whether they are likely to hit us, we do something which tends to distract from the other activities just mentioned. By contrast, thinking or reasoning—the formation of beliefs or intentions on the basis of reasons for them—can occur in a way which does not compete with looking, recalling, or visualizing for the scarce resource of conscious attention.

Secondly, deliberation is a form of *activity*. The deliberator is not just a forum for discussion or a battleground between contending inclinations: he is the author, the agent of the deliberation (Shoemaker 1996: 28). In deliberation we are trying to do something: to prove a theorem, to make a decision, and so forth. And when these activities involve deliberation, they are *intentional* under that description. I can't unintentionally deliberate about what to think or do.

Thirdly, deliberation is an activity which aims at *resolving* a certain issue (Stroud 2000: 30), (Moran 2001: 59 and 131). In this chapter I shall focus on deliberation which governs belief and action, on theoretical and practical deliberation. A deliberator does not merely inquire what he ought to believe or to do; he means to make up his mind on the point. Of course, he is perfectly capable of thinking about what he ought to *have* believed or to *have* done. He is also capable of thinking about what someone else ought to believe or to do. But such appraisal is not deliberation about what to believe or do. Appraisal does not fail merely because its object refuses to comply whilst deliberation which leaves one with an open mind on the point is unsuccessful deliberation.

What exactly is involved in making up one's mind about something: what is it to be convinced of something or to have decided to do it? A full answer to this question is beyond me, but one point should be made: belief and intention both act as a block on further deliberation.[1] Suppose I am convinced of the honesty of my accountant. To have such a belief is not just to think that the evidence currently favours his honesty: that would be consistent with having an open mind on the question, with carefully collecting and assimilating further information and being thoroughly on one's guard. Believing my accountant to be honest, I simply don't consider whether a certain anomaly in the company's

---

[1] See (Harman 1986) for belief and (Bratman 1987) for intention.

books should undermine my faith in him: I ignore it or explain it away on the assumption that he is honest.

The point is quite general. To have made your mind up about an issue is incompatible with further deliberation: deliberation aims to resolve the matter, and you can't aim to resolve a matter that has already been resolved. Having made up my mind to lie to the tax inspector this year, I do not reopen the issue of whether to lie to the tax inspector. I may construct various lines of thought to support my belief in my accountant, but, so long as my continued belief is not meant to depend on the success of these efforts, this thinking will not constitute deliberation.

Neither beliefs nor decisions are immutable. Certain events may arouse my suspicions; may sow doubts. They won't do this *via* a process of deliberation—I can't (seriously) consider whether these events show my accountant to be dishonest without already having ceased to trust him—rather, it is by undermining this conviction that they make such deliberation possible. This refusal to consider whether my accountant is dishonest may be perfectly reasonable, even in the face of a not insignificant amount of evidence. But as it mounts up, there will come a point when my belief should be undermined by the evidence before me; either I must change my mind or at least open my mind on the issue. At some point, conviction wilts and the blockage is removed.

How exactly does this happen if not via a process of deliberation? It can happen by means of reasoning, which is not deliberation about my accountant's probity because it is not an intentional action performed with the aim of settling what to think about this issue.[2] Perhaps unconscious reasoning makes some action of his strike me as suspicious, and that undermines my conviction. Or else I might be reasoning perfectly consciously about my accountant's honesty, say with the aim of convincing someone else, and then find myself in difficulties. Or else I might be deliberating about some apparently unrelated matter and arrive at a conclusion which, I then realize, throws doubt on my accountant's honesty. In no case do I reason with the intention of making up my mind about this matter.[3]

I hope I have said enough to distinguish deliberation from plain reasoning at least. Why should deliberation, as so far described, require the ability to think of yourself? One possibility is that the deliberator, whether theoretical or practical,

---

[2] Considering this example in earlier work, I said that such belief revision cannot be the product of reasoning (Owens 2000: 144–5). I wrote this because I had not clearly distinguished reasoning from deliberation.

[3] Later on I shall ask whether I can revise a belief or decision, not by reconsidering the first-order issue but rather by considering the higher-order question as to whether this belief or this decision is a reasonable one.

makes up his mind by considering certain psychological states, namely his own beliefs, desires (etc.) so conceived. This would imply that a deliberator must indeed be self-conscious. On this view, when I deliberate, I must do so by considering the fact that *I* (the deliberator) am someone who believes that p or desires that q.[4]

To test this hypothesis, let's examine an example of deliberation and see what it involves. I am driving past a friend's house wondering whether he is home. I could stop, get out of my car, and ring the front doorbell, but I'd prefer not to go to all that trouble unless he is indeed at home. So I drive slowly by, scrutinizing the front of the house. First I notice that the garage door is closed. That would tend to indicate that he isn't at home, for I know that he closes the garage door only when the car has gone. As a check, I glance at the front door and find it open. I know that the front door would never be left open unless there were someone in the house and that someone is very likely to be him, the probable absence of his car notwithstanding. So I decide to stop and knock on his door.

This story involves stretches of conscious deliberation. Not that I need have rehearsed this paragraph to myself whilst making the decision. It does not matter what, if any, words sounded in my mind's ear; my attention was occupied with trying to work out whether my friend was at home in just the way described. My deliberation involved experience, belief, and decision, all states with intentional content, but none of these contents referred to experience, belief, or decision. First, I saw a closed garage door. From this I concluded that my friend's car was not in the garage. This didn't lead me to infer that my friend was away. Instead, I turned my attention to the front door, saw an open door, formed the view that my friend was likely to be at home, and so decided to get out of my car. These various states of mind concern the condition of two doors, what else was likely to be true given the condition of those doors, and how to act given what was likely to be true.[5]

This very typical instance of deliberation employs no psychological concepts. That might lead us to conclude that deliberation deploys psychological concepts only when it happens to be about someone's psychology. Such a conclusion would not be far wrong, but we need to be careful; facts about my psychology do sometimes contribute to deliberation about non-psychological phenomena.

---

[4] (Korsgaard 1996: 92–3) might be read as suggesting that we think of deliberation in this way.

[5] Considering a similar example (Peacocke 1996: 129–30) argues that reasoning leads to 'the revision of beliefs in the light of thought about relations of evidence and support but the thoughts it involves all seem to be thoughts about the world, not about the thinker's thoughts'. See also (Peacocke 1998: 73).

Suppose I have doubts about whether my visual experience of the front door was accurate (I was distracted by driving). Then I might use the fact that I am enjoying that experience under those conditions as a piece of (inconclusive) evidence to be weighed against other forms of evidence: I might treat my experience, so conceived, as a more or less reliable indicator of how things are. But this is not the role my experience normally plays in the formation of beliefs based on experience.

Something stronger is true of belief itself. Take my belief that my friend never leaves his door open when he is away from home. When I infer that he is in fact at home, I base my inference on the fact that he behaves in this way, not on the fact that I believe he behaves in this way (Moran 2001: 83, 128–9). In the eyes of someone who has no idea about the habits of my friend, the fact that I believe this might play an important role in establishing that he is at home. But, for me, it plays no such role. Perhaps there are cases in which the fact that I currently believe p can serve as evidence, in my own eyes, for the truth of certain other propositions, but there belief is not playing its normal role in inference (deductive or otherwise).

What of desire? When I desire something, there generally seems to me to be something good about it and when deciding whether (or how) to satisfy my desire, I am focused on that good, not on the desire which registers it (Stroud 2000: 34–5). In the above example, I am focused on how to get to meet my friend, on how to bring about that desirable outcome, not on my desire for it. If there seems to be nothing good in what I desire, the fact that I nevertheless desire it may come to be an element in my deliberations: perhaps I must work out how best to placate this desire or distract myself from its suggestions. But here the desire is not treated as a consideration internal to my deliberations, one which counts in favour of the course of action it suggests but rather as a potential obstacle to my acting on the conclusion of my deliberations. In so far as I simply *act on* the desire, the fact that I have this desire is not an element in my deliberations.

To sum up, if deliberation requires that the deliberator think of himself, this isn't because the deliberator must be thinking of himself as the owner of certain psychological states.

3.2 Practical and Theoretical Deliberation

We have been asking what the deliberator considers in the course of his deliberations, rather than how this deliberation is initiated and controlled. Yet deliberation is an action with a characteristic goal. The successful deliberator establishes a certain relationship between himself and the world: *knowledge* in the case of theoretical deliberation; *agency* in the case of practical deliberation. Doesn't this imply that the deliberator must intend that he (thought of as the agent of this deliberation) come to know or decide on something?

On this hypothesis, a theoretical deliberator aims to remove *his own* ignorance on a certain point and a practical deliberator is out to settle how *he himself* will act. But must deliberation involve the deliberator intending to establish a relation between himself, conceived of as the agent of the deliberation, and the world? To tease out the content of the aim which the deliberator must set himself, let's attend to the form of the question which a deliberator seeks to answer.

Williams suggests that practical and theoretical deliberation differ in this regard (Williams 1985: 68–9). Take an epidemiologist trying to work out whether there will be an avian flu pandemic. His deliberation begins with the question 'Will there be an avian flu pandemic?' and it ends once that question is answered. Neither the question nor the answer requires either the first-person concept or the notions of knowledge and ignorance to formulate them. True, the issue will not arise for the scientist unless he is ignorant of the answer and wishes to know it, but it does not follow that his inquiries are guided by thoughts about what *he* knows. The scientist could instead ask himself an explicitly normative question: 'Ought I to believe that there will be an avian flu pandemic?'. But, as Williams says, for the purposes of theoretical deliberation, this question is equivalent to 'Ought *one* to believe that there will be an avian flu pandemic?'.

It would be different were our scientist advising a government minister on this matter. Then his actions would be guided by thoughts about the minister, about what the minister knows and what he does not know, as well as by thoughts about avian flu. Here the scientist must deploy his knowledge that he, the deliberator, is distinct from the person whose ignorance he is trying to cure. It does not follow from this that, when the scientist is trying to cure his own ignorance, his deliberations must be guided by the thought that the deliberator and the person whose ignorance he is trying to cure are the same person, namely himself.[6] Why need he think that in order to estimate the threat posed by avian flu?

Now consider the deliberations of the minister who must decide what preparations to make for a possible pandemic. When a practical deliberator asks himself a normative question, the form of the normative question is not 'what ought to be done about this?', something which any bystander might ask, but rather 'What should *I* do about it?', a question which can sensibly occur only to one who might have some influence over the matter.[7] A practical deliberator is conscious of

---

[6] *Pace* (Shoemaker 2003: 399–400).
[7] The first-person plural might be more appropriate both in this case and in others.

the fact that *his own* actions are the focus of attention rather than someone else's. 'Practical deliberation is in every case first personal and the first person is not derivative or naturally replaced by *anyone*' (Williams 1985: 68).[8]

Williams is surely right that theoretical deliberation makes no essential use of the first person. What of practical deliberation? Perhaps we need the first-person concept here only because we have gratuitously introduced normative concepts. Can't the minister avoid normative concepts altogether in setting the theme of his practical deliberation simply by asking himself what *to do* about avian flu? True, that is a question which only one with influence over what is done on the matter can sensibly ask themselves. But only someone with influence over what is thought about avian flu can sensibly ask themselves what *to think* about it. And if you can decide what to think about avian flu without thinking of yourself, why can't you also decide what to do about avian flu without thinking of yourself?

Still, a contrast remains, a contrast at the level of what I shall call *reflective* deliberation. Someone who thinks about what he *ought* to do with a view to thereby determining what he will do, someone who engages in practical deliberation by thinking about *reasons* for action, must deploy the first-person concept. Not only must he know that the point of view from which these deliberations are being conducted is the point of view of the agent whose actions are the object of these deliberations. He must link the point of view of the deliberator with the point of view of the agent by means of the *I* concept. He must think of them both as *his* point of view. A theoretical deliberator can weigh the reasons for and against various answers to his question without doing any such thing. Or so, at least, I shall argue.

This claim about reflective practical deliberation must be distinguished from some superficially similar observations. It is widely agreed that agents need information in an egocentric form: they must think of places as 'here' and 'there', times as 'now' and 'then' if they are to be able to act on what they know (Perry 1979). For example, I may have a complete map of the library and be able to point to the place I want to be on the map, but unless I know where that place is in relation to a place thought of as *here* I won't be able to use the map to get to where I want to be. This is true enough, but it imputes no relevant form of self-consciousness to an agent. Thinking of oneself as an agent is a quite different matter from having information about one's environment in an egocentric form.

---

[8] Williams says various other things (e.g. that action is motivated by desire and that the deliberator must be thinking about his own desires in deciding what to do) that I do not endorse. The explanation of this practical-theoretical asymmetry, which I shall later offer, would not serve Williams's metaethical purposes.

A cat needs to be able to think of places in this egocentric way in order to get around the world, but cats presumably don't think of themselves as the agents of their actions because they don't know what an agent is (Burge 2013: 387).

Some writers have claimed that the *I* concept is crucial to our practical thinking because agents such as humans don't just engage in present activity; they plan their future agency, they form future-directed intentions and thereby exercise a type of control over their own agency which most animals lack. These writers maintain that one who intends to act in a certain way must identify the agent who has the intention with the agent who is to carry it out by means of the *I* concept: intentions to act have a *de se* content.[9]

This may be so, but I am not concerned with what is involved in exercising control over our future action by forming intentions. Rather, I am focused on what is involved in controlling *both* our intentions *and* those actions not foreshadowed in our future-directed intentions by means of practical deliberation. It may be that someone who wishes to control certain future actions by forming intentions must do so by thinking of these actions as *his* actions. But this will not explain why someone who is deliberating about whether to form a certain intention must do so by thinking of it as *his* intention. Nor will it explain why someone who is deliberating about how to act must do so by thinking of what he does as *his* action. In so far as we are rational, we can exercise an immediate and direct influence over both action and intention by deliberating about what *we* should do, influence of a kind which we do not have over what other people do.[10] That sort of influence is not exercised by forming future-directed intentions to decide.

Later I shall argue that, whilst deliberation about the reasons we have to perform various actions has, insofar as we are rational, an immediate and direct influence over what we decide to do, the same is not true of deliberation about the reasons we have to form various beliefs. That is the truth in Williams's claim that the *I* concept is indispensable in practical but not in theoretical deliberation. But before exploring that idea, let us ask what other forms of cognitive self-control there are besides reflective and unreflective deliberation.

---

[9] For different versions of this claims, see (Velleman 1996: 69–72) and (Burge 2013: 412–14).

[10] We exercise this influence over our own decisions by assessing the rationality of carrying out those decisions and *not* by assessing the rationality of causing ourselves to take them. There may be cases in which it would be rational for me to cause myself to take a decision which it would not be rational for me to execute (Kavka 1983). In these cases, I would argue, the decision it is rational for me to induce is not a rational decision and so rationality alone does not guarantee that I can get myself to take it, but only that I can decide to do something to get myself to take it (Owens 2000: 81–2). In trying to get myself to take this irrational decision, I am in much the same situation as I would be were I trying to get someone else to take an irrational but advantageous decision. I have no immediate influence.

3.3 Reflective Maintenance: Shoemaker

We are on our way to concluding that only practical deliberation requires the deliberator to think of himself as the agent of his deliberation, at least when it is deliberation about reasons. If so, practical but not theoretical deliberation will fit Descartes' specification. But perhaps we have been looking in the wrong place for Descartes' all-purpose tool of cognitive self-control.

At least during the destructive phase of the *First Meditation*, Descartes' meditator is not in the business of making up his mind about any first-order matter. Rather, he is reviewing the beliefs he already has with a view to getting rid of them if they don't hold up to rational criticism. So the meditator is not engaged in deliberation as we defined it. Rather, he is 'bracketing' his current beliefs (and decisions) in order to consider whether those beliefs (and decisions) are reasonable, and an unfavourable assessment is meant to have an adverse impact on these beliefs (and decisions), at least in so far as he is rational. People are capable of *revising* their beliefs and intentions as well as of forming them, and it looks as if such revisions sometimes come about by means of higher order normative assessments rather than first-order deliberation. Perhaps this is the point at which Cartesian self-control is exercised. Should this checking process involve deployment of the first-person concept, Descartes will have what he wants.

So let us ask what is involved in the revision of a propositional attitude. Shoemaker urges that the revision of belief and intention *always* requires something more than first-order deliberation, that it always requires us to think about our beliefs and intentions:

> If the beliefs and desires are all first-order beliefs and desires i.e. beliefs and desires that are not themselves *about* the agent's beliefs and desires, then one thing they do not rationalise is changes in themselves. For such changes to be rationalised, the beliefs and desires would have to include second-order beliefs and desires—desires to promote consistency and coherence in the system of beliefs and desires, and beliefs about what changes in the beliefs and desires would be needed in order to satisfy the second-order desires, which in turn would require beliefs about what the current beliefs and desires are.
>
> (Shoemaker 1996: 33)

Here Shoemaker implies that any reasoned change in belief (or desire/intention) must involve such higher order states. This can't be right. As already noted, reasoning can *determine* what I believe without being *about* what I believe (Moran 2001: 110–12).

Suppose I discover a great deal of evidence for p where p is inconsistent with something I already believe: q. The inconsistency here is not very subtle and requires no great logical acumen to detect. Here, reasoning will lead me to abandon the belief that q once I adopt the belief that p; I am prepared to reason from the evidence for p to the truth of p only if I am also prepared to abandon my belief that q. *Pace* Shoemaker, these manoeuvres do not require me to think about my beliefs. What such reasoning depends on is my knowledge that p and q cannot both be true. In the course of the reasoning which leads to the adoption and abandonment of these beliefs, I am exclusively concerned with such things as the truth of p and q and the facts which serve as evidence for each of them. Such evidence does not (normally) include facts about what I believe or don't believe.

Still, people don't just pose questions about the world; on occasion they also ask themselves about their own beliefs. Perhaps Shoemaker is looking for a way in which the rational person can deliberately revise their own beliefs and intentions, and he correctly sees that first-order deliberation cannot provide it. Here, Shoemaker invokes what one might call a process of *reflective maintenance*. This process is driven by a desire 'to promote consistency and coherence in the system of beliefs and desires'. Clearly, we need beliefs about psychological states in order to pursue the goal which this desire sets but must we think of them as *our* beliefs and desires to keep them coherent? Do rational beings exercise a form of control which is special to *their own* beliefs and intentions when engaged in reflective maintenance?

Take a closer look at Shoemaker's second-order desire. There is no personal pronoun in the specification of its object: the content clause mentions '*the* system', not 'his system' or 'my system'. If reflective maintenance is an activity motivated by this desire, second-order beliefs employing the first-person concept are not required to guide this activity towards its goal. Someone interested in promoting consistency and coherence in a given system of beliefs and desires must be able to discriminate between the components of that system and the components of other systems. But, for all we have been told, one might do this whilst thinking of the system in question as D.O.'s system or simply as *this* system. One need not think of it as a system composed of *my* beliefs and desires (Moran 2001: 112).

Was this just a slip on Shoemaker's part, a slip which can be repaired by giving the desire which drives reflective maintenance an egocentric content? Perhaps reflective maintenance should be defined as cognition motivated by a desire for consistency and coherence in *one's own* system of beliefs. But why suppose that rational people have such an egocentric desire simply in virtue of being rational? If rational people value consistency or coherence in their own case, this is because they value consistency or coherence as such. As Burge says, 'an individual's assessment of some judgement as irrational carries with it some *prima facie* grounds not only that it be altered—but *prima facie* grounds to alter it, regardless of who the source of the judgement is' (Burge 2013: 392). True, rational people with a command of the first-person concept will form the derivative desire for consistency and coherence amongst their own mental states. But what lies behind this egocentric desire is the desire for coherence as such, a desire which may cause me to scrutinize my own beliefs but which may equally lead me to argue with other people about the rationality of their beliefs and attempt thereby to change them for the better.

Of course, for all sorts of practical reasons, I will normally take a special interest in those beliefs and desires which are, in fact, my own (and I can't do much to help others until my own house is in some kind of order). Yet, on occasion, it will seem more important to resolve (by reasoning from premises which I believe they accept) an incoherence in someone's else's beliefs than it does to attend to a problem with mine. The idea that rational people have a special form of control over (and thus a special responsibility for) their own cognition which they don't have over other people's seems to have escaped us (Moran 2001: 112–13, 118–19).

I don't deny that reflective maintenance is a real phenomenon. I do deny that the capacity for reflective maintenance is what gives each of us some special control over and responsibility for our own mental lives which (as the likes of Descartes suppose) we have simply in virtue of being rational. Why should the satisfaction of the desire for coherence, etc. which motivates reflective maintenance always be the rational person's highest priority? They may decide that pursuing coherence isn't feasible in this instance. Furthermore, at any given moment, it might be more important to devote their limited energies to monitoring and repairing another's mental states—or to something else altogether. Yet one's own rationality depends on the rationality of one's mental life in a way that is not contingent on the urgency of one's desire for coherence or the feasibility of acting on it.

3.4 Reflective Reasoning: Burge

Like Shoemaker, Burge focuses on the process of assessing and revising one's propositional attitudes in the hope of discovering an instrument of cognitive self-control which deploys the first-person concept. In this section, I allow that his view works well when applied to action and intention, but I conclude the chapter by casting doubt on whether we have the same sort of control over belief.

Burge distinguishes two types of reasoning (Burge 2013: 73–5). First, there is *plain reasoning*. In plain reasoning, we form and change our attitudes on the basis of reasons without thinking of them *as* reasons; in the process we assess truth, falsity, evidential support, entailment, etc. amongst propositions but do not assess the truth or reasonability of attitudes. Then there is *critical reasoning*. In critical reasoning one thinks of reasons *as* reasons, that is as reasons for attitudes; one thinks about the different sorts of propositional attitude, of the rationalizing connections between them and of whether the resulting attitudes are justified or correct. Critical reasoning involves thinking about thoughts, but Burge leaves open the possibility that a creature might engage in such reasoning without being able to think of any of its thoughts as *my* thoughts (Burge 2013: 389–92 and 397–8). Still, he insists, any critical reasoner who lacks the first-person concept lacks a full understanding of what he is doing.

For critical reasoning to be a genuine instrument of cognitive self-control, we must be able to engage in it intentionally, i.e. engage in it with the intention of thereby revising the attitudes under review, should that prove necessary. And this entails having a certain understanding of what critical reasoning involves. Burge calls critical reasoning that meets this condition *reflective reasoning*. But why does a full understanding of critical reasoning require deployment of the first-person concept? What exactly is someone without it failing to grasp?

> Acknowledging, with the *I* concept, that an attitude or act is one's own is acknowledging that rational evaluations of it which one also acknowledges provide immediate ... reason and rationally immediate motivation to shape the attitude or act in accordance with the evaluation. Unless further evaluations of the attitude must be taken into account, there need be no further intervening reasoning involved for it to be rational to have the reason affect the attitude or act. The first-person concept fixes the locus of responsibility and marks the immediate rational relevance of a rational evaluation to rational implementation on the attitude being evaluated—to epistemic or practical agency. (Burge 2013: 391–2)

The key claim here is that 'there need be no further intervening reasoning involved for it to be rational to have the reason affect the attitude or act'. What 'further reasoning' does Burge have in mind?

Here, Burge is thinking of the further reasoning that would be involved in working out how to reform someone else's propositional attitudes. As we have seen, Burge assumes that all rational beings have an interest in the elimination of irrationality. But when the attitude in question is thought of third-personally, further issues arise. First, there has to be some chance of affecting the offending attitude. Second, one has to decide whether this chance is worth taking. This will involve a stretch of practical reasoning, reasoning about the cost and effectiveness of various means (Burge 2013: 84–5 and 393).[11]

---

[11] It will also mean discovering what the other person's propositional attitudes actually are, which may, Burge says, involve reasoning (Burge 2013: 83–4).

Suppose somebody has an unreasonable attitude. Rational beings as such must regard this fact as providing *prima facie* grounds for reform, but there are at least two ways in which such reform might fail to take place without them having shirked their responsibilities. First, they might simply be unable to do anything about it. Second, they might decide that there was no reasonably priced means of reforming it. Either way, there is a gap between the fact that this attitude is unreasonable and it's being the case that one ought to change it.

But now suppose that the unreasonable attitude is one's own. According to Burge, this immediately closes the gap. No rational subject can be relieved of the responsibility of reforming their own attitudes. If there is reason to reform an attitude and that attitude is one's own, and one makes a reasonable evaluation of it, one must acknowledge that reason. Furthermore, that very acknowledgement should suffice to ensure the abandonment of the attitude. One who knows (a) that an attitude is unreasonable, and (b) that this attitude is their own, also knows (c) that they *can* revise it. There is no question of having to discover some method or technique of self-manipulation in order to rid oneself of it. A reasonable person can't decline to relinquish an irrational attitude on the grounds that there is no suitable way of so doing:

> If in the course of critical reasoning I reasonably conclude that my belief that a given person is guilty rests entirely on unreasonable premises or bad reasoning, then it normally follows immediately... that it is reasonable to give up my belief about guilt or to look for new grounds for it. (Burge 2013: 82)

Burge does not deny that one can find it hard to rid oneself of an irrational belief or even fail to know of it altogether. Suppose I maintain that my brother had nothing to do with my father's death but my analyst convinces me that I do in fact believe his behaviour drove my father to an early grave. Even once I have been brought to acknowledge this conviction, I may find it very hard to relinquish it. Perhaps hypnosis is required. Then it will be a question of how costly and effective the hypnosis is. Clearly, such behaviour exhibits a deep sort of irrationality and, Burge suggests, one might not regard such attitudes as truly *one's own* (Burge 2013: 83, see also Moran 2001: 93–4).

Burge's central idea is that each of us has a special power over and responsibility for our own attitudes, and the function of the *I* concept is to mark that locus of power and responsibility. Each of us knows that we have the power to rid *ourselves* of an unwarranted belief or of a senseless intention simply by judging that we ought not to have this belief or this intention (Burge 2013: 394–5). But we are unable to rid *other* people of their unwarranted beliefs or intentions simply by judging that *they* ought not to have those beliefs and intentions. This asymmetry of power (and thus of responsibility) can be grasped only by someone in possession of the *I* concept. The critical reasoner who lacks the *I* concept may discover that certain beliefs or intentions happen to be immediately responsive to his evaluations of them, whilst the process of reforming other beliefs and intentions requires further action on his part. But from the perspective of this reasoner, it is a brute contingency that certain psychological states are responsive in this way, not something he can be sure of simply in virtue of being rational (Moran 2001: 131–2, 145–6). Such a critical reasoner cannot understand why his reasoning has the influence that it does.

Burge concludes that a critical reasoner without the *I* concept can't intend to engage in that special cognitive activity in which we engage when checking and revising our own first-order attitudes. Without the *I* concept, one is incapable of reasoning with this intention because one can't conceptualize the owner of the object reviewed—a psychological state—in a way which gives one's reasoning the right sort of authority over it, i.e. one can't conceptualize that owner as being identical with the occupant of the point of view from which the review is being conducted. And unless the critical reasoner conceptualizes the object of review in a way which reveals the basis of his authority over it, he can't intend to change the object in the way a rational person does, i.e. simply by exercising that authority. Our subject may reason critically, and that reasoning may have an impact on the states reviewed, but he won't know that he can do this in the way that fully rational people know that they can influence their mental lives. Rather, he will be engaged in something more like reflective maintenance.

3.5 Reflective Deliberation

Burge's line of thought suggests an explanation of the asymmetry between theoretical and practical deliberation which I derived from my discussion of Williams. This may surprise for two reasons. First, Burge is concerned with reflective reasoning, with the appraisal and revision of attitudes already formed. Williams was concerned with deliberation which aims to form such attitudes. Second, where Williams saw an asymmetry between theoretical and practical deliberation, Burge sees none between reflective reasoning about beliefs and reflective reasoning about intentions. Yet, as I shall urge, Burge is wrong on the latter point, and once we have seen why, we are in a position to explain the asymmetry.

Let us begin with the first point. Williams argued that the practical deliberator must link by means of the *I* concept the perspective from which the deliberation is conducted with that of the agent who performs the action decided upon. This is so, I argued, where practical deliberation takes a reflective form, where it is deliberation about reasons for action. When practical deliberation takes that form, the deliberator is invoking the peculiar authority (the direct and immediate influence) that his practical deliberation has over his own actions. Now Burge suggests that someone deliberately engaged in reflective reasoning about decisions already made is invoking the special authority which his reflective reasoning has over those decisions. I suggest that authority which an agent's practical deliberation has over his (potential) actions is the very same authority his reflective reasoning has over his (actual) plans and projects. Now, where practical deliberation turns reflective, where it involves thinking about the reasons for potential *attitudes* like decision, it involves hypothetical reflective reasoning (an appraisal of hypothetical decisions). I conclude that a reflective practical deliberator must invoke the very same authority which Burge identifies and thus must deploy the *I* concept.

Turning now to the asymmetry between theoretical and practical deliberation, we must first note an important fact about practical deliberation: it is a psychological process which consumes time, energy, conscious attention, and other resources in limited supply. When assessing the quality of someone's deliberation from the outside, we ask whether it is properly sensitive to the amount of time and energy, etc. that can be devoted to resolving the issue at hand. In particular, when considering whether it was right for someone to conclude their deliberation by taking a decision at a given moment (rather than doing this earlier or later or not at all), we ask whether this was sensible given that they couldn't go on amassing relevant considerations indefinitely or assessing those they already knew of.

Surely, facts relevant to the assessment of decisions already taken should also be considered when taking them. Recall our earlier example. At some point, I need to decide whether to get out of the car to visit my friend or drive on—I can't go on deliberating about this forever—and a good deliberator not only takes the right decision but knows when to take it. Having judged that now is the moment of decision, a rational agent will take the required decision; simply in virtue of being rational, our agent has the power to decide whether to stop the car by judging that he ought *now* to make up his mind about whether to stop. But to make this judgement he must think not only about the merits of the action to be decided upon but also about the constraints on the process of decision-making.

Let us turn now to theoretical deliberation. When we assess such deliberation from the outside, the same points seem to apply. Consider the belief I form about how likely my friend is to be at home. I could form a view about this just by looking at the garage door or I could decline to form a view even after I have seen both the garage door and the front door. What makes it appropriate for me to form a view when I do is how much the issue matters and how easy it would be to gather and absorb more evidence. In this case, the belief has a largely practical significance, but the same question—how much evidence should I require?—will arise for any belief, and non-evidential considerations are needed to answer it. Yet on one point, theoretical deliberation differs crucially from practical: though such non-evidential considerations seem highly relevant to the assessment of belief, they won't figure in the subject's theoretical deliberations. Why not?

The reason is that a subject can't influence what he believes (as he *can* influence what he does) by reflecting on the process of deliberation itself. Take practical deliberation once more. Suppose our agent is trying to decide whether to lie to the taxman. He is inclined to think that lying is the best option here, but he also knows that further information might come along which will change his mind, not by convincing him that his situation has changed but rather by showing him that his original judgement was wrong: perhaps there was some aspect of the situation he overlooked or some consideration he gave insufficient weight to. Our agent has the capacity to get himself to wait a bit longer before taking a decision simply by judging that he has not yet got sufficient evidence about his current situation to make up his mind, given the importance of the issue, etc. Of course, our agent has a choice about whether to exercise this capacity to determine whether he makes his mind up; he might have moved straight from the present appearance that things favour lying to a decision to lie.[12] Still, that would be his choice.[13]

The same is not true of belief. Return to the issue of whether there will be an avian flu pandemic. Suppose our subject believes that there won't because he has been told this by a friend whose judgement he trusts and who has had more time to think about these matters. The rest of us can wonder whether this testimony gives our agent sufficient evidence to form a view, given the importance of the issue, the limitations on their cognitive resources, and so forth. Couldn't our subject raise this sort of question with himself before forming a view, and couldn't his answer determine whether he finds what he has been told convincing, at least in so far as he is rational?

It seems not. True, one can make an assessment of how reasonable such belief would be as easily in the first person as in the third person, but when it comes to actually forming the belief, one is left unmoved by *reflection* on time and

---

[12] Indeed, at some point in the hierarchy of possible levels of reflection on such choices he *must* fail to exercise this capacity, but there is no particular point at which this must happen.

[13] Following (Korsgaard 1996: 92–3), (Moran 2001: 140–2) makes a related point. Neither author sees a difference between practical and theoretical reasoning.

cognitive resources, on considerations which concern how reasonable it would be to form any view at all, given the amount of evidence we have. No doubt believers have some sort of sensitivity to such non-evidential factors—how else could they form reasonable beliefs?—but that is quite different from saying that your *judgements about* such matters determine when you are convinced on the further question at issue. Rational people can't control their convictions by deliberating about whether they should make up their minds or not, given the importance of the issue and so forth. At least they can't do this simply in virtue of being rational.

From the point of view of the theoretical deliberator there is no role for a self-conscious decision about whether to believe: the moment of conviction is simply the moment at which the evidence (seems to) establish the truth. The subject may deliberate about how reliable the evidence is and, in so far as he is rational, such deliberations will help to determine whether or not he believes it. What need not have any influence on belief is the judgement (however right) that he has heard enough and should now make up his mind. By contrast, the practical deliberator can get himself to take a practical decision simply by reflecting on the reasons for making up his mind now and then judging that the time has come to take a decision.[14] And exercising this capacity intentionally involves deploying the first-person concept. There is no analogue of this in theoretical deliberation.

Now we have our explanation of the asymmetry suggested by Williams. That asymmetry shows up when the deliberator engages in 'normative ascent', when his deliberations take the form of thinking about reasons. In the practical case, such normative ascent gives the rational agent a reflective purchase on his decision-making. To get this purchase, the agent must consider not just the reasons which count in favour of various courses of action but also the deliberative process itself, the constraints it labours under, and how these should influence his decision-making; the subject must think of himself as both deliberator and agent. Seeing himself as both deliberator and agent, the rational subject must think of the process of deliberation as no less a part of the subject matter of deliberation than the action to be decided upon. He must integrate the point of view of the agent whose actions are being decided upon with the point of view from which the deliberation is being conducted. And to do this in a way that he knows will be immediately efficacious, he must use the *I* concept. The deliberator could register the pragmatic constraints on the deliberative process by using impersonal formula like 'this process must come to an end now', but such formula would not reveal his rational authority over the process.

---

[14] This judgement about when to decide is not a belief. See Chapter 7: Section 7.4.

By contrast, the theoretical deliberator gains no purchase on the process of belief formation by going in for normative ascent. The subject engaged in first-order theoretical deliberation is not required to connect up the standpoint of deliberation with any other standpoint. In posing himself the deliberative question, he need not think of these deliberations as part of the very world whose character he is investigating. And since rationality alone does not enable the theoretical deliberator to govern his beliefs by thinking about the constraints on the deliberative process, he cannot exercise rational control over his beliefs by instead thinking about how reasonable they are (or would be). The theoretical deliberator lacks that capacity to control his beliefs by reflecting on the reasons for them which Burge attributes to him and which the practical deliberator has.

3.6 Conclusion

We have failed to find a source of mental self-control which meets Descartes' specification. Deliberation controls the formation of both belief and intention but only what I called reflective practical deliberation must deploy the *I* concept and no form of deliberation gives us direct control over the revision of either belief or intention. Reflective maintenance controls the revision of both belief and intention, but this control is not direct, nor need it involve deployment of the first-person concept. Finally, reflective reasoning is an instrument of direct control and requires the *I* concept, but it is an instrument we can deploy to control intention and action, not belief. Descartes was right to think that, where our mental life takes the form of free agency, we have a distinctively first-personal method of controlling it. But much of our mental life manifests our rationality without being a form of free agency. Therefore, what makes us responsible to the norms of reason cannot be some instrument of mental self-control which we have in virtue of being self-conscious.[15]

---

[15] Many thanks to Michael Martin, Nishi Shah, Paul Snowdon, and Matthew Soteriou, and to audiences in Manchester, Portland, and Fribourg.

4

Value and Epistemic Normativity

Most writers would agree that beliefs are governed by norms, that there is a right way and a wrong way of forming and relinquishing beliefs. 'Being governed by norms' has at least two connotations. First there is the idea that these norms should *guide* beliefs' comings and goings. Second there is the idea that where these norms are violated, it is (generally) appropriate to *criticize* the believer for this. Discussion of the form of guidance appropriate to epistemic normativity must be left for another occasion. Here I assume only that the acquisition and extinction of belief should in some sense be guided by these norms. As to criticism, those who violate epistemic norms are stigmatized as irrational, but what does that criticism involve and why is it appropriate?[1] Criticism seems like an appropriate reaction to an (illicit) threat to some human interest, either one's own or someone else's. So where epistemic irrationality is criticizable, we should expect belief and its rationality to be something that matters to us, something that we value, something whose presence or absence bears on our interests.

In this chapter I attempt to ground epistemic normativity in human interests, in facts about what is good for us. One might try to demonstrate that it is in our interests both to have beliefs and to conform those beliefs to epistemic norms. Yet it would frequently be in our interests to adopt quite irrational beliefs or to relinquish perfectly rational beliefs (e.g. to boost our confidence and avoid depression). Some writers have concluded from this that it is a mistake to ground epistemic normativity in value.[2] I instead infer that the authority of epistemic norms cannot lie in the value of actually conforming to them. Rather, it lies in the value of being *subject* to those norms, whether or not you actually conform to them.[3] Before making that case I shall explore some more familiar ways of grounding epistemic norms in value.

---

[1] Elsewhere I've argued that when we stigmatize someone as irrational we are blaming them (see Introduction: Section I.5 and Owens 2000: Chapter 8), but here I remain neutral on the nature of rational criticism.
[2] For example (Raz 2011: 41–7) and (Shah 2013: 316).
[3] This is my solution to the problem of authority raised in Chapter 2.

4.1 The Bayesian Challenge

Let's begin with this claim:

Evidence: Believe that p only if you have sufficient evidence for the truth of p.

Evidence for a proposition is any indication that the proposition is true. Where you have no evidence at all or the evidence you have is insufficient, your belief is irrational. I am hoping something like *Evidence* will prove attractive to anyone who acknowledges the existence of norms of rationality governing the formation of belief. To keep *Evidence* as uncontroversial as possible, I leave it entirely open what it is for someone to 'have' evidence for a proposition, what form of psychic contact or availability is involved. I also leave it open what is involved in p's being evidence for q: the indication relation may be a priori or a posteriori, necessary or contingent. Evidence may not even be distinct from the thing it is evidence for: perhaps some propositions are self-evident in that our grasp of them is a sufficient indication of their truth. *Evidence* simply requires that you believe only where you have a sufficiently strong indication of the truth of what you believe.[4]

Though I have tried to make *Evidence* as vague and inoffensive as possible, some will still baulk. Bayesians will agree that anything worth calling a belief must be based on some indication of the truth of the proposition believed, but *Evidence* goes further. It postulates a dichotomy between belief and its absence and it postulates a threshold of evidential sufficiency which the believer must cross before they are entitled to be convinced of p's truth. The difference between conviction and agnosticism so understood is like the difference between standing to someone's right or to their left, a difference marked by a (perhaps rather vague) boundary. Bayesians recognize no such boundary.

On the Bayesian model, being a good believer involves proportioning one's level of confidence in p to the strength of one's evidence for p, believing p to the appropriate degree (and not-p to a reciprocal degree). There is no need to settle on an 'all-out' belief in either proposition:

One could easily enough define a concept of acceptance which identified it with high subjective or epistemic probability (probability greater than some specified number between one-half and one), but it is not clear what the point of doing so would be. Once a subjective or epistemic probability value is assigned to a proposition, there is nothing more to be said about its epistemic status. Bayesian decision theory gives a complete account of how probability values, including high ones, ought to guide behaviour, in both the context of inquiry and the application of belief outside of this context.

---

[4] There may also be norms requiring us to believe in the face of sufficient evidence.

So what could be the point of selecting an interval near the top of the probability scale and conferring on the propositions whose probability falls in that interval the honorific title 'accepted'? (Stalnaker 1984: 91)

Stalnaker asks: what is the point of forming beliefs? What good do they do us? What function do they perform in human life? Without an answer to these questions, we have no reason to take the norms associated with belief seriously and thus have no reason to form psychological states that involve our subjection to them.[5] Bayesians like Stalnaker do have definite views about what constitutes good evidence, views which fill out the Bayesian injunction to proportion one's beliefs to the available evidence; they acknowledge norms of coherence, norms whose authority is grounded in the practical needs to which Stalnaker alludes (i.e. the guidance of behaviour and inquiry). But these norms do not include anything like *Evidence*.

In the next section, I'll consider a response to Stalnaker's challenge that derives *Evidence* from another norm, namely the requirement that our beliefs be true:

Correctness: Believe that p only if p is true.[6]

The response is a two-stage affair. First, postulate (*pace* Stalnaker) a psychological threshold between believing and not-believing such that (as *Correctness* says) we should be on the belief side of the threshold only in respect of true propositions. Second, argue that because belief is governed by *Correctness* it is also governed by *Evidence*. In Section 4.2 I'll establish that even granted *Correctness*, we have no reason to think that belief is also governed by *Evidence*. The way to *Evidence* is not via *Correctness*.

4.2 Alethic Conceptions of Belief

Some maintain that *Correctness* captures the distinctive normative character of belief (Shah and Velleman 2005: 499). It certainly differentiates merely imagining

---

[5] Some contend that certain norms are constitutive of belief, that to have a belief at all is to be subject to standards like *Evidence* (e.g. Shah and Velleman 2005: 510). On this constitutivist view, to believe that p *just is* to be required to have sufficient evidence for p and so there can be no question about whether belief ought to be governed by this norm. I doubt that answers Stalnaker's question. He can simply ask after the point of forming beliefs so conceived. Perhaps we are compelled to believe regardless, but then we should do whatever we can to stop ourselves from forming beliefs.

[6] Bayesian degrees of confidence are not governed by *Correctness*. Your confidence in p is meant to reflect the level of evidence you have for p and so, unless that level of evidence is 1, coherence requires you to have a reciprocal degree of confidence in not-p. By contrast, a rational person will believe either p or believe not-p or neither (Ross and Schroeder 2012: 17–19).

that p from believing that p; there is no requirement that we imagine only what is true. It also imposes a requirement of consistency on our beliefs; since reality is consistent, an inconsistent set of beliefs must include false beliefs. But *Correctness* and *Evidence* seem quite distinct, for you might conform to *Correctness* without conforming to *Evidence*: good luck can ensure that you get the truth by accident. And you might also conform to *Evidence* without conforming to *Correctness*: reasonable error is ubiquitous.

It is natural to suppose that *Correctness* and *Evidence* are connected as follows: the best way of conforming to *Correctness* (i.e. to believe only truths) is to conform to *Evidence* (i.e. to believe only on the basis of sufficient evidence). For the purposes of our discussion, I'll imagine that the rational believer is trying to conform to *Correctness* by consciously following *Evidence*, but nothing hangs on the nature of the guidance mechanism. Our conformity to these norms is always non-voluntary and may well be unconscious.[7]

Let's begin our discussion of this proposal by asking why we should take *Correctness* seriously. In line with our general hypothesis about value and normativity, that should involve there being value in having a true rather than a false belief. Now, if it matters to you to have a belief on a certain issue, isn't it better that the belief in question be true rather than false? In a particular case there may be various advantages to having a false belief, advantages that might outweigh the value of truth: still, isn't there something to be said in favour of getting it right? You may not care whether the number of stars in the galaxy is odd or even, which is why you have no view on the matter, but where you do care enough to form a view, mustn't you see some point in getting it right, some interest that is served by having a true rather than a false belief?

There are two problems with this account of the normative force of *Correctness*. First, once the side effects of having a true rather than a false belief are taken off the table, the value of truth becomes rather obscure. Why should you wish, for its own sake, to be right rather than wrong? Suppose I believe on whatever grounds that I'm going to die tomorrow. Is there something to be said in favour of my death, namely, that it will vindicate my belief, that it will at least prove me right? Does my belief give me (or anyone else) any reason at all to ensure that I do die?[8] This sounds like a strange idea, but we may have misconstrued our interest in truth. Perhaps the value lies in our beliefs *tracking* the truth, in being

---

[7] We have no choice about whether to form beliefs on a certain matter, at least once the evidence is in, and we also have no choice about whether to retain that belief so long as the evidence remains (Raz 2011: 44) and (Shah 2013: 316–17).

[8] The question is pressed by (Raz 2011: 45) and (Piller 2009: 196–200).

sensitive or responsive to how things are in the world rather than in a brute match between world and content, however achieved. Let's suppose that this is so; the project of grounding *Evidence* in the value of truth now confronts a second difficulty.

Where I do see some point in getting it right, how much trouble should I take to get it right? Suppose I am trying to spell 'assessment' correctly, then I must see some value in spelling it correctly, but it remains a question exactly how hard I should try. If time is short and I must issue a written warning that you are about to be assessed, it would be silly for me to worry *too* much about precisely how many 's's the word contains. My goal of good spelling must be balanced against the other goals I am trying to achieve, and here correct spelling may count for rather little. All things considered, it may be sensible for me to write the word at a speed that makes it rather unlikely that I shall achieve my goal of spelling it correctly. This prudent haste is perfectly consistent with the fact that I was trying to spell it correctly.

This isn't how it is with belief. A believer is, we may suppose, trying to get it right, but one shouldn't weigh the value of truth against other relevant values in order to determine whether or what to believe. Take my belief that I'm going to die tomorrow and suppose that there is some value in my tracking the truth. Given that I am going to die, this means that there is some disvalue in my thinking I'm going to live, but there is also a great deal of disvalue in my believing I'm going to die: all the pain of anticipation. Now suppose that we are trying to settle what I ought to believe. Should we weigh the value of my getting this right against the disvalue of acquiring a painful belief? If so, we might conclude that I should remain agnostic in the face of overwhelming evidence of death or even become convinced that I'm going to survive given only the most tenuous grounds for hope. As a verdict on the rationality of belief, this can't be right. We can't allow the postulated value of truth-tracking to be weighed against the disvalue of future pain.[9]

This second difficulty should make us wonder how much guidance *Correctness* really gives us about when to believe.[10] Whilst being guided by *Correctness* clearly involves being sensitive to the evidence at least to some extent, it need not involve

---

[9] Note that this second difficulty can be generalized to threaten any attempt to ground the authority of an epistemic norm in the value of our conformity to it. Take *Evidence* and suppose there is some intrinsic value in basing one's beliefs on sufficient evidence. Whatever that value may be, we can't determine what it would be reasonable for someone to believe by weighing the desirability of their believing in accordance with *Evidence* against the desirability of their forming beliefs in other ways.

[10] As William James observed, *Correctness* does not actually require us to form any beliefs: you could conform to it by believing nothing at all (James 1956: 17–19).

being sensitive to the evidence in anything, like the way in which belief is sensitive to evidence. Consider suspicion.[11] Suspicion, like belief, is governed by *Correctness*:[12] to suspect that OJ murdered his wife is to be mistaken should he be innocent (however justified the suspicion and reasonable the error), but the evidence required for reasonable suspicion that p clearly differs from that required for reasonable belief in p.[13] The same applies to hope and fear. Where p is false we speak of false hopes and fears that p; such hopes and fears are no less mistaken than incorrect beliefs. This is so even though false hopes and fears may, like incorrect beliefs, be perfectly reasonable, being well grounded in evidence. Yet both reasonable hopes and reasonable fears are built on much less evidence than is required for reasonable belief. So *Correctness* fails to capture the norms distinctive of belief, since *Correctness* does not tell us what constitutes evidence sufficient for the formation of belief.[14]

I'll conclude this section by asking whether we might avoid these problems by strengthening *Correctness* as follows:

Knowledge: Believe that p only if your belief would constitute knowledge of p.

Knowledge entails *Correctness* since knowledge entails truth. Perhaps knowledge is the value for which we have been searching, a value that can underwrite the authority of both *Correctness* and *Evidence*. Suspicions, hopes, and fears do not require knowledge. On the contrary, ignorance is a presupposition of suspicion, hope, and fear.

I agree that *Knowledge* is a norm that applies uniquely to belief (and belief-involving states). You can't think it reasonable for you to believe that p if you take yourself to be ignorant of whether p (Owens 2000: 40–1). Furthermore, this norm

---

[11] In Chapter 2 I used the example of a guess or conjecture to make the point. (Shah and Velleman 2005: 498 n.7) expressed doubts about whether guessing is a propositional attitude like belief. Suspicion is immune to such doubts. Note that to suspect that p is not just to hypothesize that p (*pace* (Shah and Velleman 2005: 512)). One can entertain and test the hypothesis that p whilst having a completely open mind about whether p is true, but if one suspects that p, one's mind is not entirely open (Greenspan 1988: 85–8).

[12] One might doubt that suspicions, hopes, and fears are subject to *Correctness* on the grounds that one can reasonably entertain inconsistent suspicions, hopes, and fears. The issue is complex, but on this point I see no difference between these attitudes and belief. To suspect that X did it and suspect that Y did it is usually a matter of suspecting a conspiracy or else of having a disjunctive expectation. Perhaps it can also be reasonable to maintain genuinely inconsistent beliefs and inconsistent suspicions, at least where the alternative is to make an arbitrary choice about which one to abandon (Chapter 2). Be that as it may, inconsistent beliefs and suspicions are on a par.

[13] Contrast the legal standard for reasonable suspicion (e.g. when arresting someone) with the legal standard for convicting them in court.

[14] This conclusion should worry anyone who wants to characterize belief in terms of *Correctness* regardless of where they think the source of the latter's authority lies.

indicates a plausible value. Isn't knowledge *pro tanto* better than ignorance, at least where it is important to have some view on the matter? This may be denied (Raz 2011: 43 n.15), but let's allow it for now. Still, given our theoretical ambitions, this is not a satisfying result, for knowledge is a value whose content can be specified only by reference to the satisfaction of the very epistemic norms whose authority we are seeking to ground in that value. Knowledge requires justified belief [15] and *Evidence* specifies just how much evidence one must have in p's favour for one to be justified in believing that p. Given this, *Knowledge* must be explained in terms of *Evidence* and not vice versa.[16] So, even assuming that knowledge is valuable for its own sake, we can't base the value of conforming to *Evidence* on the value of conforming to *Knowledge*.

We can restate the point just made in terms of truth-tracking rather than evidence. Knowledge of p involves more than a simple match between the content of my belief and the character of the world; knowledgeable belief must track the truth, and a belief tracks the truth where it is based on some reliable indicator of its own truth. Such tracking is plausibly worth having; the problem is that one can have more or less of it. Reasonable suspicion tracks the truth to a certain extent, whilst reasonable belief hugs the truth more closely. We must explain the point of tracking truth in the way that (reasonable) belief tracks truth rather than in the way that (reasonable) suspicions, hopes, and fears do; we must say why people should want to get at the truth *in this particular way*.

We have been assuming that both truth and the value of truth can be understood without using normative notions. In that respect, *Correctness* is well placed to explain the content of other norms of belief formation and, for all I have said here, such an alethic account might well be part of the story about norms like *Evidence*. But it can't be the whole story and we can't complete that story just by reverting to *Knowledge*, for knowing that p involves having a justified belief in p, and to be justified in believing p is at least to conform to relevant epistemic norms such as *Evidence*. So the idea that knowledge has value seems to presuppose rather than support the idea that conformity to such epistemic norms has value. In Section 4.3, I'll consider one attempt to explain, rather than assume, the value of knowledge.

---

[15] At least this is so when we are dealing with creatures for whom the question of justification arises. Perhaps cat-knowledge does not require justification. I have no view about whether human knowledge can be *analysed* in terms of justification and other factors.

[16] Some epistemologists have attempted to explain the relevant notion of tracking or reliability in terms of non-normative notions such as probability, counterfactual sensitivity, and so forth. I can't examine these efforts here and only note that none have garnered general agreement. I shall assume that the notion of epistemic justification and, in particular, the notion of sufficiency invoked by *Evidence* cannot be analysed in non-normative terms.

4.3 Pragmatic Conceptions of Belief

While constructing an account of belief and knowledge, Edward Craig tells us that, 'Fortunately there is a firmly fixed point to start from. Human beings need true beliefs about their environment, beliefs that can guide their actions to a successful outcome' (Craig 1990: 11). For Craig, the value of true belief lies in its motivating successful agency, agency that achieves its objectives. Craig goes on to argue that true beliefs amounting to knowledge are precisely those most likely to guide action to a successful outcome, and so we can add that the value of knowledge lies in its role in motivating successful agency.

This suggestion about the source of epistemic normativity has indeed been an intellectual fixture, at least since the advent of Pragmatism. It is endorsed by American Pragmatists like Peirce, James, and C.I. Lewis; British Pragmatists like Ramsey and Braithwaite; and by many more recent writers.[17] Stalnaker clearly considers the 'guidance of behaviour' to be a core function of belief, and the same applies within the recent literature on 'pragmatic encroachment'. For example, Fantl and McGrath maintain that 'the importance of the concept of knowledge' resides in the fact that 'it sets a meaningful lower bound on strength of epistemic position: your epistemic position regarding p must be strong enough to make it rational for you to act as if p is true' (Fantl and McGrath 2007: 581), while Stanley and Hawthorne claim that 'Where one's choice is p-dependent, it is appropriate to treat the proposition that p as a reason for acting iff you know that p' (Hawthorne and Stanley 2008: 578). The differences between these formulations will not matter here; I shall treat them both as characterizing knowledge by citing a norm that connects knowledge with agency. If we also assume that something like *Knowledge* is correct, we can derive a claim about belief, namely

> *Pragmatism*: We are entitled to believe that p iff we are entitled to act as if p is true (or take p as a reason for action).

I want to highlight two attractions of *Pragmatism*. The first is that it connects belief to what many take to be the ultimate source of any form of normativity, namely, our ability to produce valuable states of affairs by means of our agency. On this view, false and ignorant beliefs are bad because they undermine our ability to pursue familiar goods like pleasure, beauty, and so forth. Agents are able

---

[17] Some of these writers may have regarded pragmatic conceptions of belief as an alternative to alethic conceptions of belief. I'll instead treat claims such as *Pragmatism* as supplementing or underwriting rather than as replacing a claim like *Correctness* or *Knowledge*. (Velleman argues that without an alethic component, we could not distinguish a belief from a fantasy and a desire from a wish (Velleman 2000: 255–77).)

to pursue those goods successfully when they can make the world satisfy the desires or fulfil the intentions on which they act. Such a match is just the converse of truth and no more requires normative notions for its specification than does truth itself.

A second attraction of *Pragmatism* is that it seems to do a good job of differentiating belief from the other propositional attitudes governed by *Correctness*. To be entitled to suspect (or hope or fear) that p is not to be entitled to act as if p is true. In certain contexts, one might be entitled to act on one's suspicions but Pragmatism states that one is always entitled to act on a (well-grounded) belief, to act as if one's belief is true, whatever the context. Thus, the norms governing belief in p will be those whose satisfaction always makes it sensible to act as if p were true. We now have an answer to our earlier question: what is the point of trying to get at the truth by forming beliefs, by coming to know the truth? Belief and knowledge provide a basis for making decisions about what to do, one on which we are entitled to rely in any context.

At this point Stalnaker would object. He maintains that we don't need such 'all-out' beliefs in order to take decisions, that we could manage well enough with Bayesian degrees of confidence in the relevant propositions without seeking to divide those propositions into those that we know and those we don't. What practical purpose is served by setting an evidential threshold above which one may believe that p and below which one may not? Why not just proportion one's belief to the evidence, proportion one's willingness to behave as if p (or not-p) to the degree of one's belief in p (or not-p) and act accordingly? Isn't that how we determine what odds to accept in a betting situation?

The pragmatist replies that we can't keep track of the evidence for and against the innumerable propositions whose truth might matter to us.[18] At some point we cease to deliberate, close the books, take a view before throwing away much of the evidence (so we don't have to store it), and act accordingly. How could it be otherwise, given the limits on our capacity to retain old information and consider the significance of new information as it arrives, while doing everything else we must do? Even where our conclusion has a probabilistic content it will still be an all-out belief, not a Bayesian level of confidence.[19] In the eyes of the pragmatist we form beliefs for much the same reason that we set ourselves to do something

---

[18] (Harman 1986: 38–42 and 46–9). For a more recent statement of the point, see (Ross and Schroeder 2012: 27–8).

[19] It should be noted that 'all-out' attitudes like belief and intention are stronger or weaker, more or less firm. What makes these attitudes 'all-out' is the presence of a line between believing and not-believing, intending and not-intending. The strength of the attitude is a function of how easy it is to get the subject back across the line, to abandon the relevant belief or intention (Owens 2000: 142–5).

by forming an intention to do it: if we are to act effectively, we cannot always remain non-committal either about how things are (or are likely to be) or about what to do in the light of this.[20] The precise point at which we should make up our minds about how things are (at which the evidential threshold for rational belief has been reached), like the precise point at which we should settle what to do, will be fixed by the need to ensure successful agency.

One might wonder whether it is always a good thing for an agent to be able to execute her intentions successfully. Doesn't that rather depend on the quality of her intentions? I shall allow that there is always *something* to be said for having this power, even if, given the idiocy of one's intentions, one would on the whole be better off without it. What of propositions whose subject matter is of no practical relevance? For instance, some of us take enough of an interest in the number of stars in the galaxy to form beliefs about such things, though we may never have occasion to act on these beliefs. The pragmatist can respond that we rightly value the higher order capacity to determine which issues are practically relevant and which are not, a capacity that requires us to know much that is practically irrelevant at the first-order level. Let's give the pragmatist a pass on this, for the charms of *Pragmatism* are in any case illusory.

I'll start with its second attraction. Is the evidential threshold for knowledge (and so rational belief) really tied to the requirements of rational agency in the way the pragmatist suggests? It is not so clear that it is always rational to act as if p simply because you know that p. In particular, this is not rational in some cases where (a) the costs of acting as if p should p turn out to be false are substantial or (b) the benefits of acting as if not-p should not-p turn out to be true are substantial.[21] In these cases, though we know that p, we decline to act on our knowledge, we refuse to take p as a reason for action and so the pragmatist cannot use *Knowledge* to explain the norms of belief.

This morning I attended an examiner's meeting at which a poor degree was awarded to one of my students. I have a clear recollection of the result and I feel sorry that the student didn't do well. The next day I must write a formal letter to the student announcing the result and before writing the letter I check the list of student marks that was circulated at the meeting. Why check? Is it because

---

[20] This is perhaps less obvious when it comes to suspicions than it is with belief and intention, since we are quicker to abandon our suspicions in the light of new evidence. Still, when you suspect me of abusing your child, you don't have an open mind about whether I have abused your child and your suspicion informs your actions (and emotions like hope and fear). Were we never entitled to form such suspicions but had to keep all the available evidence in play until there was enough for belief, our lives would be very different.

[21] After laying out the case for (a) in Chapter 7: Section 7.3, I read (Brown 2008: 175–82), from whom I borrow the exam result example.

I suddenly experience doubts, fearing that I might have mixed this student's mark up with the many others that were discussed at the meeting? That *might* be how it is; equally well it might not. Perhaps I instead reason as follows: though I know perfectly well that the student did poorly (still feel sorry about this and so forth) I also recognize that my memory is fallible, a further check can easily be made and given what hangs on the letter, I should make the check before writing it. The precaution seems eminently sensible.

I am sensible not to act on my recollection that the student did poorly because the costs of being wrong are substantial. The same point is made by cases in which I risk missing out on a considerable though unlikely benefit if I act on my belief. Suppose someone offers to pay me £10 million in return for a stake of ten pence if it turns out that I was not born male. I know that I was born male and much of the rest of what I know about myself would make little sense were I not. Nevertheless, I might reasonably accept the bet (Hawthorne 2004: 176). Can the mere fact that I have been offered this bet render one of my securest convictions unjustified? Must I confess ignorance of my original gender because it is silly to miss out on this bet?

In response, the pragmatist might weaken their position thus:

Default Pragmatism: To be entitled to believe that p is to be entitled to use p as a default assumption in one's practical reasoning.[22]

In answering a question (whether practical or theoretical) we take various things for granted. The default pragmatist suggests that there are some propositions that we are entitled to take for granted in answering any given question unless we see a special reason to do otherwise, namely the propositions we are entitled to believe. And the propositions we do believe are those we actually do take for granted unless an alarm goes off, an alarm set to register situations in which it would be sensible to check or else to take a risk on it, etc. *Default Pragmatism* allows that one can fail to act as if p once an alarm goes off, whilst continuing to believe that p, provided one continues to be disposed to act as if p (without further consideration of whether p) when no alarm is sounding. Once the alarm has gone off one presumably considers what to do on the basis of other beliefs (some of which concern evidence for or against the truth of p), these other beliefs being used as default assumptions in the present context. That's what happens when one decides to purchase the lottery ticket or to check the list of exam results.

---

[22] See Chapter 7: Section 7.3. Something like *Default Pragmatism* (though not under that name) is defended in (Ross and Schroeder 2012: 8–10 and 19–22).

I don't doubt that we rely on our beliefs in determining how to act unless there is a special reason to do otherwise. The problem with this claim is that it does not distinguish belief from a range of other attitudes. Some of these attitudes are like belief in that they are governed by evidential norms. If I suspect you of abusing my child then I'll refrain from placing them in your care, but I might not report you to the police: the consequences of so doing are such that they constitute a reason for not acting on a mere suspicion. Other such attitudes seem not to be governed by evidential norms. The lawyer is obliged to act as if her client is innocent, regardless of the strength of the evidence against him. Call this attitude *acceptance*. True, she will not act on this assumption outside certain professional contexts, but, equally, there are many contexts in which we are not prepared to act on our suspicions or indeed on our beliefs.

For the default pragmatist, belief and suspicion are at bottom forms of acceptance. The difference between belief, suspicion, and the lawyer's acceptance lies in the range of contexts in which one is disposed to act on the relevant attitude. Wouldn't that suffice to explain why the evidential norms governing these attitudes differ? Indeed, but this explanation makes the difference between belief, suspicion, and acceptance out to be a matter of degree: it is just that we are both inclined and (with the relevant evidence) entitled to place greater reliance on the former. The idea that there is a categorical distinction between knowledge and ignorance—the idea that Fantl and McGrath, Stanley and Hawthorne etc. seemed to be trying to capture—has now escaped us. What remains is a continuum of propensities to assume that a certain proposition is true for the sake of action. So long as belief in p was taken to involve being disposed to act as if p *in all contexts*, belief occupied a very special position on this continuum. Having removed belief from that position, the default pragmatist is without an account of why the (range of) dispositions denoted by the word 'belief' should be of any special interest to us. Pragmatism starts to look like a more psychologically realistic form of Bayesianism.

In this section, I have been focused on the pragmatist's claim to be able to differentiate belief from other attitudes governed by *Correctness*. In Section 4.4, I'll present my own account of this matter and then I'll query *Pragmatism*'s other attraction, the idea that belief's role in the guidance of agency is the ultimate ground of epistemic normativity because it is the source of belief's value.

4.4 Belief and the Passions

What is the point of believing things, of seeking to know them as opposed to merely suspecting them? In the rest of this chapter, I'll suggest that the value of belief and knowledge lies in its enabling a form of emotional engagement with the world (suspicion underwrites a rather different form of emotional engagement). We'll reach this conclusion by arguing that the evidential threshold at which it becomes rational to believe and so to claim knowledge of p is the point at which it would be appropriate to have a range of emotional attitudes towards p (rather than the threshold at which it would be rational to act as if p were true). The evidence required by *Evidence* must suffice to make it reasonable for me to feel a certain way.

Emotions come in at least two varieties. More numerous are those with the following feature: where the emotion in question has a propositional object, the subject of the emotion can feel that way only if they believe the proposition in question. It follows that they are entitled to feel that way only if they reasonably believe the proposition in question. Where I am angry that p I must believe that p, and my anger is reasonable only if p is a proposition in whose truth I reasonably believe. Suppose I am angry that Tom stole my bike. My anger is reasonable only if it is reasonable for me to believe that Tom stole my bike. Call such emotions *doxastic* emotions. Doxastic emotions include regret, resentment, horror, disgust, fury, sorrow, embarrassment, disappointment, shame, and on the positive side delight, gratitude, pleasure, and pride.[23]

The claims just made might be further explained. Perhaps I can't even be angry that p unless I *know* (and thus believe) that p.[24] On this view, emotions like anger might better be called *epistemic* (rather than doxastic) emotions. Advocates of this view allow that anger can be misdirected; Tom may not have stolen my bike, and even if Tom did steal my bike, I may not know this (perhaps this news came from an informant who, though credible, is only repeating a rumour that happens to be true). But if anger is an epistemic emotion, it would be wrong to say that I am *angry that* Tom stole my bike since I cannot be angry about things of which I am ignorant. Rather, I am angry *in the belief* that Tom stole my bike (Unger 1975: 189–96).

I register no objection to claim that anger is an epistemic emotion, but nor do I wish to rely on it here because my point does not turn on the correct usage of idioms like 'angry that p'. Perhaps 'I am angry that Tom stole my bike' can just mean 'I am angry in the belief that Tom stole my bike'. This would be enough to

---

[23] Though my list of doxastic emotions is taken from Gordon, Gordon describes anger etc. as a *factive* emotion, where a factive verb is one that applies only where its propositional complement is true. That does not capture the connection to reasonable belief that interests me. And he applies the label 'epistemic emotion' to the non-doxastic emotions (Gordon 1987: Chapter 2).

[24] I endorse this view in Chapter 7: Section 7.3. Here I remain agnostic.

explain why I can't reasonably be angry that Tom stole my bike unless I reasonably believe that Tom stole my bike. Furthermore, given that I can't reasonably believe that p where I think I'm ignorant of whether p, it would also explain why I can't think my anger at Tom is reasonable unless I think I know that Tom stole my bike. These implications are enough for my purposes and I shall continue to call anger, etc. doxastic emotions.

Non-doxastic emotions include hope and fear together with their variants such as worry. These emotions are like their doxastic cousins in that they may take a propositional object and where this is so, they too are governed by *Correctness*; a false hope (or fear) is a mistaken hope (or fear). But hope and fear exclude knowledge.[25] One is merely hopeful (rather than joyful) or fearful (rather than devastated) precisely when one does not take oneself to know the final outcome.[26] Once I realize that the prize is going to someone else, I can no longer hope to win it, nor can I hope to win it once it is revealed that I have won it.

Both doxastic and non-doxastic emotions come in degrees: joys and regrets, hopes and fears are all stronger or weaker and all more or less intense, but this similarity conceals an important difference. The strength of a non-doxastic emotion varies in two dimensions, the strength of a doxastic emotion in only one. Consider hope and fear. Hoping that you'll win involves suspecting that you'll win as well as wishing to win (and fearing that you'll lose involves suspecting that you'll lose as well as wishing you won't).[27] The more you wish to win, the more you hope that you will win. In this respect hope is like joy: the more you want the prize, the more you'll enjoy getting it. But the strength of your hopes also varies as your suspicion that you'll win waxes and wanes. As the evidence that you will win piles up, your hopes rise; as doubts intensify, your hopes fade. There is no corresponding dimension of variation in the case of joy. For joy there is an evidential threshold: either the evidence fails to convince you that you have won, in which case joy is ruled out or else it succeeds in convincing

---

[25] Wollheim criticizes Gordon's account of what I call non-doxastic emotions on this point. He argues that one can be frightened or terrified of what one *knows* will happen (e.g. death). Sometimes it is the uncertain timing, character, or consequences of one's death that one fears, but one can also be terrified of death as such. Perhaps emotions anticipating unpleasant outcomes like 'fear', 'terror', and 'dread' take both doxastic and non-doxastic forms, a difference not clearly marked in English. See (Wollheim 1999: 106–10).

[26] Note that one can have doxastic emotions involving propositions with a probabilistic content or a modal content, e.g. I can be pleased that I have a 90 per cent chance of winning the lottery or pleased that I might win the lottery.

[27] Gordon tells us that to hope that you'll win the prize you must (a) be in doubt as to whether you have won it and (b) wish to win it (Gordon 1987: Chapter 4), yet isn't hoping to win a matter of being in some degree hopeful that you will win, of having hopes of winning that might be dashed? Mere doubtfulness about winning seems less than hopeful.

you and then you should experience joy in the degree made appropriate by the desirability of its object (Adler 2002: 217).

Someone can be angry or happy at the fact that p, or proud of it, or grateful for it, only if they believe that p. This suggests the following hypothesis: often we want a view about whether p in order to fix our emotional bearings, to avoid having our feelings baffled by ignorance. In eliminating uncertainty we learn how to feel, not just how to act. Emotional bafflement (as well as practical uncertainty) renders doubt painful and drives inquiry. True, we might sometimes prefer to stick with those emotions—hopes and fears—that presuppose uncertainty rather than learn the truth. But very often we're anxious to discover whether we have a fatal illness and not just so we can make the appropriate arrangements. We want to know how to feel about our situation.

The pragmatist might respond that these roles are complementary: belief both sets our emotional bearings and guides our practical deliberation, but, as we saw earlier, there are cases in which feeling as if p would be sensible though acting on one's knowledge of p would not and vice versa. I felt sorry that my student had done poorly in their exams even as I checked to make sure that they had. Here I feel sad because they have done poorly, but I'm hardly checking the list because they have done poorly. Furthermore, I can feel either pride or shame that I was born a man even as I accept the bet, and I can feel this way only because I believe that I was born male. Pride and shame need not come and go in response to such offers; rather, they are part of a more permanent background, dependent on relatively stable convictions which structure our emotional lives.[28]

I've suggested that the value of belief and knowledge lie in their enabling certain forms of emotional engagement with the world. On my hypothesis, the difference between knowledge and ignorance matters to us because the capacity to have doxastic emotions matters to us. This leaves it wide open exactly why various aspects of the world should concern us in this fashion. Some facts might engage our emotions for instrumental reasons, others because of their intrinsic interest (e.g. the number of stars in the galaxy). Either way, we are curious only where our emotions are at least potentially aroused. Yet aren't many facts rather unlikely to engage our emotions? I read the newspaper in a calm and detached frame of mind, generally believing what I read. Here, I form views on matters of apparent indifference, and they are no less governed by epistemic norms than those I form on matters close to my heart. So how, it may be asked, can epistemic

---

[28] I agree with Fantl, McGrath, Stanley, and Hawthorne, etc. that how much evidence I need for knowledge of (or reasonable belief in) a proposition depends on how much its truth matters to me, but I deny that either is a function of its transient practical significance (Chapter 7: Section 7.3).

norms derive their authority from the value of my emotional engagement with the relevant subject matter?

There is such a thing as mild curiosity. Some facts interest us for their own sake and not just because of their impact on our lives or their wider moral or scientific importance. We want to know because the matter interests us, without provoking anything like anger, disgust, or even hope and fear. We are faintly pleased or slightly amused when we discover what is happening on the other side of the world. Such mild curiosity is often quite enough to explain why I both entertain suspicions on a certain matter and/or want to know the truth about it: no more intense or practical concern is required.[29] But suppose I am indeed totally incurious about the exact number of pencils currently on my desk. If I do form a view about this, aren't I still subject to criticism should that view be based on insufficient evidence? I doubt it. Epistemic norms apply only where deliberation is a possibility, where there is some opportunity (usually not taken) to weigh the evidence, consider defeaters, etc.[30] This possibility exists only where it would make sense to deliberate, and it makes sense to deliberate only where there is some basis for curiosity on the point (which might just be curiosity about whether my perceptual mechanisms are working properly). Since there is *ex hypothesi* no basis for curiosity in the pencil situation, any attitude that I acquire on the matter can only be the spontaneous output of an automatic perceptual mechanism. As noted at the outset, I'm interested in norms that can guide belief formation, thereby providing grounds for a specific form of criticism: attitudes formed by reflex will not be stigmatized as irrational.

A second question now arises. Is it always in my interests to enjoy apt rather than inapt emotions, even on topics of indisputable significance? So long as life is good, the menu of apt emotions adds relish to the dish; once our fortunes turn, an appropriate emotional engagement with what is happening seems to make life worse rather than better. My friend dies and I am devastated. Wouldn't it be better for me if I somehow didn't learn of this or even deceived myself on the point? Won't my remaining friends feel more sorry for me once I'm forced to face the truth? Of course I shouldn't visit my friend if they aren't going to be there and

---

[29] Where something matters much more to one person than another, does that entail that the relevant evidential threshold for reasonable belief varies also? If so that would disrupt the workings of testimony, for in order to determine whether some competent and sincere person is a credible source on the point, I'd have to go into how much it happens to matter to them. I agree that the threshold cannot be determined in such an individualistic fashion. What sets the threshold is the social significance of the issue where this social significance is a matter of emotional significance of this sort of issue within the relevant community (Chapter 7: Section 7.3).

[30] For discussion of what deliberation involves, see Chapter 3: Section 1.

such practicalities might come to matter more than peace of mind, but then again they might not. In any case, how can this terrible knowledge *as such* be good for me? That is the topic of the Section 4.5.

4.5 Epistemic Norms and Normative Interests

The obvious way to connect epistemic norms with value would be to argue that beliefs conforming to norms such as *Evidence* have a value that beliefs violating such norms do not. As we have seen, this isn't a promising line to take. Sometimes there is no evident value or interest in conforming your beliefs to norms like *Evidence*, and where there is such an interest it is often outweighed by considerations recommending breach of the norm. I shall instead argue that what is good for us is not conformity to epistemic norms, it is rather the fact of being *subject* to those norms, of being in a position where it makes sense for us to be guided by them and are otherwise vulnerable to criticism. The validity of the norms itself has value; hence the value of belief, of the psychological state in virtue of which we are subject to them. In this final section, I will try to characterize norms like *Evidence* in a way that makes our interest in them clear and do so without instrumentalizing them, without identifying some non-normative value which conformity to them promotes.

Following the lead of Section 4.4, one might argue for this as follows: (i) we value for its own sake the capacity to engage emotionally with the world in certain ways; (ii) belief is required for that capacity; (iii) to believe is to be subject to norms like *Evidence*; therefore (iv) there is value in being subject to those norms. Here a valuable capacity is partially constituted by a belief that in turn subjects us to certain norms. Unfortunately, the argument is flawed: from the fact that A is valuable for its own sake and the fact that A involves B (even constitutively) it does not follow that B is valuable for its own sake. For example, the fact that goods like forgiveness or repentance both constitutively require a wrong does not show that there is any good in the wrong, and we should regret the wrong even as we celebrate the reaction. But, I shall urge, the present case is different: there is something good both in having the capacity to engage emotionally with the world and in being subject to the norms which possession of that capacity involves. We should not regret these things even as we regret some of the emotions they require of us.

Consider (i). What I am supposing to be of value here is not, say, the experience of an apt grief but rather the capacity to engage emotionally with my friend's fortunes. To grasp the point, let's first set aside several things that the phrase 'capacity to engage emotionally with the world' might cover but which are not in question. First, there is our capacity to enjoy the non-doxastic emotions: hope, fear, and their variants. Second, there are those simulacra of the doxastic emotions stimulated by reading novels and watching films or plays, emotions such as 'grief' and 'admiration' for the characters portrayed. Our life is surely enriched by these psychological phenomena and a good story about my friend would move me, but that story could not satisfy my curiosity about what is now happening to them unless it enabled me to engage emotionally with the relevant bits of the world.[31]

A specific piece of knowledge (such as knowledge of what is happening to one's friend) enables me to engage the fact known with a range of doxastic emotions. I maintain that, at least on issues that matter to us (like the fate of our friends) we have reason to value this specific topic-focused capacity and that is the ground of the value of particular items of knowledge. This need to engage emotionally with particular facts is registered in a feeling of frustration whenever our emotions are baffled by ignorance, when we are rendered incapable of pride, shame, joy, grief, and so forth because we don't know the truth. It makes sense to want to know whether you were admired or despised by your long-dead brother, whether you are soon going to die yourself and so forth, even if there is little you can or would wish to do about it. You want to know how to feel about the past or the future. A hedonist might respond that what you really want is to avoid the pain of the frustration caused by ignorance, but, if so, that could be achieved by popping a pill. Since the pill isn't the thing, the desire to know must be something more than the desire to avoid the psychic costs of ignorance; rather, it is a desire for some good whose absence is registered by these costs. It is also something other than the need for good news rather than bad. Of course, you wish it to be the case that your brother admired you and that you'll lead a long and happy life, but, quite apart from that, you have some desire simply to know where you stand (and for its own sake).

These facts may seem puzzling. To know that my friend has died is to be placed in a situation in which a feeling of devastation is apt or even required of me and my life goes much worse should I feel an apt devastation rather than a quite inapt indifference. So why should anyone wish (for my sake) that I know whether my friend has died, when this knowledge will require me to feel devastated? Why should anyone wish that I be subject to a norm that I conform to only at great

---

[31] There is a familiar controversy over whether imaginative literature, films, etc. generate genuine anger, fear, and so forth, given that they do not create the relevant beliefs. I'm inclined to side with writers like (Walton 1990: 195–204) and (Velleman 2000: 270) who argue that they do not, but for present purposes I could retreat to the claim that certain valuable *forms* of anger and fear, etc. are baffled by ignorance.

cost to myself? The worry is not just that the benefits of knowledge will be outweighed by the costs, that all things considered it would be preferable not to know at all, that I would on the whole be better off were I to remain blissfully ignorant of my friend's death. The worry is rather that, at least if the intrinsic value of knowledge (and belief) lies in their emotional significance, knowing lacks *all* intrinsic value because to know is to be required to have a feeling that there is no (non-instrumental) good in having. Since devastation as such has no advantages over peace of mind, how can knowledge derive its value from the fact that it requires this of us?

We are assuming that human interests ground normativity in one way only, namely, by ensuring that it is good for us to conform to the norms in question. Suppose instead that human beings have normative interests, that amongst the basic goods of human life are normative phenomena themselves: obligations and permissions but also standards of aptness and appropriateness for beliefs, feelings, and so forth. Then a psychological state could derive at least part of its value from the fact that it subjects us to certain norms, even though conformity with those norms may sometimes have nothing to be said for it. In this respect, knowledge (and belief) are not unusual. I would argue that friendship itself derives part of its value from the fact that it subjects friends to certain norms, even though conformity with those norms may do them no good in any given instance.

Many writers agree that having friends is good for you and not just because friends provide you with help and support. Friendship is good for its own sake and thereby enriches your life. One prominent feature of friendship is that it brings into play a whole set of norms. Becoming John's friend changes the normative situation between us, creating reciprocal rights and obligations, and altering what feelings are appropriate or even required. It is once John has become a close friend that I should be devastated by his death, that I would be a bad friend if I weren't. What attitude should I adopt towards the norm of friendship that requires me to feel devastated should John die? I might regard this norm as an unfortunate aspect of an otherwise good thing, a feature perhaps inextricably bound up with the depth of our friendship but not as itself making any positive contribution to its value. Were that my attitude, I might well regret that my friendship with John would require me to feel devastated should he die. But isn't regret an inappropriate reaction to the realization that I am so required? Wouldn't it show that I failed to value the friendship and the bonds of loyalty it involves correctly? The point is *not* that I should feel glad when this norm comes into play because John dies. When this comes about I am sorry mainly for John but also for myself and others would surely pity me. What is not regrettable is the underlying fact that, because of our friendship, I would be required to feel this way should John die. On the contrary, that normative fact is part of the good of a deep friendship, a friendship which serves our interest in being subject to such norms (Owens 2012: 111–17).

I've spoken of the norm requiring me to feel sad at John's death 'coming into play' when John dies, but that isn't quite right, for I'm subject to that norm only once I discover that John has died. In the context of friendship, knowledge establishes a normative connection between John and myself, making devastation the appropriate reaction to John's death. Friendship does not always require me to find out whether John is still alive whatever the cost, but it makes perfect sense for me to wish to know whether he is still alive, and to wish to know this because he is my friend, because his death will have a certain emotional significance for me. I may value the knowledge that requires a certain reaction of me even as I regret the feeling of devastation it demands and even though there are times when I deliberately remain in ignorance of his fate so I can focus on other things. And I value the relevant knowledge for its own sake because it partly constitutes (and does not merely cause me to acquire) a capacity for engagement that I value for its own sake.

I've said that believing involves being subject to various norms. Clearly, there is more to belief than that: believers have a certain psychology, they are disposed to think and behave in certain ways and they are subject to epistemic norms only in virtue of that psychology. A rock or an amoeba lacks the responsibilities of a believer because it lacks the required psychological sophistication. Furthermore, epistemic norms have their value (and so their authority) only in that specific psychological setting; the value and validity of these norms is dependent on the non-normative context in which they find application. For example, the argument of Section 4.4 suggests that belief and its norms might be no good to a pure Bayesian agent, one that has the internal machinery needed to weigh evidence and act accordingly but can feel nothing. In this respect, epistemic norms are once more similar to norms of friendship. The latter apply and have value only against the background of a relationship that they partially constitute, a relationship also constituted by certain habits of feeling and behaviour. Beings incapable of acquiring such habits would have no interest in these norms.

My central contention is that belief and knowledge can be valuable for their own sake because they serve certain normative interests. Some of these interests come into play in special contexts like that of friendship. Others have wider application, like my interest in being able to engage emotionally with whether I have won a certain prize. Unless I know the relevant facts, I am not subject to these norms, I am not emotionally engaged with the relevant subject matter and the value of knowledge lies in its making this connection. By explaining where the value of belief and knowledge lies, we have thereby established the authority of the norms that govern believing (e.g. *Evidence*) and a similar story may be told about those governing suspicion. When something engages our curiosity, we'll often value the capacity to entertain hopes and fears about it even whilst we remain ignorant of the ultimate truth. Suspecting, like believing, involves being subject to norms specifying what evidence provides adequate grounds for suspicion, and the value of suspicion is, in part, the value of being subject to those norms.

I'll conclude the chapter by considering two objections to my account of the value of knowledge. First, one may wonder whether the above line of thought really establishes the value of knowledge (over ignorance) as well as that of belief (over agnosticism). The objector is correct that I have been moving freely between the two, a liberty to which I felt entitled so long as I was discussing a Bayesian who denies the value of both belief and knowledge and on much the same grounds. But once the Bayesian has been answered in respect of belief, one might wonder why *Knowledge* is true, why a belief must constitute knowledge. Suppose I truly believe that I have won the prize. Whether or not this belief constitutes knowledge, it still gives me the capacity to engage emotionally with a fact about myself, a capacity quite distinct from my capacity to engage emotionally with an acknowledged fiction like a play or a film.[32] To form the belief that I won is to subject myself to various norms of evidence, etc., norms to which I must subject myself if I am to be in a position to react with pride (and so forth) to my win. And if the latter capacity has a value (one that the capacity to engage with films and fiction lacks) then I have an interest in entering a psychological state that subjects me to the norms that govern belief formation. Why should we suppose that I have any further interest in knowledge?

I agree that belief is better for me than mere agnosticism whether or not that belief constitutes knowledge and that this would be enough to answer Stalnaker's challenge, vindicate *Evidence* (though not *Knowledge*) and bring my main line of argument to a successful conclusion. Whether the argument can be extended from belief to knowledge depends on a question left hanging earlier: can I be angry that Tom stole my bike only once I *know* that he stole my bike? If the answer is 'yes', merely believing this, however truly or justifiably, will not put my anger into emotional contact with the fact: it will leave me angry only in the belief that Tom stole my bike. But if the answer is 'no', then, for all I have said, knowledge has no value beyond the value of true belief.

---

[32] (Wollheim 1999: 105–6) makes a parallel point about anger.

Second objection: isn't the value of knowledge, however understood, often outweighed by other values? Mightn't I be better off with the irrational belief that my friend is still alive, even if I do miss out on some valuable form of emotional engagement with the world? But the norms of belief formation and retention surely apply to such cases as much as to those in which the balance of advantage lies with belief in accordance with the evidence, and they alone determine whether belief is rational. Recall the objection I raised in Section 4.2 against those who sought to ground the authority of *Correctness* in the value of true belief. We imagined someone weighing the value of truth against whatever values would be served by false belief in order to determine what the subject should believe, all things considered. This procedure might endorse quite irrational belief. For the same reason, it may be thought, the value of knowledge cannot be the source of the authority of our epistemic norms. The strictness of these norms remains to be explained.

Here it is crucial to distinguish two different issues: (a) whether you should subject yourself to certain epistemic norms, and (b) whether you should conform to those norms given that you are subject to them. The question raised by (a) is a practical question, a question about what one ought to do. Where (a) is the issue one should indeed weigh the value of being subject to those norms, the value of being able to engage emotionally with the relevant facts, against the disvalue involved in actually conforming with those norms. If I have an important exam tomorrow and I have reason to suspect that something terrible has happened to John (something that I can do nothing about) it may be perfectly sensible for me to wait before looking into the matter, before acquiring the capacity to engage emotionally with his fate and so placing myself in a situation where I might be required to believe the worst. That capacity is valuable for its own sake, but its value not absolute. Here ignorance may be the better option.

The question raised by (b) can also be understood as a practical question, as asking whether you ought to do something to ensure that your beliefs conform to the norms to which they are subject, perhaps by taking some training in scientific methodology or visiting your analyst to address your tendency to wishful thinking. Here the practical considerations just rehearsed again apply and it may well be that you ought not to take such steps (the analyst costs money) and should instead allow your mental processes to run their perhaps irrational course, accepting the resulting criticism. Here the value of conforming to epistemic norms must be weighed against other relevant values to determine what one should do all things considered.

Once these practical questions have been settled and your beliefs are fixed, there is no further issue about whether these beliefs are subject to epistemic norms. The value relevant to the authority of epistemic norms over believers is the value of our being subject to those very norms (rather than the value of conformity with them), and that value is not to be weighed against the disvalue of conformity in order to determine whether we are vulnerable to criticism should we fail to believe in accordance with those norms: the emotional costs of conformity may give the believer some excuse for wishful thinking, but they provide no justification for it. Epistemic norms are indeed strict in that any believer is subject to those norms regardless of the costs of conformity.[33]

---

[33] I am grateful to audiences at Columbia University, the universities of Geneva, Fribourg, Luxembourg, Southampton, and Kings College London. Many thanks also to Alex Gregory, Mark Schroeder, Nishi Shah, Matthew Silverstein, Sharon Street, David Velleman, Clayton Littlejohn, and Jose Zalabardo for comments on drafts.

PART II
Scepticism

5

Scepticisms
Descartes and Hume

I shall maintain that the root of scepticism, at least as we find it in Descartes and Hume, is the demand for certainty. Recent writers are likely to dismiss this demand for certainty: in their view, inconclusive evidence is quite sufficient both to justify belief and to give us knowledge (should the proposition in question turn out to be true). Recent debate focuses, rather, on the possibility that we might have no evidence at all for our beliefs, that our belief-forming processes might be completely unreliable, undermining both knowledge and justification. It is the sceptical hypotheses which generate this worry—ordinary error does not—and so it is they alone, not the prosaic fact of our fallibility, which provide grounds for a real sceptical doubt.

Descartes and Hume are standard reference points for discussion of the sceptical hypotheses. Yet, I shall argue, in both Descartes and Hume, the sceptical hypotheses are secondary; what is really doing the work is their demand for certainty.

Furthermore Descartes, at least, suggests a way in which this demand might be motivated. Both philosophers do indeed raise 'the problem of the external world', but this is only one aspect of their scepticism; we can't dispatch either the Cartesian or the Humean sceptic just by demonstrating that thought or experience presupposes the existence of an external world. Their sceptical problem is more than the problem posed by the sceptical hypotheses.

5.1 Cartesian Scepticism

A reader of Descartes' *First Meditation* encounters the dreaming hypotheses after only five paragraphs and the evil demon is not far behind. This suggests that these thought experiments do indeed play a central role in his case for scepticism, that Descartes' scepticism rests on an appeal to the idea that, for all we know, most of our beliefs are false. But the first two paragraphs of that Meditation imply a quite different argumentative strategy.

At the very outset, Descartes sets himself to demolish all of his opinions:

> But to accomplish this, it will not be necessary for me to show that all my opinions are false, which is something I could perhaps never manage. Reason now leads me to think that I should hold back my assent from opinions which are not completely certain and indubitable just as carefully as I do from those which are patently false. So, for the purpose of rejecting all my opinions, it will be enough if I find in each of them at least some reason for doubt. (Descartes 1984: 12)

To undermine all my beliefs, I don't need to suppose that they are all false (i.e. I don't need a sceptical hypothesis); it is enough if, in the case of each of my beliefs, there is some reason to doubt that belief. Given the demand for certainty we need only the universal possibility of error, not the possibility of universal error, to destroy all conviction (Williams 1978: 54).

Now one might try to establish the fallibility of each of our claims to knowledge by going through them one by one, highlighting ways in which we might be wrong. Take beliefs based on experience: you think that the trousers match the shirt, but the shop lighting could be misleading you; you expect that your friend will soon walk through the mist towards you, but this anticipation could be turning a swirl into a silhouette. In each and every case, there will be local sources of error which you didn't eliminate. But, as Descartes notes, to tackle our convictions individually in this way 'would be an endless task' (Descartes 1984: 12). He circumvents this difficulty in the case of beliefs based on experience by locating a source of sensory illusion which is, potentially, present in every case.

At this point, Descartes introduces the dreaming hypothesis. In the past, I have been tricked into thinking that I am sitting in my chair reading a book when in fact I am sound asleep. Couldn't such a thing be happening now? This is a question I can put to myself whenever I base a belief on sensory experience and so it is a ubiquitous source of error. Note, I need not entertain the hypothesis that I am permanently asleep in order to raise this doubt. All I need is the thought that, on any given occasion, I could be asleep. On this construal, the dreaming hypothesis is not, as yet, a sceptical hypothesis, an hypothesis which implies the total unreliability of our senses.

Next, Descartes slides from this less radical way of taking the dreaming hypothesis to a more radical one. At first, he asks us to recall particular past occasions on which we confused sleeping with waking experience. Such memories presuppose the idea that we are often awake; what they call into question is our ability to tell, on any particular occasion, whether we are awake on that occasion. But in the very next paragraph, Descartes raises the possibility that 'I do not even have such hands or such a body at all' (Descartes 1984: 13). At this point, the dreaming hypothesis turns into the thought that I am permanently asleep and that most everything I learn through the senses is false. But why does Descartes introduce such an outlandish hypothesis if he could, as he hoped, find some grounds for doubting each of our beliefs which was not a reason to think them all false?

5.1.1 The Role of the Sceptical Hypotheses

Descartes wishes to articulate a form of scepticism which calls all of our convictions into question and those convictions include some very general beliefs about the world, e.g. that there are objects independent of our mind, somehow arranged in space and time. Reflection on local sources of perceptual error cannot throw these into doubt: the possibility of perceptual error due to bad lighting, etc. depends on the world being approximately as we think it is. In order to undermine these very general convictions, we do need the idea that our experiences are all produced in some entirely deviant way, e.g. by an evil demon (Descartes 1984: 13–15): sceptical hypotheses are required to undermine our belief in the external world as such.[1] That is their job.[2] But, in Descartes view, sceptical hypotheses are *not* required to undermine our convictions about the shape, colour, and location etc. of any particular item which we take ourselves to perceive. Ordinary sensory fallibility is quite sufficient for that.

Many philosophers tend to read Descartes' reminder of the facts of sensory illusion (at the start of the *First Meditation*) as a mere softening up exercise. On their view, these facts cannot do any sceptical work by themselves since they do nothing to show that sensory experience is, in general, unreliable about the shape and position of things: the general unreliability of the senses is suggested only by the sceptical hypotheses. So the possibility of local perceptual error is not enough to throw doubt on the idea that our senses give us knowledge of our local environment, as well as of the general character of our world. But Descartes' demand for certainty extends to all belief, however specific, not just to our foundational (methodological) convictions.

Reviewing the argument of the *First Meditation* in the *Sixth*, Descartes remembers that, while trusting the senses 'I had many experiences which gradually undermined all the faith I had had in the senses' (Descartes 1984: 53), and he

---

[1] Does contemplation of this 'metaphysical possibility' actually undermine Descartes' belief in an external world, at least temporarily? This is something Descartes goes both ways on, and commentators have also divided on the issue (Descartes 1984: 11, 16, and 243).

[2] At this point, my reading of Descartes differs from that presented in (Owens 2000: 85).

then quotes examples of towers which looked round at a distance but square from close up, and so forth. Only then does he mention that 'to these reasons for doubting I recently added two very general ones' (ibid.) viz. the dreaming and the evil demon argument. It is clear that, in Descartes' view, sensory knowledge had been thoroughly undermined before the sceptical hypotheses were introduced. And we can't regain our faith in our senses until we have shown how all these local sources of error can be corrected for and eliminated, a task which Descartes undertakes in the *Sixth Meditation*.

I conclude that the sceptical hypotheses play a secondary role in Cartesian scepticism. Its primary motor is the demand for certainty and that, together with well-known facts about our fallibility, is quite sufficient to undermine the great majority of our beliefs. The sceptical hypotheses are needed only to deal with a special class of highly general beliefs: they make room for a doubt about the existence of an external world which, when combined with the demand for certainty, should suffice to destroy our faith in it. So the task of establishing the coherence of the sceptical hypotheses matters much less to the Cartesian sceptic than that of motivating the demand for certainty. I think the latter, at least, can be done, and I will attempt it (with the resources available to Descartes) in Section 5.3.

Descartes tells us that he has gone to great trouble to formulate the strongest form of scepticism so that by answering it, he can rid us of the sceptic forever (Descartes 1991: 333). And what most obviously distinguishes Cartesian scepticism from its ancient predecessors is precisely its use of the sceptical hypotheses (Burnyeat 1982: 43–50). But we should not think that Descartes has invented a new, more powerful kind of doubt, unavailable to the ancients. The sceptical hypotheses do not raise doubts of a kind we never had before; rather, they extend the old sceptical doubts as far as they can possibly go. The strongest doubt is just the most extensive doubt and the mechanism for generating this doubt is a traditional one: pointing out the possibility of error. This mechanism is no more powerful than the demand for certainty which lies behind it.

For now, we should be impressed by how little else the Cartesian sceptic need assume once the demand for certainty is in place. This infallibilist demand has often been associated with a foundationalist conception of human knowledge which portrays properly justified belief as the product of an inference from a class of propositions of which we are certain (e.g. propositions about the character of our experience). Perhaps Descartes is a foundationalist, but all the Cartesian sceptic needs is the requirement that we have conclusive grounds for each of our beliefs and the observation that our grounds are always inconclusive. He need presuppose nothing about the theoretical structure or character of these grounds.[3] In fact, he may allow these grounds to have no systematic structure or character at all. What matters is simply whether they are conclusive or not.

5.1.2 Hume's Misreading of Descartes

Hume begins the section of the *First Enquiry* entitled 'Of the Academical or Sceptical Philosophy' with the following description of Cartesian scepticism:

> It recommends an universal doubt, not only of all our former opinions and principles, but also of our very faculties; of whose veracity, say they, we must assure ourselves, by a chain of reasoning, deduced from some original principle, which cannot possibly be fallacious or deceitful. But neither is there any such original principle, which has a prerogative above others, that are self-evident and convincing: or if there were, could we advance a step beyond it, but by the use of those very faculties, of which we are supposed to be already diffident. The Cartesian doubt therefore, were it ever possible to be attained by any human creature (as it plainly is not) would be entirely incurable; and no reasoning could ever bring us to a state of assurance and conviction upon any subject. (Hume 1975: 149–50)

In Hume's view, Cartesian scepticism has three elements: (a) the demand that our use of any belief-forming faculty be justified without prior reliance on that faculty; (b) the demand that this justification give us certainty that the faculty in question is veracious or reliable; and (c) the demand that all such justifications be based on a single foundational and self-evident principle.

In this passage, Hume means to be putting Cartesian scepticism to one side so he can raise his own, rather different sceptical problem. He rejects the three-part demand, which he associates with Cartesian scepticism, and he does so by rejecting the first demand (which is implicit the other two), the idea that we should not employ any cognitive faculty until we have first assured ourselves of its veracity. But, as we shall see, Hume is wrong to attribute this idea to Descartes. In fact, Descartes and Hume share much the same conception of what a reasonable method of belief formation must be like and the conception which they share is fundamentally infallibilist.

On Hume's interpretation, a Cartesian doubt can be raised prior to any reasoning and inquiry: it requires no grounds whatsoever. But this fails to make sense of Descartes' text. Consider the following statement about beliefs based on clear and distinct perceptions:

> If this conviction is so firm that it is impossible for us ever to have any reason for doubting what we are convinced of, then there are no further questions for us to ask: we have everything that we could reasonably want. What is it to us that someone may make out that the perception whose truth we are so firmly convinced of may appear false to God or

---

[3] For a different reading of Descartes, see (Williams 1986) and (Stroud 1989: 34–9).

an angel, so that it is, absolutely speaking, false? Why should this alleged 'absolute falsity' bother us, since we neither believe in it, nor have even the smallest suspicion of it?

(Descartes 1984: 103)

Here, Descartes is insistent that we can't induce a doubt about a belief that was based on the method of clear and distinct ideas without discovering some grounds for doubt: we must employ some method of reasoning (even the very one in question) in order to get a doubt going.[4]

Hume distinguishes '*antecedent*' scepticism from another form of scepticism which is '*consequent* to science and enquiry' (Hume 1975: 149–50). Real doubts, the kind of doubts the sceptic seeks to generate, are consequent on inquiry, not antecedent to it. They arise once we begin thinking and reasoning. Hume is surely right that consequent scepticism is the real threat to belief; he is wrong only in failing to see Cartesian scepticism as consequent. Descartes never claims blankly that our beliefs may be false, that our methods of belief formation might lead us astray; he always tells a story, based on what he takes himself to have learnt of the world by using those very methods, about how reasoning involving them may actually have led us astray. Even the evil demon hypotheses works as a sceptical device for Descartes (in so far as it does) because he takes himself to know that there are powerful spiritual beings, as the brain in a vat hypothesis works for us because experience has taught us about the physical basis of our mental lives.

Furthermore, Descartes' response to scepticism makes sense only if his scepticism is of the consequent variety. The passage about 'absolute falsity' just quoted occurs in the *Second Replies* where Descartes is rebutting the allegation that he was 'guilty of circularity when I said that the only reason we have for being sure that what we clearly and distinctly perceive is true is the fact that God exists, but that we are sure that God exists only because we perceive this clearly' (Descartes 1984: 71). Descartes denies that doubt about what we clearly and distinctly perceive is psychologically possible *at the time at which we are clearly and distinctly perceiving it*: doubt can arise only in retrospect when we come to reflect on how we formed this belief, a process of reflection which will inevitably employ the very method in question. The point of proving God's existence is to quiet any such retrospective doubts by establishing that the method of clear and distinct ideas is self-confirming. We can use the method to prove the existence of an omnipotent and benevolent deity and God's existence in turn guarantees that this method is reliable.

---

[4] (Frankfurt 1970: 25) construes this paragraph as an indication that Descartes has abandoned the correspondence theory of truth and opted for a coherence theory. But the paragraph fails to support this reading: Descartes does not say that the notion of 'absolute falsity' is incoherent, just that its possibility does not matter to us. Nor should we attribute a controversial theory of truth to Descartes if we can avoid so doing.

Were Cartesian scepticism of the antecedent variety, the fact that our fundamental methods of belief formation are self-confirming would mean nothing: a completely erroneous method (e.g. counter-induction) might be self-confirming. But a scepticism which is 'consequent to science and inquiry' may be answered in this way.[5] Once convinced, by the method of clear and distinct ideas, of the presence of an omnipotent and benevolent God, we can see that the course of future inquiry could not undermine that method. And, for Descartes, this should soothe any doubts about it. The method gives us the certainty that knowledge requires.

5.2 Humean Scepticism

Hume makes fun of the idea that we should 'have recourse to the veracity of the Supreme Being in order to prove the veracity of our senses' (Hume 1975: 153); he thinks Descartes' theological reasoning can deal neither with the antecedent, nor the consequent sceptic, and it is hard to disagree. Hume then deploys several different sceptical arguments which seek to demonstrate that our belief-forming processes are indeed self-undermining. These arguments form the substance of Humean scepticism. Like Descartes, Hume himself is no sceptic[6] and like Descartes, he deploys sceptical reasonings in order to teach us something about belief. The lesson he has to teach us—that belief is not governed by reason[7]—is not Descartes', but his way of addressing the issue, by means of consequent scepticism, is remarkable similar.

Before looking at the details of Hume's sceptical argument, I want to articulate the conception of rational belief he shares with Descartes. For both of them:

(1) Reason controls belief by means of the subject's judgements of the quality of their reasons for belief.

---

[5] Thus, I agree with Frankfurt that Descartes' argument 'is an attempt to show that there are no good reasons for believing that reason is unreliable' (Frankfurt 1970: 175). But whilst Frankfurt's view is that Descartes feels able to respond to scepticism in this way only because he has endorsed a coherence theory of truth, I hold that pointing out the self-confirmatory character of reason would constitute an adequate response to (consequent) scepticism, regardless of our theory of truth, because it deprives us of any reason to believe that reason is unreliable. On this point, see (Curley 1978: 105–18) and (Williams 1978: 198–209).

[6] (Hume 1975: 161) distinguishes what Hume calls 'excessive' or 'Pyrrhonian' scepticism from 'mitigated' scepticism and Hume appears to endorse the latter. In this chapter I am concerned only with what Hume calls Pyrrhonian scepticism, the view that we should suspend judgement on all matters. For discussion of mitigated scepticism, see (Stroud 1999) and (Fogelin 1993: 108–13).

[7] Hume uses the word 'reason' in a number of different senses. In this chapter, I am interested in that use of the word on which reason is contrasted with imagination and with its associates habit, instinct, and custom.

(2) Reason controls belief where these reflective judgements can motivate appropriate first-order beliefs.

(3) Reason controls belief where the subject's judgement that they have conclusive grounds for a belief can motivate the corresponding belief (or where the subject's judgement that their grounds are inconclusive can motivate suspension of belief).

The most controversial element here is (3), the idea that the subject cannot feel justified in having a given belief, in claiming knowledge, unless it seems to him that he has a conclusive reason for that belief. Descartes distinguishes knowledge from mere conviction as follows: 'there is conviction when there remains some reason which might lead us to doubt, but knowledge is conviction based on a reason so strong that it can never be shaken by any stronger reason' (Descartes 1991: 147). The aim of his war against the sceptic is precisely to turn our convictions into knowledge. Hume has a similar notion of knowledge, a similar conception of the aim of rational belief. Indeed, the first of Hume's sceptical arguments is meant to turn on nothing more than the fallibility of our belief-forming mechanisms.

5.2.1 Scepticism about Reason and the Senses

In the section of the *Treatise* entitled 'Of Scepticism With Regard to Reason', Hume attacks the very citadel of reason—deductive inference (taken to include mathematical reasoning)—but not by requiring some antecedent proof that deductive inference is a reliable cognitive mechanism. Who would be surprised to find that we couldn't establish the veracity of deductive inference without making use of deductive inference? Instead, Hume allows us to employ deductive inference *ab initio* and then argues that it undermines itself.

Hume's line of thought goes as follows: once we have experienced the fallibility of any form of reasoning, deductive or inductive, reason itself requires us to make a judgement about how likely that reasoning is to deliver the right result 'as a check or controul on our first judgement or belief' (Hume 1978: 180). This higher order judgement is itself known to be fallible on similar grounds and so we must make a further judgement about how likely it is that our assessment of the chance of error will be correct before we can reach any conclusion at all:

But this decision, though it should be favourable to our preceding judgment, being founded only on probability, must weaken still further our first evidence, and must itself be weakened by a fourth doubt of the same kind, and so on *in infinitum*; till at last there remain nothing of the original probability, however great we may suppose it to have been, and however small the diminution by every new uncertainty.   (Hume 1978: 182)

Hume concludes that reason subverts itself. This argument has great generality: it applies to any form of reasoning of which we have had enough experience to realize that it is fallible. But it rests on some rather dubious probabilistic reasoning, and by the time Hume came to write the *Enquiry*, it had been dropped in favour of other sceptical arguments of rather narrower scope but with a similar form.

Take the habit of basing belief on experience. Hume attaches no great significance to the facts of sensory illusion which are:

> only sufficient to prove, that the senses alone are not implicitly to be depended upon; but that we must correct their evidence by reason, and by considerations, derived from the nature of the medium, the distance of the object, and the disposition of the organ, in order to render them, within their sphere, the proper *criteria* of truth and falsehood. There are other more profound arguments against the senses, which admit not of so easy a solution.
> (Hume 1975: 151)

These remarks might seem to put a great distance between Hume and Descartes, at least on my reading of Descartes. But no; Hume asserts that sensory fallibility is not worrying *only* because he thinks we can always correct for it. Descartes would agree; he spends much of the *Sixth Meditation* telling us how to avoid sensory error altogether. This is no more than a pious hope on both their parts. It is hard to see how, even in a case where we put our minds to it, we could eliminate all possible sources of local perceptual error; *a fortiori* in the generality of cases, given the constraints on our time and imagination.

Putting this to one side, what is the 'more profound argument' that Hume mentions? It is based on an assumption which Hume thinks the 'slightest philosophy' will confirm, namely 'that nothing can ever be present to the mind but an image or perception, and that the senses are only the inlets, through which these images are conveyed, without being able to produce any immediate intercourse between the mind and the object' (Hume 1975: 152).

Given this assumption, Hume's sceptical reasoning runs as follows:

> It is a question of fact, whether the perceptions of the senses be produced by external objects, resembling them: how shall this question be determined? By experience surely, as all other questions of a like nature. But here experience is, and must be entirely silent. The mind has never anything present to it but the perceptions and cannot possibly reach any experience of their connection with objects. The supposition of such a connection is, therefore, without any foundation in reasoning. (Hume 1975: 153)

Humean scepticism about the senses is clearly consequent. The Humean sceptic is not requiring, in advance of any reliance on sensory experience, that we justify such reliance by ruling out the possibility of illusory experience. Rather, he is using sensory experience to undermine sensory experience as follows.

Having begun by basing your beliefs on sensory experience (correcting it with a bit of inductive reasoning) you quickly learn (e.g. by pressing your thumb against your eyeball) that the objects of vision are not external items. So, by what means do you know of such external items? Certainly not by direct experience. Perhaps then by inductive inference from the occurrence of the image you directly experience to the presence of a material object which resembles it: after all, I take myself to know that the sun will rise tomorrow in advance of any experience of its rising tomorrow. But, however cogent it is in general, inductive inference cannot help in this instance because we have no past experience of the connection between sensory images and external objects on which to base such an inference. Therefore, we must admit that our own recognized procedures of inquiry will not support it.

Does Hume's deployment of this argument make him a sceptic? No. Hume himself is not *endorsing* the theory of perception which this argument invokes. In fact, he says, it contradicts 'the universal and primary opinion of all mankind' (Hume 1975: 152). Hume simply observes that this theory is among 'the obvious dictates of reason' which 'no man, who reflects, ever doubted' (ibid.). The universal and primary opinion reasserts itself whenever we cease to reflect, and Hume offers no view on which opinion is right: he merely maintains that each is convincing in its own sphere and that they are in tension with one another.

So what is Hume trying to achieve with these sceptical arguments? Hume is seeking to establish that reason does not govern belief. Reason is a faculty that works by means of reflection, by means of judgements about the probative force of our grounds for belief. If reason controls belief then we can determine what we believe simply by making a judgement about what we ought to believe. In order to establish that reason does not control belief, all Hume must do is to present certain lines of thought which human beings happen to find compelling, arguments which tend to convince us (given the way we are made) that our belief in an external world is unjustified, and then observe that our belief in this external world is impervious to such argumentation (Hookway 1990: 106).

Humean scepticism about the senses presupposes the coherence of the idea that we could have all the sensory images we do without there being any external items corresponding to them. But Hume has no special interest in the sceptical hypotheses. He is happy to employ any argument which appears to convince us that our beliefs are unjustified, whether or not it depends on a sceptical hypothesis. If reflection on past experience of our fallibility alone will do the job, fine. If we happen to find the sceptical hypotheses threatening, that's just fine too. The crucial thing about any sceptical argument is that it should impress us, at least at the level of reflection. The problem with antecedent scepticism is that it doesn't work even at that level: no one feels obliged to justify their belief-forming procedures *in advance* of making any use of them (a point Descartes would fully endorse).

This reading of Hume is confirmed by what he says in the *Treatise*. Hume foresees the following objection, directed not at the particular sceptical argument he has just put forward but against the whole idea of a sceptical argument: 'If the sceptical reasonings be strong, say they, 'tis a proof, that reason may have some force and authority: if weak, they can never be sufficient to invalidate all the conclusions of our understanding' (Hume 1978: 186). Here is Hume's answer to the objection:

Reason first appears in possession of the throne, prescribing laws, and imposing maxims, with an absolute sway and authority. Her enemy, therefore, is obliged to take shelter under her protection, and by making use of rational arguments to prove the fallaciousness and imbecility of reason, produces, in a manner, a patent under her hand and seal. This patent has at first an authority, proportioned to the present and immediate authority of reason, from which it derived. But as it is supposed to be contradictory to reason, it gradually diminishes the force of that governing power, and its own at the same time; till at last they both vanish away into nothing, by a regular and just diminution.   (Hume 1978: 186-7)

Hume starts from the idea that belief is governed by reason, that every human being, at least in so far as they are rational, has the ability to motivate belief simply by forming a view about what they have reason to believe. Hume then takes any judgement of the form 'I have reason R to believe that p' and seeks, by some line of thought or other, to induce the countervailing judgement that R is no reason to believe in p. To give us a recipe for doing this in the case of every such judgement would be to abolish reason's reflective control over belief by means of reason alone. Reason stultifies itself. And the sceptic can demonstrate that reason's reflective control is self-undermining in just this way without undermining himself.

5.2.2 Scepticism about Induction

Until now, I have ignored the very sceptical argument for which Hume is most famous. This is no accident. Hume's discussions of inductive inference in the *Treatise* (Hume 1978: 86-94) and the *Enquiry* (Hume 1975: 25-39) pose a problem for my reading of Hume because they both suggest that his scepticism about induction is a form of antecedent scepticism. How can we reconcile this fact with Hume's firm rejection of antecedent scepticism later on in the *Enquiry*? The answer to this question reveals the role played by certainty in Hume's conception of reason.

Hume's argument against induction takes a form which is familiar to us all from undergraduate textbook discussions of scepticism. He starts with a set of data which we are assumed to know without inference. Since Hume has not yet introduced scepticism about the senses, he permits us to rely on the deliverances of both sensation and memory. Hume then points out that the inference from the fact (which we know through the senses) that the sun rose this morning to the fact that it will rise tomorrow morning is non-demonstrative. Demonstrative inferences are monotonic—a valid demonstrative argument for a given conclusion gets no stronger with the addition of further premises—but clearly, the more times we have seen the sun rise, the more confident we should be in inferring that it will rise tomorrow. So inductive inference is non-monotonic and therefore non-demonstrative.

What sort of reasoning is involved in inductive inference?

> To say it is experimental, is begging the question. For all inferences from experience suppose, as their foundation, that the future will resemble the past... If there be any suspicion that the course of nature may change, and that the past may be no rule for the future, all experience becomes useless and can give rise to no inference or conclusion. It is impossible, therefore, that any arguments from experience can prove this resemblance of the past to the future; since all these arguments are founded on the supposition of that resemblance. (Hume 1975: 37–8)

Hume concludes that inductive inference cannot be regarded as reasoning but must be treated as a product of non-rational custom and habit.

The form of Hume's argument here clearly suggests an antecedent scepticism about induction. Hume makes no attempt to demonstrate that inductive inference is self-undermining. Indeed, he implicitly concedes that induction may be self-confirming, that by using induction we could (pretend to) establish the uniformity of nature. His complaint is that such a procedure would be circular, the very complaint Descartes' critics brought against his theological argument for the reliability of his method of clear and distinct ideas. How can this be reconciled with Hume's scornful dismissal of any sceptic who demands that we test the reliability of each of our belief-forming faculties before placing any reliance on it?

In fact, Hume does not make the quite general demand implicit in antecedent scepticism: he permits us to rely *ab initio* not only on demonstrative reasoning but also on the deliverances of sense and memory. Clearly, he sees some difference between these methods of belief formation which do not require prior vindication, and inductive inference, which does. The difference is not hard to find. Those methods of belief formation which are acceptable *ab initio* all *purport* to give us conclusive reasons for belief. This is clearly true of demonstration, but, for Hume, it is equally true of sensation and memory. Hume remarks that an inductive inference must be based on 'an impression of the memory or senses, beyond which there is no room for doubt or inquiry' (Hume 1978: 83). Both memory and the senses appear to bring the object of belief itself before the mind, and so there is no apparent room for error, no grounds for a prior doubt. Of course, once we have relied on sensation for a bit, we discover that it misleads us on occasion, but we don't need experience of error to know that induction might mislead us: induction never even purports to give us conclusive reasons for belief. We know a priori that inductive reasoning is non-monotonic, that the cogency of an inductive inference is a matter of degree. That is why scepticism about induction does not need to undermine induction from within; that is why antecedent scepticism about induction is effective (at the level of reflection). The grounds for a real doubt are already present at the very outset.

Descartes and Hume both distinguished beliefs produced by reason from beliefs produced by the imagination (i.e. by instinct, custom, and habit), an imagination which we share with the beasts. In their view, a method of belief formation presents itself as a method of reasoning only if it appears to justify certainty about its conclusions. Any method of belief formation which fails to promise certainty must first be vindicated by a proper method of reasoning before we can rely on it. And if this can't be done, we must admit that to form beliefs by that method is to yield to the workings of our imagination. Since induction could not be so vindicated, Hume made the required admission: 'the experimental reasoning, which we possess in common with the beasts, and on which the whole conduct of life depends, is nothing but a species of instinct or mechanical power *that acts in us unknown to ourselves*' (my italics) (Hume 1975: 108). And he thought the same applied to any method of belief formation. For Hume, 'belief produced by reason' is an empty category; for him, our beliefs are governed by the very principles of instinct and imagination which rule the mental lives of the beasts.

5.3 Descartes, Freedom, and Certainty

Why did Descartes think that no rational believer could convince himself of anything by reflection on inconclusive evidence for it? Descartes' *Fourth Meditation* contains a discussion of intellectual freedom and his theory of error. Many commentators have found this part of Descartes' text hard to construe and it plays rather a peripheral role in their account of Cartesian scepticism (e.g. (Williams 1978: Chapter 6) and (Wilson 1978: 139–50)). But I shall argue that it is the *Fourth Meditation* which motivates Descartes' demand for certainty.

5.3.1 Theodicy

At first glance, the *Fourth Meditation* is no more than an exercise in theodicy. Descartes is out to explain how an omnipotent and benevolent God could allow us to acquire false beliefs. He treats this as a specific form of the problem of evil and deploys several of the traditional responses to this problem. Of particular interest is the so-called 'free will defence', according to which evil is the result of an exercise of man's free will and is therefore not God's responsibility. Descartes applies the free will defence to false belief, saying that error comes of our choosing to form a view when we have no conclusive grounds for belief (i.e. no clear and distinct perception).

It is Descartes' theory of judgement which allows him to employ the free will defence to explain away the evil of error.[8] For Descartes, judgement is the result of an interaction between two different faculties: the will and the understanding. The understanding proposes a proposition for our approval and then the will assents to it or not as the case may be:

the will simply consists in our ability to do or not do something (that is to affirm or deny, to pursue or avoid); or rather, it consists simply in the fact that when the intellect puts something forward for affirmation or denial or for pursuit or avoidance, our inclinations are such that we do not feel we are determined by any external force.

(Descartes 1984: 40)

We act when the will leads us to make true a proposition proposed to us by the understanding; we believe when the will leads us to accept as true a proposition proposed to us by the understanding.

This theory of judgement is implausible. In the practical case, we are able to choose among courses of action which the understanding presents as equally desirable; more controversially, we are able to choose a course of action even if the understanding presents it as less desirable than some alternative. But there is no analogue of either ability in the theoretical sphere. Belief or judgement are not subject to the will in the way Descartes appears to think (Owens 2000: Chapter 5). To use an ancient example, I won't be able to form a view about whether the number of stars is odd just because the evidence is evenly balanced and I decide to form a view on the matter. I can assent to a proposition only where the understanding's estimate of the evidence tells in its favour. So it is unclear what role is left for the will. God can't pass the buck to us for all our errors just by observing that we freely chose our erroneous beliefs.

But Descartes needs his theory of judgement for reasons which have nothing to do with letting God off the hook. He, like most other Enlightenment philosophers (Hume excepted), is a firm adherent of two ideas: (a) each individual is responsible for the rationality of their beliefs and is at fault where their beliefs are unjustified, and (b) such intellectual responsibility requires intellectual freedom,

---

[8] For an illuminating account of Descartes' theory and its relationship to Augustinian and Stoic views of judgement, see (Menn (1998): 307–18).

we can be held to account for our beliefs only insofar as they are under our control. Whether or not we are responsible for all the errors we commit, we certainly are responsible for those of our erroneous beliefs which are unjustified and the very idea of belief-justification requires the existence of intellectual freedom. The problem with which Descartes grapples in the *Fourth Meditation* is a problem for anyone who shares these two assumptions.

5.3.2 Freedom and Certainty

In the course of expounding his theory of error, Descartes forges a link between freedom and certainty. Speaking of a truth clearly and distinctly perceived, Descartes says:

> I could not but judge that something which I understood so clearly was true; but this was not because I was compelled to judge by an external force, but because a great light in the intellect was followed by a great inclination in the will, and thus the spontaneity and freedom of my belief was all the greater in proportion to my lack of indifference.
> (Descartes 1984: 41)

In this case, I feel no indifference because I have a conclusive reason: I could not be clearly and distinctly perceiving the truth of this proposition unless it were true. Aware that I have a conclusive reason, I adopt the belief in perfect freedom, exercising only liberty of spontaneity and not liberty of indifference. But if this is perfect freedom, how are we free to commit error?

Descartes wants to insist that we are responsible for our erroneous convictions. I commit errors in cases where I form a belief even though 'I do not perceive the truth with sufficient clarity and distinctness' (Descartes 1984: 41). And I commit such errors freely because (given Descartes' theory of judgement) I have the power to choose a belief even where the evidence alone should leave me indifferent. No doubt feeling the tension between this statement and the idea that true freedom requires the absence of such indifference, Descartes adds that 'the indifference I feel when there is no reason pushing me in one direction rather than another is the lowest grade of freedom' (Descartes 1984: 40). I am accountable for error because I am misusing my free will when I affirm something on the basis of inconclusive evidence.

There is an obvious conflict in Descartes' thinking here. On the one hand, he says a fully rational person could not get themselves to assent to a proposition just by reflecting on inconclusive evidence for it; rather, they would remain indifferent and suspend judgement:

> this indifference does not merely apply to cases where the intellect is wholly ignorant, but extends in general to every case where the intellect does not have sufficiently clear

knowledge at the time when the will deliberates. For although probable conjectures may pull me in one direction, the mere knowledge that they are simply conjectures, and not certain and indubitable reasons, is itself quite enough to push my assent the other way.

(Descartes 1984: 41)

Reason alone would not enable us to motivate belief in p by reflection on inconclusive evidence for p, even when the balance of inconclusive evidence tips firmly in the proposition's favour. So, Descartes adds, no one could assent to such a proposition in perfect freedom. But Descartes also maintains that by exercising the will's liberty of indifference, we can come down in favour of p and should be held to account if we do. So we must be free to believe in the face of uncertainty after all.

Can we rescue Descartes from this difficulty by dropping first his theory of judgement and second the idea that justified belief requires justified certainty? Suppose Descartes were to agree that judgement does not involve an act of will, that we control our beliefs by means of reflection on inconclusive evidence rather than by means of the will, that we control our beliefs where our judgement of the balance of evidence for and against a given proposition can determine what we believe. Perhaps this would be enough to ensure that people are responsible for their unjustified errors at least (though God is left to carry the can for the rest).

My analysis of Cartesian scepticism and my account of Descartes' conception of reason gives such reflective judgement a key role. So the notion of reflective control, even when stripped of its association with the will, should fit snugly into Descartes' system. But even once we have excised Descartes' theory of judgement from the rest of his thought, we have yet to dispose of his demand for certainty. As we have seen, the *Fourth Meditation* links freedom with certainty (or lack of indifference) and it is a link which survives the rejection of Descartes' will-based theory of judgement.

5.3.3 Reflection and Certainty

In the *Fourth Meditation* Descartes gives us rather good grounds for thinking that rational people cannot motivate belief by reflection on inconclusive evidence alone. It is fairly clear what is supposed to be troubling the believer confronted by inconclusive evidence which favours p but who finds himself 'indifferent' between p and not-p: he could get himself to regard this inconclusive evidence as sufficient for belief in p only by bringing to mind *pragmatic* considerations (Owens 2000: Chapter 2). To determine whether a given level of evidence is sufficient to justify belief, he must contemplate the importance of the issue, the cognitive resources he can afford to devote to resolving it, and so forth.

When taking a practical decision, we often remind ourselves of the pragmatic constraints on the process of deliberation in an effort to force a decision—'I must settle now which train to get and then get on with thinking about other things'—and reflection on such considerations does motivate decision in a rational person. But our rationality alone won't guarantee that we can get ourselves to believe something simply by judging that the evidence favouring it is sufficient to establish its truth, given the importance of the issue, etc. Trying to make up my mind about the guilt of the man before me, I can reflect that (given the time constraints) I must now deliver a verdict, and if I am rational, this reflection will make me announce a verdict. But my rationality alone can't guarantee that such reflections will issue in a belief on this subject.

Its looks as if a rational believer, as such, can't get himself to believe that p simply by judging that the balance of inconclusive evidence favours p. The only apparent cure for the impotence of reflection is to strip away the pragmatic constraints on belief and seek to ground our convictions in evidence alone, thereby securing our intellectual freedom, the foundation of epistemic responsibility. This is exactly what led Descartes to think that justified belief requires possession of a conclusive reason. If we allow anything less than conclusive grounds to motivate the formation of belief then pragmatic considerations must be allowed to determine what level of inconclusive evidence is sufficient; and once they are permitted to intrude, reflective control over belief is lost. That, I suggest, is the root of the Cartesian idea that we are fully free in forming a belief only when we are certain.

My reading of Descartes explains why he draws such a big distinction between what is required for knowledge of what we should do and what is required for knowledge *tout court*:

> As far as the conduct of life is concerned, I am very far from thinking that one should assent only to what is clearly perceived. On the contrary, I do not think that we should always wait even for probable truths; from time to time we will have to choose one of many alternatives about which we have no knowledge. (Descartes 1984: 106)

But why? If both practical and theoretical judgement involve the will's assenting (or not) to the deliverances of the understanding, are they not on a par? Why shouldn't practical judgement require ideas as clear and distinct as theoretical judgement? The answer is that, though action is under our reflective control whether or not we have conclusive reasons for our deeds, only conclusive reasons can give us reflective control over belief.[9]

---

[9] My account of Descartes' obsession with certainty is at variance with those to be found in the contemporary scholarly literature. I discuss some of these accounts in (Owens 2000: Chapter 4).

For Descartes, certainty is a control issue, and what scepticism exposes is the limits and the presuppositions of rational control. Having noted (in the passage quoted earlier) that inconclusive evidence leaves the rational believer indifferent as to what he ought to believe, Descartes completes the passage by linking this fact with the psychological efficacy of the sceptical doubt:

> My experience in the last few days confirms this: the mere fact that I found that all my previous beliefs were in some sense open to doubt was enough to turn my absolutely confident belief in their truth into the supposition that they were wholly false.
>
> (Descartes 1984: 41)

Here, Descartes is alluding to a passage in the *First Meditation* where, in order to rid himself of habitual beliefs which creep back whenever his guard is lowered, he decides to accept the truth of the sceptical hypothesis:

> I shall never get out of the habit of confidently assenting to these opinions, so long as I suppose them to be what in fact they are, namely highly probable opinions—opinions which, despite the fact that they are in some sense doubtful, as has just been shown, it is still much more reasonable to believe than to deny. In view of this, I think it would be a good plan to turn my will in completely the opposite direction and deceive myself, by pretending for a time that these former opinions are utterly false and imaginary.
>
> (Descartes 1984: 15)

Gassendi refused to believe that Descartes could do this and Gassendi is surely right that we cannot convince ourselves of the truth of a sceptical hypothesis by a simple act of will (Descartes 1984: 180). But Descartes' deeper point is correct: I may judge that my former opinions are highly probable but this *judgement* will not ensure that I retain those beliefs so long as the possibility of error remains in view. A rational believer who sees that the evidence is inconclusive will have an open mind about what he ought to believe. If I continue with my old beliefs, this is only because of the force of unreflective habit, a cognitive inertia which is the enemy of rational control. Descartes may be right about this even if he is wrong to suppose that this epistemic indifference can be resolved by an act of will.

To sum up, both Descartes and Hume wanted to know whether belief was subject to reason, and each philosopher addressed this issue by asking whether we could control our beliefs through reflection on the quality of our reasons for them. Lately, their concerns have been buried under a host of semantic and metaphysical questions about the coherence of the sceptical hypotheses. I don't deny that these questions are deep and interesting but Cartesian scepticism raises other profound issues. In particular, it should make us wonder whether reason really does require some form of intellectual freedom, whether epistemic rationality and responsibility are present only where our beliefs are under the control of reflection. Perhaps this assumption is just false.[10] Perhaps that is the lesson of Cartesian scepticism.[11]

---

[10] This assumption about freedom and responsibility is clearly present in Descartes' ethical thought. See *The Passions of the Soul* (e.g. Descartes 1985: 384), a work whose Stoicism ought to be more central to the interpretation of Descartes' philosophy.

[11] Many thanks to Chris Hookway, Robert Stern, and Robert Hopkins for their comments on an earlier draft of this chapter.

6

Descartes' Use of Doubt

In Part Two of the *Discourse on the Method* we find a remarkable resolution:

> regarding the opinions to which I had hitherto given credence, I thought that I could not do better than to undertake to get rid of them, all at one go, in order to replace them afterwards with better ones, or with the same ones once I had squared them with the standards of reason. (Descartes 1985: 117)

Two questions arise. What are these 'opinions' to which Descartes had hitherto given credence? And what are the 'standards of reason' by which they should be judged?

Early on in the *First Meditation*, Descartes tells us that his opinions come 'either from the senses or through the senses' (Descartes 1984: 12). Those that come *from* the senses Descartes calls the 'teachings of nature'. For example, nature teaches that there are objects in the world around me resembling the ideas I receive from the senses in respect of shape and colour, etc. (Descartes 1984: 26). Those opinions that come *through* the senses are the opinions of others, heard and then preserved in memory (Descartes 1985: 218–20). From childhood, Descartes absorbed the teachings of both nature and society and far into adulthood he holds these opinions to be 'most true' (Descartes 1984: 12). So Descartes' 'opinions' comprise almost all of the beliefs he finds himself with at the outset of his inquiry.

Descartes is dissatisfied with these opinions. For example, he remarks that 'When I say "Nature taught me to think this", all I mean is that a spontaneous impulse leads me to believe it, not that its truth has been revealed to me by some natural light' (Descartes 1984: 26–7). Clearly, he thinks there is a higher standard to which he should conform and he states it in the *First Meditation*:

> Reason now leads me to think that I should hold back my assent from opinions which are not completely certain and indubitable just as carefully as I do from those which are patently false. So, for the purpose of rejecting all my opinions, it will be enough if I find in each of them at least some reason for doubt. (Descartes 1984: 12)

It looks as if Descartes means to abandon almost all of his beliefs until he can find reasons for holding them which render those beliefs 'certain and indubitable'.

There has been much debate over how to interpret these statements. It has been maintained that Cartesian certainty is an ideal which believers should aspire to rather than a standard which every reasonable belief must meet. And indeed, towards the end of the *First Meditation*, Descartes allows that the beliefs he is setting out to undermine are 'highly probable opinions—opinions which, despite the fact that they are in some sense doubtful... it is still much more reasonable to believe than to deny' (Descartes 1984: 15). This statement is important because it shows that the Cartesian sceptic allows that we have substantial, if inconclusive evidence for our various opinions. But Descartes does not here say that belief in p is reasonable provided the evidence makes p highly probable (*pace* (Broughton 2002: 46, 87–8), (MacArthur 2003: 169)); he merely says that if the evidence makes p highly probable then belief in p is more reasonable than belief in not-p, a point which interests him because he is about to consider whether to adopt the supposition that his opinions are actually false. For all the quoted passage tells us, in the absence of certainty, agnosticism may be the only option that is reasonable *tout court*. As we shall see, when Descartes considers this very point in the *Fourth Meditation*, that is exactly what he says (see also (Descartes 1984: 53)).

It has also been maintained that the standard of certainty is meant to apply to belief only in a certain special context, in the context of scientific inquiry, or in the course of our search for knowledge (see (Frankfurt 1970: Chapter 2) and (Wolterstorff 1996: 180–218); compare (Broughton 2002: 7–18, 42–61), (Burnyeat 1997: 118–20), and (Wilson 1978: 42–9)). This reading gains support from Descartes' repeated insistence that his Method of Doubt has no application to practical affairs:

As far as the conduct of life is concerned, I am very far from thinking that we should assent only to what is clearly perceived. On the contrary, I do not think that we should always wait even for probable truths; from time to time we will have to choose one of many alternatives about which we have no knowledge. (Descartes 1984: 106) (See also (Descartes 1984: 15, 248, and 243)).

Some interpreters conclude, with Frankfurt, that the doubts of the *First Meditation* are 'purely methodological' or that the rule of certainty is not intended by Descartes as 'an ordinary rule for conscientious believing' (Broughton 2002: 46).

In this chapter, I shall argue that Descartes acknowledges the existence of a number of representational states governed by rather different normative standards. Belief or judgement is only one of these states, a state governed in all contexts by the rule of certainty. It is against our beliefs or judgements that the sceptical reflections of the *First Meditation* are directed. But when it comes to practical affairs, it is often appropriate to invoke another sort of representational state in the process of deciding what to do. These states—conjectures—are not governed by the rule of certainty and are thus immune to the sceptical reflections of the *First Meditation*.

Many commentators suppose that the whole of Descartes' sceptical argumentation in the *First Meditation* turns on the radical hypothesis that we are always dreaming or on the idea of an all-powerful deceiver. But if, as I maintain, it is the simple demand for certainty which drives Descartes' scepticism, these hypotheses must play a rather more specialized role. Reviewing the argument of the *First Meditation* in the *Sixth*, Descartes remembers that, while trusting the senses 'I had many experiences which gradually undermined all the faith I had had in the senses' (Descartes 1984: 53) and he quotes examples of towers which looked round at a distance but square from close up, and so forth. Only then does he mention that 'to these reasons for doubting I recently added two very general ones' viz. the dreaming and the evil demon argument. Elsewhere, I have argued that the latter are introduced for a very specific purpose, to directly undermine our general belief that there are objects distributed in a space around us. And they do this in just the way that ordinary sensory error undermines our convictions about what is now before us, by depriving us of certainty on the point (Owens 2000: 119–24 and Chapter 5: Section 5.1.1).

This chapter has two parts. In the first two sections I give Descartes' reason for thinking that belief labours under the stringent epistemic requirement enunciated in the *First Meditation*. Descartes must tell us why a failure to satisfy the demand for certainty could move a reasonable person to abandon belief and, I shall argue, the *Fourth Meditation* contains a persuasive answer to this question. In the last two sections, I shall show that, for Descartes, there are ways of representing the world to which this answer does not apply and so which are not subject to the demand for certainty.

6.1 The Role of Reflection

Having dissolved most of our convictions in the *First Meditation*, in the *Second* and *Third Meditations* Descartes draws our attention to beliefs which, it seems, can't be undermined in the same way, to beliefs which are certain. By the time we get to the *Fourth Meditation*, Descartes is ready to step back and give an account of how our faculty of judgement works: with the experience of epistemic failure followed by some epistemic success behind us, we are now in a position to describe the mechanism which underlies all this. The *Fourth Meditation* is the obvious place to look for Descartes' account of why reasonable belief requires certainty (Owens 2000: 57–8 and Chapter 5: Section 5.3).

Here is what we find. Descartes starts by considering a case in which:

[A] my intellect has not yet come upon any persuasive reason in favour of one alternative rather than the other. This obviously implies that I am indifferent as to whether I should assert or deny either alternative, or indeed refrain from making any judgement on the matter. (Descartes 1984: 41)

Descartes immediately takes things further:

[B] What is more, this indifference does not merely apply to cases where the intellect is wholly ignorant, but extends in general to every case where the intellect does not have sufficiently clear knowledge at the time when the will deliberates. For although probable conjectures may pull me in one direction, the mere knowledge that they are simply conjectures, and not certain and indubitable reasons, is itself quite enough to push my assent the other way. (Descartes 1984: 41)

From this, Descartes at once draws the following conclusion:

[C] If, however, I simply refrain from making a judgement in cases where I do not perceive the truth with sufficient clarity and distinctness, then it is clear that I am behaving correctly and avoiding error. But if in such cases I either affirm or deny, then I am not using my free will correctly. (Descartes 1984: 41)

Without 'certain and indubitable reasons', we lack 'sufficient clarity and distinctness'. In this section, I'll offer a reading of the above passages, postponing objections until the next.

In **Passage [A]**, Descartes says that if the evidence in favour of p is no greater than that in favour of not-p this 'obviously implies that I am indifferent' as to whether p. Is that really so? Wishful thinkers and careless believers are often heedless of the evidence. Why shouldn't 'I' be one of them? Here, Descartes is drawing our attention to the following fact: someone who judges that the evidence in favour of p is no stronger than that against it ('my intellect had not yet come across any persuasive reason') cannot get himself to believe that p by judging that he *should* believe that p given this evidence ('I am indifferent as to whether I should assert or deny either alternative'); reflection on such evidence will leave him feeling indifferent between the two propositions. This person is in the same situation as someone asked to form a view about whether the number of stars is odd or even; he might find himself with an ungrounded belief on this matter, but he couldn't arrive at it by reflecting on what he thought of as *reasons* for belief.

Here, Descartes is not setting up his own epistemic standards, rather, he is getting his standard from a fact about belief, namely, that when human beings reflect on which of two equally well supported but incompatible propositions they ought to believe, that process of reflection generates no inclination to believe either. Where there are motivational forces at work apart from reflection, a view may still be formed, but, so far as reflection on what strikes him as a good reason goes, the believer will be left agnostic on the matter. What should convince us of this is each person's 'experience in his own case'; though 'self-evident', these facts about our motivational psychology cannot be proved 'by rational argument' (Descartes 1984: 259).

We are still a long way short of any demand for certainty, but **Passage [A]** does tell us something about the workings of Cartesian scepticism. Descartes sets out to undermine our beliefs by demonstrating that, as presently constituted, they fail to live up to a requirement which we ourselves acknowledge. And if the demand for certainty is to be the motor of an effective scepticism, it is essential that Descartes proceed in this fashion. Should he appeal to some standard of justification to which ordinary believers are not in some sense already committed, their doubts are more likely to focus on Descartes' standard than on the beliefs he disparages.

Let's examine the rest of the quotation. **Passage [B]** suggests a much stronger requirement on reasonable belief: that belief in p must be supported by 'certain and indubitable reasons', i.e. *conclusive* evidence for p. Again, this claim is supported with an assertion about what happens when we *reflect* on our grounds: 'although probable conjectures may pull me in one direction, the mere knowledge that they are simply conjectures, and not certain and indubitable reasons, is itself quite enough to push my assent the other way'. This confirms our earlier hypothesis that Descartes is testing the adequacy of certain reasons by asking whether reflection on them can motivate belief. He now suggests that reflection on merely probable grounds cannot do the trick. On this reading, it comes as no surprise when, in **Passage [C]** Descartes moves from these points to the conclusion that certainty is, in fact, the normatively correct standard for belief.

One might well wonder about the plausibility of the claims Descartes makes about reflective indifference. Do I really feel indifferent about whether to believe p or not-p when the evidence strongly (though not conclusively) favours p? Don't I often form the belief that p in these circumstances because I think I have sufficient evidence for p? I shall tackle this worry in Section 6.2, but first I want to connect the above passages from the *Fourth Meditation* with the doubts of the *First*.

The 'I' of the above passages is an engaged epistemic deliberator trying to work out what he should believe about a certain matter on the basis of the evidence before him; he is not evaluating beliefs which have already been formed. Yet in the *First Meditation* Descartes does appear to be subjecting beliefs which he has already to an unfavourable evaluation. For Descartes, these tasks are connected: the way to evaluate a belief in p which is based on evidence e is to ask yourself whether you could have formed a belief in p simply by reflecting on the probative force of evidence e. That is the test the meditator applies so destructively in the *First Meditation*. Descartes demands that the conclusions of the epistemic evaluator be grounded in the more fundamental perspective of the epistemic deliberator, and his attempt to live up to this demand leads to scepticism.

In the *Seventh Replies*, responding to Pierre Bourdin, Descartes sums up his procedure in the *First Meditation* with a homely analogy:

Suppose [Bourdin] had a basket full of apples and, being worried that some of the apples were rotten, wanted to take out the rotten ones to prevent the rot spreading. How would he proceed? Would he not begin by tipping the whole lot out of the basket? And would not the next step be to cast his eye over each apple in turn and pick up, and put back in the basket only those he saw to be sound, leaving the others. (Descartes 1984: 324)

Frankfurt (1970: 19–20) takes this passage to be confirmation of his view that Descartes' 'rejection' of all his beliefs is purely methodological and so need not be based on any prior examination of the grounds for them: it is little more than the decision to undertake such an examination. But there is a two-stage process here of which tipping the apples out is only the first.

In the *First Meditation*, Descartes initially asks us to evaluate our current beliefs from the perspective of someone who is trying to decide whether or not to form them. This procedure does indeed involve the sort of methodological distancing which Frankfurt equates with the Doubt. Having got us to adopt this perspective, Descartes reminds us of various sources of error which are usually ignored when such beliefs are formed and asks whether we can explicitly discount them from our new perspective. The answer is that in good conscience we cannot, and so, as epistemic deliberators, we find ourselves unable to endorse our own beliefs. It is at *this* stage, only a little further on in the *First Meditation* that Descartes invites us to abandon these beliefs.

But why adopt this rather roundabout procedure? Why proceed via the standpoint of the epistemic deliberator? Why not just appeal directly to our intuitions about what one is and is not entitled to believe? To put the question another way: why does the *First Meditation* take the form of a meditation? Why insist that its sceptical argumentation must be stated in the first person? When Descartes addresses these questions (Descartes 1984: 110–13) he insists that the meditation form is indispensable, but he is less clear about the reason for its indispensability. I shall side with (Foucault 1998: 405–6) and against, for example (Wilson 1978: 4–5) in maintaining that Descartes' use of the first person is essential to the *cogency* of the sceptical argumentation in the *First Meditation*.

6.2 The Need for Certainty

Imagine you are expounding the *First Meditation* in Epistemology 101. In an attempt to get your students to take Descartes seriously, you say 'Here is this man standing before this barn. He doesn't bother to go around the back of the barn to establish that it is not a mere facade. He concludes simply from the look of it that it is indeed a barn. Isn't he being unreasonable in ignoring the possibility that what's before him is a mere facade?' That way of putting the point won't do the trick. The students will respond that, by the standard usually applied to such situations, the man would be unreasonable *not* to ignore this possibility (unless he has grounds for thinking he is on a film set, etc. etc.). And Descartes has yet to show why the standard we normally apply is, in fact, inappropriate.

To rescue the lecture, first let's try to say *why* the laxer standard seems appropriate. Some might maintain that there is nothing to add here: it is just a fact that our epistemic norms don't require that check. I agree that explanation must end somewhere, but need it come to a halt quite so quickly? Isn't there a story to be told about why we don't demand that our subject check that every barn he sees has a back before concluding it is a barn? Human beings need beliefs, they need to have convictions about a whole range of matters—to satisfy their curiosity, to ground their emotional lives, as well as for more practical purposes. That's why it would be unreasonable to demand the elimination of every possible source of error. Asked to defend our conclusion that the subject's conviction was reasonable, we would note that someone with a finite capacity to collect, store, retrieve, and evaluate evidence can't always be holding out for more: at some stage, he must form a view on the basis of the evidence he has now got if he is ever to form a view at all.

Given this, how do we present the sceptic's point in a way that might carry conviction? Do as Descartes suggests and get the students to look at things from the standpoint of an epistemic deliberator. Suppose you start with no view about whether there is a barn before you and then try to get yourself to form a view by reflecting just on what you see from the spot on which you are standing. Try telling yourself the very story you told a moment ago, all that stuff about the constraints you labour under and your need to make up your mind. It doesn't seem to have the required impact; it doesn't seem to be the sort of thing which could (just insofar as you are rational) convince you to form a view about whether there is a barn before you.

We are now in a position to support the claims Descartes makes about indifference. First, it *is* true that I feel reflective indifference in the face of inconclusive evidence, at least once I am clear that I would need to invoke pragmatic considerations to make up my mind. However much the inconclusive evidence is stacked in favour of p and against not-p, I could always wait for more, and purely evidential considerations will never explain why I don't wait for more. To motivate belief, to explain why we make up our minds, we need to invoke pragmatic considerations, but *reflection* on such considerations does not make one's mind up: in that sense, it leaves one feeling indifferent, just as Descartes says. Our minds may be made up because of these pragmatic constraints, but *reflection* on these considerations won't move us.

Descartes puts his sceptical argumentation in the form of a meditation precisely to bring this fact home to us; the inefficacy of reflection on pragmatic considerations is evident once we are persuaded to adopt the essentially first-person standpoint of the epistemic deliberator. That's why Descartes is so insistent that the reader must 'join me in meditating' (Descartes 1984: 112) if he is to rid himself of the prejudices and preconceptions which he brings to the *Meditations*. We'd miss his point if we simply evaluated beliefs we had already formed from the outside, as it were.

Does the above line of reasoning make an appearance in Descartes' text or is it something we must attribute to him to make sense of what he does say? Before answering, let me first rephrase the points just made. In the eyes of an 'external' evaluator there are two distinct questions one can ask about a prospective belief: (a) should the believer form a view about whether p; and (b) given that he should form a view, should he believe that p or that not-p? But from the first-person standpoint of the epistemic deliberator, this distinction evaporates. For the prospective believer themselves, there are not two separate questions: should I now form a view about whether p? if so, which view should I form? Insofar as reflection on certain considerations persuades him that he ought to form a view on whether p is true, such reflection can do so only by persuading him of the truth (or falsity) of p. In getting us to meditate, Descartes makes this fact plain.

This line of thought comes close to the surface of Descartes' text a little earlier on in the *Fourth Meditation* where he gives his theory of error:

When I look more closely at myself and inquire into the nature of my errors...I notice that they depend on two concurrent causes, namely on the faculty of knowledge which is in me, and on the faculty of choice or freedom of the will; that is they depend on both the intellect and the will simultaneously. Now all that the intellect does is to enable me to perceive the ideas which are subjects for possible judgements; and when regarded strictly in this light, it turns out to contain no error in the proper sense of that term.
(Descartes 1984: 39)

To get error, I must endorse or assent to the ideas served up by the intellect when those ideas are, to some degree, obscure or confused and assent is an act of will.

Coming to believe p involves settling on p (rather than not-p) as the better option and settling on now (rather than later) as the time to make up your mind about whether p is true. Following Descartes, we might call the faculty which tackles the former issue 'the intellect' and faculty which resolves the latter issue 'the will'. Now suppose *pace* Descartes that reasonable belief could be based on a sufficiency of inconclusive evidence. Then there would always be two questions to address. First, what is the data served up by the intellect? Does it make p look more or less plausible than not-p? Evidence alone seems relevant here. Second, is the data served up by the intellect sufficiently convincing and the issue sufficiently pressing to make it reasonable for us to form a view on the matter right now?

The fact that Descartes gives the will a role to play in the process of belief formation might make it look as if he thought that the formation of a belief requires us to attend firstly to the clarity of the ideas served up by the intellect and secondly to those other considerations which determine whether it would be sensible to make a decision now, to assent to the proposition which the intellect presents to us. But while Descartes allows that there are indeed two independent sources of epistemic *motivation* here, this does not mean he thinks there are two different kinds of *reason*. When it comes to judgement (rather than conjecture), the will has no reasons for assent except those derived from the intellect:

> the scope of the will is wider than that of the intellect; but instead of restricting it within the same limits, I extend its use to matters which I do not understand. Since the will is indifferent in such cases, it easily turns aside from what is true and good, and this is the source of my error and sin.   (Descartes 1984: 40–1)

The *only* reasons for belief are served up by the intellect or, to put the point in Descartes' words, 'it is clear by the natural light that the perception of the intellect should always precede the determination of the will' (Descartes 1984: 41).

Given this, if the intellect gave us only probable evidence we would never be entitled to form beliefs. Possessing merely probable evidence and reflecting on what he ought to believe, the believer could answer the question as to *how much* probable evidence is sufficient to justify belief only by going beyond the deliverances of the intellect, only by employing his will in a way that seems illicit not only to Descartes but also to the believer himself. As we have seen, a rational believer cannot control his beliefs by making judgements about what he should believe given the non-evidential constraints on his mental life.

The only way for the believer to retain reflective control over his mental life is to insist on certainty; mere probability, however great, will never do for belief. Practical affairs might require us to make assumptions about how things are, assumptions whose truth the understanding does not assure us of; here the will must go beyond the deliverances of the intellect. But to allow our will to play an independent role in determining our judgements is to enter a region in which it seems *to ourselves* that we have nothing to go on in the way of reasons for belief, though we may still find ourselves with (irrational) convictions. In that sense, our will is *indifferent* whenever the intellect is uncertain.[1]

We have arrived at the conclusion that certainty is required for justified belief. Isn't this rather alarming? Is it ever possible to meet this standard? I don't find a clear answer in Descartes. In some moods he appears to think that one can and should confine one's beliefs to matters about which one can be absolutely certain. The *Sixth Meditation* contains an attempt to show how careful checks can enable us to avoid making erroneous judgements based on the deliverances of the senses. For example, speaking of the judgements we make about the shape and size of particular objects, he remarks that:

Despite the high degree of doubt and uncertainty involved here, the very fact that God is not a deceiver, and the consequent impossibility of there being any falsity in my opinions which cannot be corrected by some other faculty supplied by God, offers me a sure hope that I can attain the truth even in these matters. (Descartes 1984: 55–6)

On the other hand, Descartes was pessimistic about the capacity of human beings to take his advice, and he ends the *Meditations* with the following words:

since the pressure of things to be done does not always allow us to stop and make such a meticulous check, it must be admitted that in this human life we are often liable to make mistakes about particular things and we must acknowledge the weakness of our nature. (Descartes 1984: 62) (See also (Descartes 1985: 289–91))

We don't make time to check the back of that barn even though true justification requires 'certain and indubitable reasons'.

---

[1] In **Passage** [A] Descartes says the absence of persuasive reasons 'obviously implies that I am indifferent as to whether I should assert or deny either alternative, *or indeed refrain from making any judgement on the matter*' (my emphasis). According to this final clause, I am indifferent not only about what to believe but also about whether to form any belief on the matter at all. Yet Descartes concludes **Passage** [C] by saying that I *ought* to suspend belief in these circumstances. So how can indifference as such be indicative of the absence of a reason? This difficulty might tempt someone to read 'indifference' as referring to a power of choice, a power which I have regardless of my reasons. But Descartes is quite clear that indifference is something which I feel 'when there is no reason pushing me one way or the other' and that 'if I always saw clearly what was true and good ... it would be impossible for me ever to be in a state of indifference' (Descartes 1984: 40). (See also Descartes 1991: 245 and 233). The way out of this difficulty is to read 'indifference' here as referring to an indifference of the intellect: our intellect provides no indication as to what we should do with our power of assent. It does not follow that the will feels indifferent between assenting and not assenting: where we have no guidance from the intellect, we see that we ought not to assent.

It is now clear why Descartes thinks that certainty is required for justified belief. But we are not yet out of the woods. Why doesn't the demand for certainty apply with equal force in the practical sphere?

6.3 Descartes' Conjectures

The (temporary) success of Descartes' sceptical argumentation leaves him facing the question: how is one to act without belief? Now, one could refuse to answer this question. One could maintain that, once theoretical reason has been undermined, there is no point in looking for *reasons* for acting one way rather than another. Instinct may ensure that one behaves in a certain fashion, but practical reasoning is at an end. This is not Descartes' view. Such an abdication of responsibility for one's mental life would be anathema to Descartes who places self-control at the centre of his ethical theory (e.g. (Descartes 1985: 384)). The temporary demise of theoretical reason leaves practical reason intact and Descartes uses the latter to govern his life as a sceptic. For example, he pursues knowledge, a pursuit which involves him making the judgement that knowledge is good and having views about how best to attain it (Descartes 1985: 124–5). Descartes' sceptical inquiry is meant to be an activity fully under his control because consciously directed at an aim which is judged to be both worthwhile and attainable.

How will Descartes behave in other matters until he recovers his earlier knowledge? Having resolved to rid himself of his opinions in Part Two of the *Discourse*, Descartes begins Part Three by sketching a 'provisional moral code' to guide him 'lest I should remain indecisive in my actions while reason obliged me to be so in my judgements' (Descartes 1985: 122). In content, Descartes' provisional moral code resembles that which guided the Pyrrhonian sceptics who wished to 'live by appearances'. But unlike Descartes, the Pyrrhonians abjured practical reasoning: they *were* guided by instinct (Empiricus 1994 1: 23–30).

Descartes sets himself to:

> obey the laws and customs of my country ... and governing myself in all other matters according to the most moderate and least extreme opinions—the opinions commonly accepted in practice by the most sensible of those with whom I should have to live.
>
> (Descartes 1985: 122)

Here Descartes is not passively acceding to the dictates of common sense and the weight of public opinion. Rather, he is actively choosing to adopt certain opinions because he judges them appropriate. But if these opinions are not beliefs, what are they?

We can discover what sort of state we are dealing with here by looking at the reasons Descartes gives for adopting 'the most moderate and least extreme opinions'. First, there is 'probability':

> since in everyday life we must often act without delay, it is a most certain truth that when it is not in our power to discern the truest opinions, we must follow the most probable. Even when no opinions appear more probable than any others, we must still adopt some.
> (Descartes 1985: 123)

It would be quite wrong to conclude from the *First Meditation* that any opinion is as probable (or improbable) as any other. As we have seen, Descartes clearly states that his 'habitual opinions' remain 'highly probable' (Descartes 1984: 15), something he could know only via the intellect. (On this point, as on the role of practical judgement, Cartesian scepticism may be closer to Academic than to Pyrhonnian scepticism (Empiricus 1994 1: 226–31).) The only serious candidates for retention are opinions which appear at least as probable as their competitors, so we are 'aiming at truth' when we adopt these opinions. But such opinions are unlike Cartesian judgements in that evidence isn't the only consideration relevant to their adoption: here the will has reasons of its own.

Descartes says that having abandoned his earlier opinions:

> I was sure I could do no better than follow those of the most sensible men. And although there may be men as sensible among the Persians or Chinese as among ourselves, I thought it would be most useful for me to be guided by those with whom I should have to live. (Descartes 1985: 122)

Now I take it that no one who forms opinions which appear improbable to Descartes will count as reasonable in his eyes. Still, a variety of opinions pass this test and Descartes proposes to adopt the opinions of those 'with whom I should have to live'. Clearly, there are good pragmatic reasons for this policy: social coordination is effected and social harmony enhanced if we all act on the basis of shared assumptions about the world. When Descartes adds that 'in order to discover what opinions they really held, I had to attend to what they did rather than what they said' he clearly has such considerations in mind.

Descartes goes on:

> Where many opinions were equally well accepted, I chose only the most moderate, both because these are always the easiest to act upon and probably the best (excess usually being bad) and also so that if I made a mistake, I should depart less from the right path than I would if I chose one extreme when I ought to have pursued the other. (Descartes 1985: 122–3)

Here, Descartes notes further relevant pragmatic considerations: he should adopt opinions which he can act on easily and without incurring great risks if they turn out to be wrong.

So what kind of beast are these opinions which Descartes recommends as a substitute for belief? They are 'conjectures' (Descartes 1984: 41) or guesses. Reasonable guesses are based on evidence. True, we can make a guess even when we have no evidence, but we can't reasonably guess that p regardless of whatever evidence we do have. In that sense guesses 'aim at the truth'. On the other hand, we don't guess just with the aim of getting it right. We'll make a guess when we expect to benefit from making that guess and so the need for social coordination, avoidance of risk, etc. will help to determine which guess we make (Chapter 1: Section 1.4 and Chapter 2: Sections 2.2 and 2.3).

Furthermore, there is no problem with controlling our guesses by reflecting on both the evidential and the pragmatic considerations which together make these guesses reasonable. Take one of Descartes' own examples. I am hungry, indeed starving, and the only food available is apples. It occurs to me that these apples may be poisoned, though there is no sign of this. Here, I tell myself that to preserve life, I must take a view and assume they are not. I can get myself to do this by reflecting on these practical necessities and on the difficulty of obtaining a cast-iron guarantee that the apples are safe. And because reflection on the probative force of these considerations does *not* (insofar as I am reasonable) leave me in a state of indifference as to what I ought to do, these considerations justify my guessing that the apples are safe and then eating them. Indeed, Descartes goes so far as to say that I would be 'insane' not to eat the apples (Descartes 1991: 189).

We might conclude, using language Descartes employs elsewhere (Descartes 1985: 130 and 289–90), that I am entitled to a 'moral certainty' that the apples are not poisonous. But matters are different when the question is whether I ought to believe that the apples are safe. Belief requires 'metaphysical certainty' (Curley 1993: 14–20). Yet most of us do not just guess that the fruit we eat is safe, we believe this and we believe this even though we acknowledge that evidence might come along which showed the fruit we eat to be unsafe. Are such beliefs reasonable? Can we get ourselves to believe that the apples are safe by reflecting that we have enough evidence to believe this, given that we can't spend our whole lives investigating the matter and so forth? Such reflections don't have the same power to convince us of the truth of this proposition as they do to get us to act on the assumption that it is true, and so (for Descartes) these considerations cannot constitute reasons for belief. One who believes that the apples are not poisonous does so because they feel an urge to believe this, not because it seems to them that they are entitled to this belief (Descartes 1984: 259).

It is now clear that the line of thought which prevented us taking inconclusive evidence as sufficient reason for belief does not apply to those conjectures we make for practical purposes. But what are the principles of reasoning we employ when formulating and revising our conjectures? And what is their status? Descartes hints at the sort of thing he has in mind when stating the second maxim of his provisional moral code:

> to be as firm and decisive in my action as I could, and to follow even the most doubtful opinions, once I had adopted them, with no less constancy than if they had been quite certain. In this respect I would be imitating a traveller who, upon finding himself lost in a forest, should not wander about turning this way and that, and still less stay in one place, but should keep walking as straight as he can in one direction, never changing it for slight reasons even if mere chance made him choose it in the first place. (Descartes 1985: 123) (See also (Descartes 1991: 97)).

This looks like a familiar principle for decision-making under uncertainty, one which can arguably be known a priori and with certainty (*pace* Gilson 1947: 243). In this it is like the principle mentioned earlier when Descartes said, 'it is a *most certain truth* that when it is not in our power to discern the truest opinions, we must follow the most probable' (my emphasis). So the demand for certainty is met by the principles of practical reason (compare (Wolterstorff 1996: 181) and (Marshall 1998: Ch. 2)).

To sum up, when Descartes says that his doubts apply to 'the investigation of truth' and not to 'the actions of life' he is not suggesting that belief should be abandoned only in science and not in life. Rather, he means us to abandon belief across the board whilst planning the actions of life with a quite different tool: conjecture. Both belief and conjecture 'aim at the truth', yet while we can use fallibilist norms to govern our conjectures, we cannot use them to regulate our beliefs. That is why the Cartesian doubt undermines our convictions without hobbling our practical reasoning.

6.4 Descartes' Suppositions

Having laid out his provisional moral code in Part Three, Descartes begins Part Four of the *Discourse* as follows:

> Since I now wished to devote myself solely to the search for truth, I thought it necessary to do the very opposite and reject as if absolutely false everything in which I could imagine the least doubt, in order to see whether I was left believing anything that was entirely indubitable.   (Descartes 1985: 126–7)

Here, Descartes is going beyond mere agnosticism. He 'supposes' that nothing is such as our senses make it appear, that all the arguments he had previously taken to be demonstrative are unsound and resolves 'to pretend that all the things that had ever entered my mind were no more true than the illusions of my dreams' (Descartes 1985: n127). It is one thing to abandon ordinary beliefs because they are uncertain, quite another to imagine or 'pretend' that these beliefs are false. Yet this pretence is also recommended towards the end of the *First Meditation* (Descartes 1984: 15).

Clearly, we must distinguish two rather different cognitive attitudes—conjecture and supposition—both of which Descartes employs during that phase of his intellectual journey which follows the abandonment of belief and only one of which is intended as a practical substitute for belief. Conjecture aims at truth in a way that supposition does not: a false guess is a failure as a guess, a false supposition need be no failure as a supposition. Whilst one can suppose for the sake of argument something that one believes to be false, one can't sincerely conjecture or guess that p when one in fact believes that not-p. Conjectures are constrained by probability, suppositions are not (Chapter 2: Section 2.2).

For action, we need probable conjecture, not mere supposition. So when Descartes lays down which opinions he should use to govern the sceptical phase of his life, he is concerned with adopting conjectures and not with making suppositions. But once he has a background of opinion in place, he opens Part Four with the announcement that it would be sensible to make certain suppositions in order to pursue one of his practical projects, the search for knowledge. As Descartes explains in the *Fifth Replies*:

it is often useful to assume falsehoods instead of truths in this way in order to shed light on the truth, e.g. when astronomers imagine the equator, the zodiac, or other circles in the sky, or when geometers add new lines to given figures.   (Descartes 1984: 242)

But how can mere supposition help him in the search for knowledge? I suspect supposition plays more than one role for Descartes, and I shall consider only the most important of them.

Imagine Descartes finds himself feeling quite certain of something, perhaps of a mathematical demonstration. Descartes tells us that 'my nature is such that so long as I perceive something very clearly and very distinctly I cannot but believe it to be true' (Descartes 1984: 48); it looks as if he can't doubt the demonstration (see also (Descartes 1984: 25) and (Descartes 1985: 207)). Yet, in the *First Meditation*, Descartes notes that 'others go astray in cases where they think they have the most perfect knowledge' and asks 'may I not similarly go wrong every time I add two and three or count the sides of a square, or in some even simpler matter, if that is imaginable?' (Descartes 1984: 14); (see also (Descartes 1985: 194)). So whilst he may be unable to doubt the demonstration now, he can see how a time may come when some more or less subtle fallacy is pointed out to him. Does this sort of reflection provoke a doubt about what is clearly and distinctively perceived?

Various answers to this question have been canvassed and a full response would involve addressing the problem of the Cartesian Circle. But on one point at least there is some agreement among commentators—things clearly and distinctly perceived cannot be doubted by the Cartesian sceptic in the sense in which those opinions which come from and through the senses can and ought to be doubted (compare (Williams 1983: 345–50) and (Wolterstorff 1996: 189)). True, Descartes speaks of doubt in both contexts and does not explicitly distinguish two forms of doubt (Descartes 1984: 101 and 308). But unless we make this distinction in reading him we will find it hard to explain his insistence that he can't fail to believe whatever he clearly and distinctly perceives. And there is a further point. Descartes must rely on his clear and distinct perceptions in order to carry out the *reductio* proofs with which he fends off these threatening suppositions. How could he believe in the cogency of such proofs unless he also believes in what he clearly and distinctly perceives? ((Wolterstorff 1996: 214–15); (Owens 2000: 126–7)).

Supposition plays a crucial role in the construction of these proofs by *reductio*. Descartes reacts to 'doubts' about what is clearly and distinctly perceived by *supposing* that the proposition in question is wrong or the argument invalid and then seeing what follows from that supposition. If some absurdity follows, then he has a demonstration that no such error exists. It is precisely this strategy which Descartes employs to deal with the most radical of his sceptical hypotheses, one which occurs in both the *Principles* and the *Meditations*:

> we have been told that there is an omnipotent God who created us. Now we do not know whether he may have wished to make us beings of the sort who are always deceived even in those matters which seem to us supremely evident; for such constant deception seems no less of a possibility than the occasional deception which, as we have noted on previous occasions, does occur. (Descartes 1985: 194) (See also (Descartes 1984: 25))

Reflection on this possibility is not meant to render our clear and distinct perceptions doubtful, which would be impossible. Rather, it leads Descartes to make the supposition that there is such a deceitful God in an effort to derive an absurdity from it, which he does (to his mind) successfully in the *Third Meditation* ((Descartes 1984: 35).

There is much more to be said on the matters raised in this section. What I hope to have established is that (a) we must not confuse the conjectures which govern the life of the Cartesian sceptic with the suppositions which he makes in the course of it, and (b) we must distinguish the doubts which force the Cartesian sceptic to adopt conjectures in place of his former beliefs from the 'doubts' which are resolved by first supposing that what is clearly and distinctly perceived might be false.

PART III
Practical Freedom

7

Freedom and Practical Judgement

Human beings can choose what to do. Human beings can also act freely. Many writers think the one fact helps to explain the other, that if spiders cannot act freely that is because they cannot choose what to do. True, most human actions are performed without first becoming the topic of choice, as when you turn the pages of this book. Nevertheless, once you have started reading, you do so freely because you have the capacity to choose whether to carry on.

I agree that our capacity for free action depends upon our capacity for choice. In particular, it depends upon our ability to arrive at a practical judgement, a judgement about what to do, and to implement that judgement in action. But to make a case for this, we must assure ourselves that practical judgement is under our control in just the sense that action and intention are under our control, for our ability to control our practical judgements can't be the source of our ability to act freely unless we control our practical judgements as we control our actions and intentions. That should make us suspicious of the idea that practical judgement is a kind of belief, for it is generally agreed that we don't control the formation of our beliefs as we control our actions and intentions.

In this chapter, I'll first ask what a practical judgement could be if not a belief. Then I'll argue that we have a capacity to make and enforce practical judgements, so understood, whenever we are acting freely. Finally, I'll seek to establish that the making of a practical judgement is free in the very sense in which actions and intention formation are free and so can indeed be the source of our practical freedom.

7.1 What is Practical Judgement?

Practical judgement is a judgement about what to do. Beginning here, many authors move on to say that a practical judgement is a judgement about what I (or we) ought to (or should) do and they come to rest with the claim that practical judgement is a judgement about what we have most reason to do, or what it would be best to do all things considered. Although these transitions are frequently made, and though I shall make them here, they shouldn't pass without comment. Some creatures might be capable of thinking about what to do without deploying normative concepts like 'should' and 'ought'. And we who can deploy such concepts might decide what we should or ought to do without thinking about reasons, values, or what was best. Nevertheless, to facilitate discussion I shall here assume that when a rational human agent thinks about what to do, they are thinking about what action reason recommends.[1]

The idea that practical judgement is a form of belief has been disputed by some who worry that a mere belief would not have the required motivational impact (e.g., Nagel 1970: 65). But many others are happy with the idea that a belief can play the motivational role of practical judgement. Scanlon tells us that we can 'explain the intrapersonal rational significance of judgements about reasons for action...without supposing that those judgements are anything other than beliefs' (Scanlon 2003: 19). Broome also sees no difficulty here: 'We often deliberate in order to arrive at a normative belief about what to do, and the point of our deliberation is ultimately to bring us to a decision—the forming of an intention' (Broome 2001: 180).

In this chapter, I shall assume that Scanlon and Broome have right on their side in maintaining that there are truths about reasons which we can know, the knowledge of which can move us to action. It might seem a short step from this to the view that practical judgement is 'just another belief' (Arpaly 2003: 61). For example, having told us that he is 'strongly drawn to a cognitivist understanding of...practical judgements', Scanlon adds, 'They strike me as the kind of things that can be true and their acceptance seems to be a matter of belief' (Scanlon 2003: 7). But mightn't practical judgements be 'the kind of things that can be true' without also being the kind of things whose acceptance is a matter of *belief*? I want to argue that, on at least one familiar construal of the term 'belief', practical judgements are not beliefs.

What are the connotations of this familiar notion of belief? I shall distinguish three. First, belief is governed by a norm of truth. Second, a belief motivates action on that belief. Third, belief is governed by a norm of knowledge. It is this third connotation that distinguishes belief from what I call practical judgement. I shall review these features in order.

Belief is subject to a norm of truth in that it is correct to believe that p only if p is true. This distinguishes belief from states like desire and intention that can be neither true nor false. It also distinguishes belief from activities like imagining, supposing, and hypothesizing, which can be more or less truthful (Shah and

---

[1] For some important qualifications of these claims, see Chapter 8: Section 8.1.

Velleman 2005: 499). For example, when I imagine that the figure is bisected, my imagining is false but not thereby incorrect. I am not wrong to make that supposition; there is no standard normative for imaginings which it violates simply in virtue of being false. By contrast, a false belief is *ipso facto* an incorrect belief. To believe something false is to believe wrongly, it is to make a mistake.

Perhaps some writers move from the premise that practical judgements are subject to a truth norm to the conclusion that they are beliefs because they assume that only belief is subject to a truth norm. Yet guessing that p and suspecting that p are both incorrect if false. If your guess or suspicion is false, you have guessed or suspected wrongly, you have made an error.[2] In this respect, both guessing and suspecting differ from imagining, supposing, and hypothesizing. A scientist employed to pursue a certain line of research might put forward an hypothesis or adopt a supposition for the sake of argument and he might be quite correct to do so even though his hypothesis or supposition is untrue.

Those who note that belief is subject to a truth norm often go on to say that beliefs must 'aim at the truth' and that this is why beliefs cannot be adopted at will regardless of evidence. Do guessing and suspecting aim at the truth in the same way? My own view is that this talk of 'aiming' adds little to our understanding of belief and so I don't propose to investigate whether it can help us with guessing and suspicion.[3] I observe only that whilst we can suppose or hypothesize that Bill Clinton is a woman just because we have been offered a large financial incentive for so doing, we can neither believe nor suspect nor guess this of Clinton simply to get such a reward (though we can *say* 'I guess'). On that point, believing, suspecting, and guessing are entirely at one. I leave it open how this similarity is to be explained and, in particular, whether it can be explained by reference to the truth norm.

So how are we to distinguish belief from other states governed by a norm of truth? A second connotation of 'belief' is practical: someone who believes that p has a default rational entitlement and a *prima facie* rational obligation to act as if p is true (that is, to do what would be reasonable on that supposition).[4] Many will

---

[2] In other respects, guesses and suspicions are quite different. Guessing is a mental action, an action sometimes but not always expressed in a speech act (Chapter 2: Section 2.2). Suspicion is more like belief—you come to suspect, you don't decide to suspect—but suspicion does not require the same evidential warrant as belief (Greenspan 1988: 90–1). (Note there is a factive use of 'guess' on which you fail to guess someone's age if you get it wrong but there is another usage, which I here adopt, on which you can guess incorrectly).

[3] I think it will help more with guessing than with suspicion. See, Chapter 2: Sections 2.2 and 2.3, and Chapter 4: Section 4.2.

[4] (Broome 2001:181–2) argues that one need not have any reason to act on one's beliefs (e.g. if they are false). I shan't discuss Broome's view here. What I presuppose is something Broome will allow, namely, that there is (in a way to be qualified) some irrationality in failing to act as if your beliefs are true.

think this claim too weak, but I shall postpone that particular discussion for a few pages. Even this weak claim is enough to differentiate belief from both guessing and suspecting. It can be reasonable to act as if your guesses or your suspicions are true, but there is no default entitlement or *prima facie* obligation to do so. Whether this is reasonable will depend on further facts about the situation.

Have we said enough to differentiate belief from other mental phenomena? I doubt it. There is a further connotation of 'belief' which makes the cut between belief and practical judgement. Belief is not just subject to a norm of truth, it is also subject to a norm of knowledge: if what you believe is something you don't know then your believing it is incorrect. To show someone that they don't know that p (perhaps because they are not justified in believing it) is to show them that they are also mistaken in believing it. To think yourself right to believe that p, you can't think you are ignorant of its truth, anymore than you can think p false (Owens 2000: 37). It might be an accident that you are right to guess that p, but it won't be an accident that you are right to believe that p.[5]

I don't deny that there are uses of the term 'belief' which would not sustain this connection with knowledge; I assert only that there is a notion of belief which does, a notion familiar from both epistemology and ordinary life. It is not clear to me whether the writers I quoted at the outset are employing this epistemic notion of belief in formulating their claims about practical judgement. But, as we shall see, clarity on this point is crucial to our understanding of practical freedom.

Some maintain that this third feature of belief is not really independent of the other two. This is wrong. One's guess or one's suspicion can be perfectly correct because true even though one fails to know that it is true. Guessing and suspecting demonstrate that something can be subject to the truth norm without being subject to the knowledge norm. Furthermore, we can at least conceive of a mental phenomenon which is governed by the truth norm but is unlike guessing, etc. in that one *does* have a default entitlement (obligation) to behave as if it were true even when one is not in any position to claim knowledge of its truth. This possible phenomenon I shall call a practical judgement.[6] In this chapter, 'practical judgement' refers to something which is like belief in that it should

---

[5] In Gettier cases you have committed an error even though your belief is both reasonable and true.

[6] 'Judgement' is sometimes used to refer either to a kind of internal assertion which manifests belief or else to a cognitive action which is a precursor of belief. For example, both (Shah and Velleman 2005: 503) and (Peacocke 1998: 88) use the term 'judgement' to denote a mental act 'aimed at the truth' which concludes theoretical deliberation and so (in a rational person) is a precursor of a belief. I doubt the existence of such 'theoretical' judgements. It may be that practical judgement is a mental action, but this point needs careful handling and I place no weight on it here.

dispose us to behave as if it is true yet unlike belief in that it is subject to the truth but not to the knowledge norm.

It is one thing to point out that a phenomenon like practical judgement might exist, it is quite another to establish a real theoretical need for it. In Section 7.2, we shall see that practical deliberation often terminates in something both subject to a truth norm and action motivating but which does not constitute a belief.

7.2 Judgement and Ignorance

I am assuming that the practical deliberator is seeking to determine what to do by determining what he ought to do, by settling what action reason recommends. But we shouldn't assume that practical deliberation concludes only when the deliberator thinks they *know* the answer. A question like 'What ought I to do?' may be answered with a guess or by the formation of a suspicion, at least where knowledge of the answer is unavailable. And, I want to suggest, a deliberator can make a practical judgement, even where he knows he has yet to dispel his ignorance about what to do.

I am trying to settle on a suitable restaurant for our anniversary dinner. We live in a large city and there are many to choose from. In the case of some, I take myself to know that there is nothing to choose between them. If those restaurants are also the best, I might simply pick one of them at random. I thereby decide *to* dine at a certain restaurant (i.e. form the intention to dine there) without deciding *that* we ought to dine there: if I went to the one I didn't choose by mistake, I wouldn't be doing anything I judged I ought not to do. On this point, my action is not guided by my judgement as to which option is best.

There are other cases in which my action *is* guided by my judgement, even though I am ignorant of which option is best. Suppose that I neither take myself to know which of the more attractive restaurants is best, nor that they are equally good. In fact, I'm pretty sure there are significant differences between them which further investigation would reveal and which might well affect my choice. But one can only spend so much time choosing a restaurant, even for an anniversary dinner, so I make reservations at the restaurant which seems the best on present showing. Here, I judge that we ought to go to this restaurant, and I do so on the basis of my beliefs about desirable features of the restaurant, but I wouldn't claim to know that this restaurant was the best or the most desirable or the one that reason favours. That I know I'm currently in no position to know.[7]

---

[7] (Holton 2009: 59–61) observes that we often make choices even though (a) we believe the options to be both significantly different and commensurable, and (b) we know that we are in no

My way of proceeding is unobjectionable. What I am doing is registering in my practical deliberations limitations on the process of deliberation itself. These limitations are hardly shameful. On the contrary, they are constraints under which all finite creatures labour and it makes perfect sense to take them into account when determining when to make up your mind. Because of them, rational practical deliberation often concludes with (and does not merely stop at) a proposition that the deliberator wouldn't claim to know.

Can we accommodate this point by instead relaxing our assumption that practical deliberation aims to discover what we have most reason to do? Perhaps I need not take myself to know that this restaurant is the best one before concluding that I ought to dine there, but don't I at least take myself to know that it is good enough for my purposes, that there is no decisive objection to it, that given the limited time and effort I can expend on the matter, this is the option I ought to go for? If so, the judgement which concludes deliberation may be a normative belief after all.

Sometimes we can indeed know that a restaurant is good enough in this sense, without being in any position to know that it is the best. But, on other occasions, the issue as to whether a restaurant is 'good enough' might be hardly less difficult to settle. For example, whether it is 'good enough' might depend on whether there is a nearby restaurant which is known to be better by my partner. Perhaps I have time to eliminate this possibility (by obliquely questioning my partner, etc.). In that case, I may know that the restaurant is good enough without necessarily knowing that it is the best all round. But suppose I don't have the chance to rule this possibility out. I might still judge that we ought to go ahead and eat there.

Nor will it help to build the constraints on the deliberative process explicitly into the content of my practical judgement. I *might* be in a position to know that, given my limited deliberative resources, the thing I ought to do is to settle on the option which currently seems best (the one which I suspect to be best). On the other hand, I might not. I might only be a position to make the educated guess that I ought to make a judgement at this stage rather than holding out for more information. When, on the basis of this guess, I judge that I ought to conclude deliberation now, this is no mere stab in the dark. But equally, I wouldn't claim to know that I ought to do this, for I know it is a real possibility that a bit more deliberative effort would yield results and so forth. Nevertheless, I judge that what I ought to do is to settle on this restaurant.

---

position to know which option is best. Holton describes these as cases of 'choice in the absence of conscious judgement' (p. 61). He says this is because he regards conscious belief as the upshot of conscious judgement (p. 57).

Someone may wonder whether these decisions about what one ought to do are genuine judgements. Are they not decisions *to* rather than decisions *that*? It is certainly true that the point of making such a judgement is not merely to evaluate the options but actually to get yourself to act. In that the judgement is like an intention. And at least where future action is in question, the skill of making practical judgements just is the skill of drafting sensible intentions. Still, this should not blind us to some obvious differences between them.

First, intentions may be reasonable or unreasonable, but it is doubtful whether they are correct or incorrect and they are certainly not assessed for truth. By contrast, the judgement that I ought to φ is evaluated not just as reasonable or unreasonable but also as correct or incorrect, and its correctness depends on its truth value. Secondly, even though a good practical judge will opt only for feasible intentions, the fact that he judges that he ought to φ no more guarantees that he will form the intention to φ than it guarantees that he will φ when the time comes. Both lapses are possible.

To sum up, in making a practical judgement I need not form a belief about which option is best or even good enough. I need not form a belief about what I ought to do. I can be living in ignorance on all these points.[8] But I may still conclude my deliberation with a *judgement* about what I ought to do and sensibly implement that judgement in decision and action. This practical judgement shares two of the features I took to be characteristic of belief: it is correct only if true and it should move me to act as if it is true. But it is not a belief, for though I think myself entitled to make it, I lay no claim to knowledge of its truth.

From what has been said so far, practical judgement looks rather like the better sort of guess, but the comparison is misleading. A practical judgement is not, like an educated guess, just a way of dealing with ignorance. If it were, it could hardly be the source of our practical freedom, for we don't think ourselves free only where we are ignorant of what to do. In section 7.3, I shall argue that practical judgement can actually countermand belief, both normative and non-normative, for it sometimes makes sense to judge that you ought to act as if what you *know* to be so isn't so. Such a practical judgement won't be based on a guess, since you can't (reasonably) guess to be false what you know to be true.

---

[8] In previous work, I left it open whether a rational person must know their reasons, whether they can be in ignorance of what rationality requires of them (Owens 2000: 15–16). I now think that whilst a rational person must act on their view of what reason recommends, one can take a view about what reason recommends without taking oneself to know what reason recommends (Williamson 2000: 180). In particular, ignorance about what one should do cannot always be dispelled by knowledge of some principle of decision-making under uncertainty.

7.3 Judgement and Knowledge

How could it ever be sensible for us not to act on what we know? To answer this question, we must ask why knowledge matters to us. I have argued that belief is not the only action motivating state subject to a truth norm. If so, why do we value knowledge? Why does it matter to us whether we can *know* the answer rather than make an educated guess at it?[9] We want to be right and someone who knows is more likely to be right than someone who doesn't, but that fact alone won't explain the importance of the boundary between knowledge and ignorance. We are much more likely to be right about some of the things we take ourselves to know than about others; furthermore, we are almost as likely to be right about some of the things we don't take ourselves to know as about many of the things we do.

Since belief embodies a claim to knowledge, to ask about the value of knowledge is to ask why we want beliefs, why we want to satisfy our curiosity, to remove our doubts, to resolve our uncertainties. Guesses and suspicions, however well founded, will never suffice, though they may carry just the information we need. One popular answer presupposes that if someone is entitled to believe that p then it must be sensible for them to act as if p is true. Things we know are, it is said, things we can (and must) assume to be true for the purposes of action.[10] On this view, 'the importance of the concept of knowledge' resides in the fact that 'it sets a meaningful lower bound on strength of epistemic position: your epistemic position regarding p must be strong enough to make it rational for you to act as if p is true' (Fantl and McGrath 2007: 581).

In discussing the motivational role of belief, I agreed that things we believe do play a special role in our practical deliberations. But I doubt this role is best captured by making unqualified claims like the following: 'S is justified in believing that p only if S is rational to act as if p' (Fantl and McGrath 2002: 78). Firstly, such claims postulate too tight a connection between belief and rational agency. It is not always rational to act as if p because you know that p. In particular, this is not rational in some cases where (a) the costs of acting as if p should p turn out to be false are substantial, or (b) the benefits of acting as if not-p should not-p turn out to be true are substantial.

Secondly, such claims focus on the connection between belief and agency to the exclusion of other equally significant features of belief. Our convictions play a crucial role in our emotional psychology. Someone can be angry at the fact that p, or proud of it, or grateful for it, only if they know that p (Gordon 1987: 47–9).

---

[9] Those interested in the value of knowledge often ask why knowledge is more valued than mere true belief. This is not the best way of putting the question if belief is subject to a norm of knowledge.

[10] Something like this is presupposed by many of those who argue that whether we know that p depends, in part, upon our practical interests in the truth of p (e.g. Hawthorne 2004: 173–81).

Often, we want to know whether p in order to fix our emotional bearings, to avoid having our feelings baffled by ignorance; in eliminating uncertainty we learn how to feel as well as how to act. Sometimes we would prefer to stick with those emotions—hopes and fears—that presuppose uncertainty rather than learn the truth. Still, the boundary between knowledge and ignorance retains its emotional significance.

In the light of these points, I propose the following as a partial account of knowledge—to know that p is at least to be justified in using p (i) as a default assumption in your practical reasoning, and (ii) to inform whatever cognitive processes guide the higher reaches of our emotional lives.[11] A default assumption is one that you can rely on when you have no specific reason not to. Memory is full of beliefs we depend on in this way, and cognition could not take its current form unless we were entitled to this reliance. Such default assumptions are indeed crucial to all practical reasoning. Even where we end up making an educated guess, we feel entitled to act on that guess (i.e. to judge that we ought to) only because of an assumed background knowledge of the situation. But it is not *always* advisable to act on these assumptions. Nor is the advisability of acting on these assumptions the only thing which makes them worth having. On my view, knowledge is valued more than an educated guess because a proposition known forms part of that framework of default assumptions which we need to conduct both our cognitive and our emotional lives.

Let's test a purely agency-based view of the value of knowledge against my own proposal by considering some examples. I have parked my car on the street outside, taking the amount of care a reasonably conscientious citizen would to park legally. When I enter the house, my partner informs me that the police have been ticketing the street this week. Before being told of this, I took myself to know that my car was parked legally, that is, I took myself to have evidence sufficient to justify my believing this. Hearing my partner's words, I reluctantly go out and recheck the position of my car and the relevant parking notices. Is this an implicit admission that I no longer know that my car is legally parked, at least until I have completed the checks, because my belief is no longer justified?[12]

Our linguistic intuitions here seem inconclusive. Being reluctant to check, I might say to my partner, 'I know I'm properly parked' and they might reply, 'Yes, I agree, but it is still worth checking'. That sounds as if my partner is agreeing that I do know and thus agreeing that they can learn from me how the car is parked whilst also suggesting that here it might not be sensible to act on

---

[11] I say 'at least' because propositions we take ourselves to know may also play a distinctive role in our theoretical reasoning, e.g. they may serve as our evidence (Williamson 2000: 203–7).

[12] A similar example is used in support of this conclusion by (Fantl and McGrath 2007: 560).

our knowledge since the costs of being wrong on this point are substantial and the check can easily be made. Is my partner merely being polite? Or are they observing quite sincerely that this is one of those cases where practical judgement should countermand the motivational effects of a default background assumption to which I am still perfectly entitled?

Suppose my partner instead says 'But do you *really* know the car is properly parked?' Now it sounds as if I *am* being invited to abandon my belief and to do so because it has become unjustified. But this isn't the only interpretation available. Perhaps my partner is highlighting the possibility that my belief is false, a possibility that would deprive me of knowledge even if my belief were still fully justified, a possibility on which I must now focus for practical rather than epistemic reasons. My partner might be seeking to influence my practical judgement without thereby changing my convictions.

Our car example is one in which I am sensible not to act on my (well-founded) assumption that p because the costs of being wrong are substantial. Similar issues are raised by cases in which I risk missing out on a considerable, though unlikely, benefit if I act on my default assumption. Suppose someone offers to pay me £10 million in return for a stake of 10p if it turns out that I was not brought up a Catholic. I know that I was brought up a Catholic and much of the rest of what I know about myself would make little sense were I not. Nevertheless, I might reasonably accept the bet (Hawthorne 2004: 176).[13] Can the mere fact that I have been offered this bet render one of my most well-founded convictions unjustified? It would sound odd for me to confess ignorance of which religion I was raised in because it is silly to miss out on this bet. On the other hand, as I place the bet, I might say to myself 'Well I guess I *might* be wrong about which religion I was born into' and then it would be slightly strange to add 'but I *do* still know'.

There is something awkward about describing yourself as acting on an assumption which you know to be false, but the awkwardness is, I reckon, just the awkwardness of explicitly acknowledging the possibility of error in a context in which you also claim knowledge. 'I know that p though I'm not absolutely sure that p' jars, as does 'I know that p though I might be wrong', but we shouldn't infer that one who takes themselves to know cannot sensibly acknowledge their own fallibility. On the contrary, rationality requires such an acknowledgement from us all and rationality permits us, on occasion, to act on it by not assuming in our practical deliberations things we take ourselves to know.

On my view, belief and practical judgement are each, in their different ways, fundamental to our lives as agents. In one way, belief is more fundamental.

---

[13] I might reasonably accept *any* such bet but not *all* such bets.

No agent could get by on judgement and conjecture alone. Without that background of default assumptions, one could make neither guesses nor practical judgements. On the other hand, it is true of (virtually?) any belief that a rational agent has the capacity to countermand its motivational effects by judging that it would be right not to act on it.

As already noted, belief and knowledge have a life outside our practical deliberations, underwriting a rich emotional psychology. For example, I can feel proud that I was raised a Catholic, or ashamed, for that matter, only if I know that I was raised a Catholic. If I don't think I know this, whilst I can think myself entitled to entertain hopes or fears on the matter, I can't think pride or shame would be in place. Yet I won't come to think pride or shame impossible just because I have been offered the bet. Pride and shame need not come and go in response to such offers; rather, they are part of a more permanent background, dependent on relatively stable convictions which structure our emotional lives as well as supplying default assumptions for practical deliberation.

Now imagine that I am rather proud to own such a fine car, the very car I parked outside the house. On this occasion my partner informs me some time after I have arrived in the house that the police are confiscating illegally parked cars and were doing so in our street only last week. Must I cease to take pride in my car until I have checked that no such confiscation has taken place? Should I be gripped by fear for my social status? A sober person would rather judge that it is sensible to check how the car is parked and then calmly leave the house, convinced that their car is still there. Such conviction would be misplaced had they parked the car less carefully, but it isn't misplaced simply because they judge that they should check.

What is true of pride (or shame if I feel bad about driving a status symbol) applies equally to anger, embarrassment, sorrow, joy, gratitude, disappointment, disgust, and much of the rest of our emotional lives. Behind these attitudes and reactions lie certain default assumptions about how the world is, assumptions which shape what we do, think, and feel in a wide range of contexts. If this cognitive background is to be so widely available, it can't be tied too closely to any one context. Even as I walk out the door to check my car, I may be using the default assumption that I have a car in various inferences (e.g. in thought about the best way to avoid tomorrow's traffic jams) as well as to take my emotional bearings. Why deny that I can be entitled to believe it, just because I am also confirming its truth?[14]

---

[14] Similarly for testimony. I shouldn't be prevented from dipping into the fund of common knowledge by some ephemeral circumstance. I would be so prevented if I couldn't now learn that p from you just because it would not be sensible for me to act on this knowledge at this very moment.

Several authors, myself included, have argued that the level of evidence required to justify a given belief depends, in part, on the needs and interests of the believer (Owens 2000: 24–7). And this raises the prospect that different subjects confronted by the same evidence for p may find themselves in a rather different epistemic situation with regard to p. Where this happens, I would maintain, it happens because of relatively permanent and pervasive differences between people, e.g. differences in social role, intellectual interests, or long-term personal relationships.[15] Our convictions are multipurpose, and changes or variations in what would justify them make sense only where a range of these purposes are affected by the relevant factors. Such variations are not brought about by transient changes in the stakes riding on particular issues.

For example, if someone is a close relative of mine, the amount of evidence I require before I begin to doubt their honesty is rather different from that required by a stranger. And if bird spotting is my main passion in life, I may not feel able to believe that a Willow Warbler has appeared for the first time in California even on the basis of several reported sightings, whilst it would be neurotic for the average newspaper reader to demand as much. In both cases, because it matters so much more and in so many ways for me to be right about this sort of thing, I am held to higher standards in forming beliefs about it.[16]

The points made in this section apply as much to beliefs about what I should do as to the non-normative beliefs on which they are based (*pace* Fantl and McGrath 2007: 571–4). Since I know my car is correctly parked, I know I would be wasting my time going to check it and so I know that I ought not to check it.[17] Yet I judge that I ought to check it. Of course, I make this judgement in the light of what I know about the (remote) chance of it being parked illegally and the trouble involved in checking. But I screen off the knowledge that it is in fact correctly parked in judging that I ought to check. Once I have checked and found

---

[15] I am less confident of the existence of relevant variations between believers than I am of the proposition that the required level of evidence is fixed, in part, by the needs and interests of believers as such. That conclusion can be established simply by asking what else could fix this level: evidence certainly can't. (Fantl and McGrath 2002: 71 and 87–8) complain that this simple argument against evidentialism tells us little about how the relevant level of evidence is fixed. I agree, but this throws no doubt on its soundness as an argument against evidentialism.

[16] My account of the role of belief in practical deliberation is, in some respects, similar to that offered in (Bratman 1999: 15–34). Bratman regards belief as providing a 'default cognitive background' for practical deliberation, whilst maintaining that we may 'posit' things we don't believe or 'bracket' things we do when deliberating about particular issues (p. 29). For Bratman, these positings and bracketings, unlike beliefs, are mental acts. Bratman's account differs from mine in that (a) he confines himself to belief's role in practical deliberation; (b) he asserts that reasons for belief are purely evidential; and (c) he does not discuss knowledge (or freedom).

[17] Where change is likely, the maintenance of knowledge requires periodic checking. This is not such a case: neither the position of your car nor the parking regulations are likely to change.

the car to be legally parked, I will admit that my belief was right and my judgement was wrong: it wasn't true that I ought to have checked. Nevertheless, both belief and judgement were perfectly reasonable.[18]

I conclude that, though people have a rational entitlement and obligation to act as if their beliefs are true, this requirement is defeasible. Does the same apply to practical judgement itself? Is the rational requirement to act as if one's practical judgement is true also defeasible? I think so. Suppose I judge that I ought not to back this inventor and finance the production of his self-cleaning shirt. Then you offer me a bet asking a small stake for a large reward should my practical judgement turn out to be false. Even if I am very confident of my practical judgement, the reasonable thing might well be to accept the bet. Here, I don't abandon my practical judgement, indeed I act on it in that I allow it to govern my investment behavior, but I don't act as if it is true when accepting the bet. There is no failure of rational self-control here because I am behaving in accordance with my higher-order judgement that I ought not to act as if my first-order judgement is true. In a rational agent, practical judgement can countermand the motivational force of both belief and practical judgement.

7.4 Practical Freedom

Let's return to the question with which I began: how does our capacity for choice underwrite our practical freedom? The initial worry that action could not be free were our actions determined by our beliefs was met with the claim that we have an independent capacity to control our actions by means of our practical judgement. But this is no advance unless we are freer in making practical judgements than in forming beliefs. Is practical judgement any better suited to be the source of our freedom? First, I'll say what a mental phenomenon must be like in order to be the source of our freedom and then I'll argue that practical judgement alone satisfies that requirement.[19]

---

[18] Given that I have argued that belief and practical judgement are subject to a norm of truth, can one reasonably believe that p and judge that not-p? Can a rational person (knowingly) tolerate a situation in which they can't possibly be obeying both of the relevant norms? I think so. Several authors have noted that, where one discovers an inconsistency amongst one's beliefs but can't tell which of the relevant beliefs is false, it may be reasonable to settle for inconsistent beliefs (Chapter 2: Section 2.1). This shows that the relationship between norms of correctness and norms of rationality is rather complex.

[19] This chapter is about the psychology rather than the metaphysics of freedom. It asks what psychological states are distinctive of free agents. Other psychologies of freedom award the palm to higher order desires or normative beliefs or yet other mental phenomena. I shall not commit myself on what sort of capacity a free agent must have to do, decide, or judge otherwise than he did. This

I'm exploring theories of free action according to which our freedom consists in our ability to use a certain psychological instrument to control our agency. Call this instrument *choice*. I am assuming that our freedom of action depends on a prior freedom of choice. But what is choice? Which bit of our psychology constitutes our choice? Is it a *belief* about our reasons, or else a *judgement* about our reasons, or else an act of *will* based on this belief or this judgement?

At the outset, I suggested that the psychological instrument of our practical freedom must satisfy a certain condition, namely that we be able to control that instrument as we control our actions by way of it—the source of our freedom of action must be free in just the way that action itself is free. In my view, practical judgement is the source of our freedom of action because practical judgement is under the control of practical judgement in just the way that action (and intention) are under the control of practical judgement. Where an action is free, this is so because (i) one can control the action (or intention) by making a practical judgement, and (ii) one can control whether one makes the practical judgement by making a practical judgement.

Some maintain that action is not truly free unless every determinant of this action is itself freely chosen. It is an open question whether this demand can ever be satisfied or even coherently stated. But there is another thought which might be what lies behind at least some people's attraction to the impossible demand:

> *Constraint*: If one has freedom of action because one has freedom of choice, choice must control choice in the way that choice controls action.

What *Constraint* requires is that the regress of control terminate in a type of mental phenomenon which controls itself in just the way that it controls action. Note that a form of choice might satisfy *Constraint* even if such choices were entirely determined by factors (our upbringing, social environment, etc.) which we did not choose.

Among the candidates for the psychological instrument of our self-control, only practical judgement satisfies *Constraint*, or so at least I shall urge. I reject the idea that (normative) beliefs are the source of our practical freedom because one can't control those beliefs by forming beliefs about what one should believe. I also maintain that, though intention controls action, intention does not (in the same sense) control itself: the will is not subject to the will. So, I shall conclude, free choice consists in the making of a practical judgement.

---

question would be the focus of any inquiry into the metaphysics of freedom. In particular, I take no stand on whether freedom as I understand it is consistent with determinism.

Let's begin with the will. Voluntarists hold that what makes us free is our possession of a will, of a capacity to control our actions by forming intentions. For voluntarists, what makes our actions free is the fact that they are subject to our will (i.e. to our intentions). What does it mean to say that an action is subject to our will, that we can perform it 'at will'? Elsewhere, I have argued that something is subject to our will when we have the capacity to bring it about simply because its occurrence seems desirable to us. Many actions are subject to our will because we can bring them about for this reason. But, in that sense at least, the will is not itself subject to the will, for we can't form an intention to φ simply because it seems desirable to form that intention and regardless of whether φ-ing would itself be desirable (Owens 2000: 78–82). In fact our will is no more subject to our will than our beliefs are subject our will. We can no more form intentions 'at will' (i.e. form whatever intention would be most desirable regardless of the apparent value of what is intended) than we can believe 'at will' (i.e. form whatever belief would be most desirable regardless of the apparent truth of what is believed).

So the will fails to satisfy *Constraint* since the will does not control itself in the way that the will controls action. Nevertheless, the voluntarist is right to observe (a) that when we form intentions we are free as we are not when we form beliefs, and (b) that nothing can be the source of our practical freedom unless it is itself free in the way in which the will is free. Even if our practical freedom does not have its source in the freedom of our will, it certainly encompasses freedom of will as well as freedom of action. Let me briefly explain why we don't control our beliefs and then contrast belief with both judgement and intention.

The intellectualist maintains that we exercise control over ourselves by making normative assessments of our states and activities, both actual and potential. This is, I think, the right conception of control, but it does not apply to belief itself (whether normative or non-normative). Why not? Given some initially plausible assumptions about the psychological capacities of a rational person, it seems that we must be able to control our beliefs by forming higher-order beliefs about whether we are entitled to them. If one first assumes that rational belief is based on reasons for belief and then assumes that in so far as belief is sensitive to the reasons for it, it must also be sensitive to our beliefs about those reasons, it seems to follow immediately that, in so far as we are rational, we must be able to control our beliefs by forming beliefs about the reasons for them. Were this so, normative belief would satisfy *Constraint* since normative belief would control itself in just the way that, the intellectualist supposes, it controls action. I agree that rational belief is sensitive to reasons for belief but I deny that that we are able to control our beliefs by forming beliefs about the reasons for them. Thus, normative belief violates *Constraint*.

As already noted, evidence alone does not settle whether someone is justified in believing what they do, and thus whether they know it.[20] One must also consider how much this sort of issue matters to the believer, how confident they need to be on the point. All forms of deliberation, whether doxastic or practical, are subject to constraints of time, energy, and cognitive resource (e.g. memory), and an assessment of the outcome of doxastic deliberation cannot fail to take these limitations into account. Furthermore, the rational believer must himself be sensitive to these limitations. Yet it is a fact that doxastic deliberators lack the capacity to get themselves to form a belief by explicitly considering such factors, by reflecting on whether they should now form a view about whether p given these limitations, the importance of the issue, and so forth. At least the deliberator does not have this capacity simply in virtue of being a rational deliberator.[21] So we can't exercise rational control over our beliefs by forming normative beliefs about them (nor indeed by making judgements to the same effect). That is what underlies the widespread idea that belief is not free.

In this respect, practical judgement differs from belief, as we can see by returning to our earlier example. There are two kinds of case to consider: those in which we don't take ourselves to know what we ought to do and those in which we do. In both, practical deliberation concludes with a practical judgement, a judgement that can supplement or countermand the operations of belief and one that is itself under the control of practical judgement. This independent capacity for practical judgement is the source of our practical freedom.

First, recall my choice of restaurant. Here I don't take myself to know which restaurant is best because I suspect that it could easily turn out that some other restaurant was much better than the one I am presently inclined to choose. I don't even take myself to know whether I ought to make the choice now (though I feel inclined so to do) because if I waited a little longer I just might learn a lot more. Here, the rational agent retains the capacity to make a judgement on the basis of what he does know about whether he ought to plump for this restaurant, a judgement which will take account of all the relevant information available to him, including the constraints on the deliberative process itself. He also has the capacity to make a higher-order judgement about whether he should make that very judgement, or hold off until he is a bit less distracted, for instance. And so on up the potential hierarchy. And, insofar as he is rational, he will act on the judgement with which he terminates the regress even though at no point does he

---

[20] This paragraph summarizes the argument of Chapter 2 of (Owens 2000).
[21] I am assuming that theoretical deliberation (i.e. the assessment of facts which provide reasons for belief) need not involve beliefs about reasons. See Chapter 3: Section 3.1.

claim to *know* either what he ought to do or what judgement he ought to make. So, unlike belief (and intention), practical judgement controls itself in just the way it controls action (and intention).

Suppose instead that I have become convinced that a certain course of action is for the best, or at least, that it is the one I ought to pursue given the various constraints I labour under. This *becoming convinced* of what I ought to do is quite unlike the making of a practical judgement about what I ought to do. I don't decide to become convinced of this in the way I decide to make a judgement about what I ought to do. Conviction is appropriate where the suspicion that I might easily learn otherwise is inappropriate and what settles this is not just the evidence but also those pragmatic considerations that determine what level of evidence would justify conviction. Yet one can't convince oneself simply by judging, however correctly, that the time has come to make up one's mind, given the constraints one labours under. Rationality doesn't guarantee that you can get yourself into a state where you think you know the answer by means of such reflections. (By contrast, rationality does guarantee that you can get yourself to make a practical judgement on the matter by noting the constraints on your deliberations.)

Suppose I am convinced that such and such is the right course of action. Do I still control my practical judgement on this point or is it now in thrall to this unfree belief? The argument of Section 7.3 preserves my judgemental control over it. It is true of (virtually?) any belief that we have the capacity to judge that we ought not, in this instance, to act as if that belief is true. And we have this capacity simply in virtue of being rational agents. Of course, our judgements are based on an assumed background of default assumptions, i.e. on a set of beliefs on which we are relying for present purposes. Nor is this cause for regret: practical freedom would have little value if its exercise were not informed by what we know. But, of each of those beliefs, it is again true that we have the capacity to judge that we ought not to act as if it is true.

I began by saying that, for practical judgement to be the source of our practical freedom, we must have the same sort of control over it that we have over our actions and intentions. I finish by noting that this condition is satisfied. Practical judgement is no more subject to the will than intention. A practical judge can't get himself to judge that p solely on the grounds that making that judgement would itself be desirable. But, as we have seen, a rational agent *can* control his practical judgements by reflecting on the constraints on the process of deliberation as well as on the merits of the options. Exactly the same is true of intention. When debating which restaurant to book I won't just be thinking about the relative merits of the restaurants but also about the need to make up my mind sooner rather than later, so that I can lay other plans for the evening on the basis of my choice and so that I can turn my attention to unrelated matters. A rational agent can get himself both to make a judgement about where he ought to eat and also to form an intention to eat there by telling himself that he has thought about the matter for long enough and must now decide (Owens 2000: 33). He can control both judgement and intention by reflecting on the constraints on the process of practical deliberation. So, practical judgement satisfies our requirement: it controls intention (and thus action) in just the sense that it controls itself.[22]

---

[22] I owe thanks to Matt Soteriou, Nishi Shah, and Richard Holton, to audiences at Amherst College, the universities of Sheffield, Leeds, and London, and to David Bell for once asking me what I thought a practical judgement was.

8

Habitual Agency

Some of what we do, think, and feel is intelligible because we do, think, and feel it from habit. In this chapter, I'll focus on habitual action. I'll argue that one way to make sense of action is by observing that the agent is in the habit of behaving that way. To 'make sense' of an action is not merely to explain it: actions that make little sense can still be explained.[1] To make sense of an action is to explain it in a way that throws no doubt on its status as intentional activity.

Here is one account of what intentional action involves:

> What marks intentional actions is that they are done because of what their agents believe the action is (including what it may bring about). That means that what the agents believe about the action leads them to do it, and guides their doing of it, all the way (that is, as far as that kind of action can be guided by its agent), and that suggests that they approve of the action, given what they believe about it. They so act because they approve of the action, and that in turn means that they think that it has some value, since value is what we approve of. (Raz 2011: 64)

Take a non-intentional action like the movement of my tongue. Moving my tongue is something that I do (unlike the beating of my heart), but I am normally quite unaware of what my tongue is doing and need see no point in its moving as it does. By contrast, when I intentionally move my tongue, the movement is guided by an awareness of what I am doing and, if Raz is right, I must see some point, some value in moving my tongue. It often matters to us whether we are acting intentionally because it matters to us whether our behaviour is an expression of our view of the merits of what we are doing. Even when we do what, on

---

[1] This notion of 'making sense' is close to Weber's *Verstehen*. 'A correct causal interpretation of typical action means that the process which is claimed to be typical is shown to be both adequately grasped on the level of meaning and at the same time the interpretation is to some degree causally adequate.' As he notes, no degree of regularity in a pattern of behaviour will render it intelligible if 'adequacy with respect to meaning is lacking' (Weber 1947: 99). Weber regards both 'affection' and 'tradition' as non-rational sources of intelligible social action (115).

the whole, we think we ought not to be doing, the action is still intentional (in Raz's view) provided we see some merit in acting as we are.

Now consider a problematic case. A man is eating sawdust. Is he eating sawdust intentionally? How could he fail to be aware of what he is doing and guiding what he is doing by means of that awareness? Still, Raz will ask whether our Sawdust Man sees any point in eating, sees any good in it. Our man probably doesn't believe that sawdust is either tasty or nutritious. Still, he craves it, and eats it because he craves it. Does that make sense of what he does? It would if he foresaw enjoying the sawdust. It would if he foresaw at least relief from his painful craving for sawdust. But suppose nothing like this is true; suppose he sees no point in eating sawdust. That would make Raz doubt that he could be eating it intentionally.

We've established that there is a difference between *explaining* a bodily movement and *making sense* of it or rendering it intelligible. We've also introduced a possible account of this difference. A *rationalist* equates acting in a way that makes sense with acting *on a reason*. Broadly conceived, a 'reason' for φ-ing is a consideration that at least appears to support the judgement that you ought to φ and does so by recommending φ-ing,[2] so you could arrive at that judgement by reasoning from the reason. A rationalist allows that you can intentionally φ without judging that you ought to φ because you φ-ed despite judging that φ-ing was, on the whole, a bad idea (i.e. you acted *akratically*). But, for your φ-ing to make sense, there must be a reason that both prima facie *recommends* φ-ing in some respect and is in some way *connected* to your φ-ing, even if not via an all-things-considered judgement in favour of it. The most obvious mode of connection is that the agent's φ-ing is motivated by an awareness of the prima facie reason (by reasoning from the reason), but, as we shall see, this is not the only possibility.[3]

In the course of this chapter, I shall examine various modes of connection between action and reason, but I shall be confining myself to only one mode of recommendation. I shall focus on forms of rationalism (like Raz's) according to which a reason identifies a good, desirable, or valuable feature of the proposed action. On this view, intentional action makes sense because of the (apparent) desirability of what is done. For such a rationalist, all rationalizing considerations

---

[2] This formulation is not meant as an analysis of any of the notions contained in it. It merely provides some information about the relationship between them.

[3] I want to leave it open to what extent and in what ways the agent might be wrong in thinking that they have a certain reason. The rationalist's point is that the agent must think that they have a reason.

(e.g. acting to fulfill a promise or to carry out a decision already made) must connect with what is good or desirable.[4]

I shall agree that, to be intentional, an action must be under the control of the agent's views about what is good or desirable, but the rationalist is wrong to suppose that the agent must see some good in the particular action they are intentionally performing. Some people wear clothes in public and tell the truth even where they see no reason to do these things and even where there is no reason to be doing them. The fact that they are in the habit of doing these things is quite sufficient to render their choosing to do them intelligible and thus to ensure that what they do counts as intentional agency. To be a creature of habit (as we all are) is not to be a slave to instinct, drive, or compulsion.[5]

Some terminology. *Actions* are forms of behaviour imputed to a whole organism, as when the organism eats sawdust or moves its tongue. I distinguish *intentional actions*, acts that it makes sense for the organism to perform, from *non-intentional actions* that may be explicable but not in a way which renders them meaningful or intelligible. I distinguish *chosen acts*, acts one has performed as a result of thinking about what to do, from *unchosen acts*, which one performs without any such thought. Finally, I distinguish acts that are the product of *deliberation*, of thinking about what one *ought* to do, from those performed without deliberation.[6] Deliberated action is a subset of chosen action, chosen action is a subset of intentional action, and intentional action is a subset of action. The point of these stipulations should become clear as the discussion proceeds.

8.1 Acting from Habit

I'll begin with two examples of habitual action. In each the protagonist is confronted with a choice and in each they make that choice without deliberation.

---

[4] Other rationalists (intuitionists, coherentists) have rather different conceptions of a practical reason, but, to limit discussion, I set them to one side. Most writers on agency have endorsed the value-based form of rationalism. Among the moderns (Hume 1978: 439) and (Kant 1996: 186) both endorse it. Among contemporaries, the list includes Anscombe and Davidson.

[5] (Velleman 1989: 202–4) describes any consideration that would render an action intelligible as a reason for that action, so he says that habits do constitute reasons. But he acknowledges that one need see nothing desirable in doing what one is in the habit of doing, so, for present purposes, he is no rationalist.

[6] There is the idea of 'acting deliberately' which seems to apply to any chosen action, but I give 'deliberation' a narrow construal, one which emphasizes the connection between deliberation and practical reasoning. The point of substance here is the claim that one can have choice and practical thinking without practical reasoning and, if so, one needs to decide how to use the word 'deliberation'. In Chapter 7 I used 'choice' to apply only to decisions based on a practical or ought-judgement. Here I am using the word 'choice' more broadly.

I'm not saying that they fail to think about what *to do*; indeed, the situation demands this of them. But they decide what to do without determining what they *ought* to do, without comparing the considerations that count in favour with those pointing the other way. Furthermore, they *couldn't* make this choice via deliberation so understood. Since, so far as they know, there is nothing at all to be said in favour of what they are doing, there is no deliberative route to the choice that they make. Yet in each case their choice and the action that flows from it might make perfect sense. They may intentionally do what they do.

Chris is walking towards a new beach his friends have recommended. As always, when prepared to swim, Chris is wearing his trunks. He arrives to find that most of the people on the beach are sunbathing naked. He faces a choice: should he join the great majority by stripping off? Chris has never stripped off in public before, whether on a beach or anywhere else. 'I don't go naked in public' he thinks and, out of habit, he chooses to remain clothed. Sarah is at a party and encounters the author of a book she has just finished. She rather imprudently lets on that she has read it and the author asks her what she thought of a chapter that, as it happens, she particularly disliked. Being unable to deflect the question Sarah faces a choice. She could lie and save the author's face. On the other hand, she could tell the truth as tactfully as possible. 'I'm no liar' she thinks and then, as is her habit, she remarks that she had some reservations about that particular chapter.

The actions of Chris and Sarah appear straightforwardly intentional. Might that be because it is at least *possible* that there is some good in what they are proposing to do? Chris *might* avoid some social catastrophe by remaining clothed, and by telling it how it is, Sarah *might* redeem the author. But this is not why they do what they do. They act out of habit and not because they judge that some good just might come of it. In any case, if the bare possibility of a good outcome were sufficient to render their action intelligible, what behaviour would be unintelligible? After all, some good *might* come of eating sawdust.

My examples are pure cases in which habit is the only operative motive. It is helpful to focus on such cases when elucidating habitual action, but habit rarely operates alone.[7] Chris may anticipate greater embarrassment if he drops his trunks than if he doesn't, but habit may be the main thing that keeps them on. And Sarah's custom of saying what she really thinks if asked a direct question is

---

[7] For rationalism's most implacable opponents, habit, custom, and practice frame every decision we make; there is no such thing as choice purely on the merits (Oakeshott 1991; Hayek 1960: Chapter 2). Perhaps they are wrong; even so, purely rational choice may be as infrequent as purely habitual choice. There is a precedent for most of what we do, and the force of precedent is often embodied in habits.

crucial to getting her to speak up, even if the hassle of devising a plausible lie has something to do with it as well. The rationalist might maintain that in these impure cases Chris and Sarah's behaviour makes sense because habit motivates them *only given* that they see some good in what they do. The possibility of the pure case suggests otherwise. No appearance of the good is required to enable habit; habit is an independent motivational force.[8]

A rationalist can respond in various ways to these observations, but before we come to grips with the main issue, I shall explain the notion of habit I am employing. In my mouth, 'habit' is cognate to 'custom', 'usage', and 'practice'. Here are three crucial features of a personal habit:

(1) A habit of φ-ing is acquired by choosing to φ on a number of occasions.[9]
(2) To φ from habit on a given occasion, I must not φ because I have on this occasion deliberated about the merits of φ-ing.
(3) To φ from habit is, at least sometimes, to choose to φ and thus to φ intentionally.

I don't deny that things lacking one or more of these features are standardly called habits. I mean only to distinguish the habits that interest me from other psychological phenomena and, in particular, from what one might call *automatic routines*.

On a broader construal, a 'habit' of φ-ing is something like a tendency to φ which is acquired by φ-ing. So understood, 'habits' need satisfy neither (1) nor (3). Several times a day I probe a gap in my teeth with my tongue. This is something I find myself *doing* (O'Shaughnessy 1980: 60–2). Furthermore, I may be doing this because I did it in the past. In that sense, my action is 'habitual'. Nevertheless, such automatic tongue movements are unintentional.[10] True, I *can* choose to move my tongue (unlike my heart), but when I do choose to

---

[8] In recent discussion of the 'guise of the good', rationalism has been subject to various counterexamples. Some of these are cases where there is no good in doing what you are doing but no particular objection to it either (doodling). In others, you act in the teeth of various objections and for no obvious reason, but you are (or at least ought to be) dissatisfied with your behaviour. Chris and Sarah ignore various objections to what they are doing, but (I shall argue in the last section) they should nonetheless be comfortable with what they are doing.

[9] To vote Republican out of habit, one must have voted for the Republicans at least once before. Beyond this, it is open how much repetition is required for habit formation. In this chapter, I shall consider only habits that are formed by choices based on reasons, but habits can also be transmitted by imitation (Reid 2010: 84–5 and Owens 2012: 157–9).

[10] Raz prefers to describe such bodily movements as 'marginal cases of intentionality, not displaying all the features of intentional actions' because they are bodily movements we are unaware of performing (Raz 2011: 73). None of this could plausibly be said of the habitual actions described earlier.

move my tongue, the movement is no longer part of an automatic routine. Furthermore, my acquisition of the 'habit' of tongue movement does not depend on my previously choosing to move my tongue because I saw some point in moving my tongue. Such routines can become established without any consideration of the merits of the movement. By contrast, the habits which interest us here were acquired because I (on several occasions) saw some point in doing the thing that I am now in the habit of doing, and they do not exclude my now choosing to do the thing from habit.

Though the idea that habitual action is automatic has become entrenched amongst philosophers of action,[11] I doubt this reflects the scope of everyday usage, even among philosophers. When my department is proposing to appoint one of its own graduates to a permanent position, some might worry that we'll get into the habit of appointing our own students. Their fear is not that the department will appoint insiders without choosing to, as part of an automatic routine, but rather that we'll cease to consider the merits of outsiders. Appointing insiders as a matter of habit does not exclude appointing them intentionally. Normally, we act intentionally from habit without thinking about it, without making a choice, but I shall focus on habitual action that is obviously intentional in that it involves a specific choice. Chris and Sarah are confronted by something out of the ordinary: they are required to decide what to do. Even if they rarely consider whether to wear clothes or speak truthfully, they do here so consider.

8.2 The Guise of the Good

Are Chris and Sarah operating under the guise of the good? Is their behaviour intentional because they act in pursuit of some desirable objective? In this section, I'll ask whether an appearance of the good enters into the explanation of what they do. My aim is not to block all the moves open to an ingenious rationalist, to demonstrate that absolutely nothing could be said for the actions that Chris and Sarah perform. Rather, I mean to contrast the difficulty of finding anything to be said for what they do with the fair certainty that it constitutes intentional agency and so to suggest that the latter need not presuppose the former.

---

[11] For example, 'an action done from pure habit is one that is not done on purpose' (Ryle 1949: 132). See also (Reid 2010: 88–91), (James 1950: 122), and (Bergson 1991: 81). Mill furnishes a precedent for my own usage: 'Many indifferent things, which men originally did from a motive of some sort, they continue to do from habit. Sometimes this is done unconsciously, the consciousness coming only after the action: at other times with conscious volition, but volition which has become habitual' (Mill 1961: 225). Another precedent may be the Aristotelian idea that virtue is a habit of choice. Velleman suggests 'custom' as a term for the non-automatic habits that concern me (Velleman 1989: 70–2 and 204).

Let's take Chris on the beach. Is there some good in his keeping his trunks on? Others have dropped theirs to get an all-over suntan, to fit in with beach custom, or simply as a pleasant change. What good could Chris see in keeping his on? He might anticipate feelings of embarrassment at being seen naked in public and avoiding embarrassment is clearly a good thing; then again he might not, being proud of his body. A different kind of person would conclude that this is not worth worrying about and do whatever suggests itself, but one can remain clothed out of habit without making even this evaluative judgement.

Sarah is unlikely to think that her choice does not really matter. Nevertheless, she also fails to deliberate about what she should do. Sarah may feel *obliged* to tell the truth, but it is at this stage an open question whether her sense of obligation highlights some desirable feature of the thing she feels obliged to do. By telling the truth she'll cause pain to the author, do nothing to improve his work, damage her own career, embarrass other members of the conversational group, etc. And in this respect there is nothing special about the obligation to be truthful. As Hume observed, fulfilling one's promises, respecting people's property rights, obeying the commands of a legitimate authority may all involve doing things that have nothing to recommend them (Hume 1978: Book 3, Part 2). Postponing further discussion of obligation until the last section, I'll focus on Chris for a bit.

It is possible to make sense of what Chris does without invoking any appearance of the good. When Chris first went swimming as a child, his parents provided him with a pair of trunks and instructed him to wear them. There are many sound reasons for obeying such an instruction and Chris took these reasons into account when deciding what to do on that first occasion. But once he had worn trunks for a bit, it is pretty unlikely that Chris thought any further on the matter until he found himself on a nudist beach. The sight of the nudist beach compels him to choose whether to wear his trunks on this occasion. How does Chris make this choice?

A rationalist would expect Chris to make his choice by deliberating, by comparing the pros and cons of sticking to his habit or of following the crowd. For such a rationalist, the choice required of Chris involves his forming a judgement about what it would be best for him to do, what he has most reason to do, or at least what reason permits him to do. In fact, Chris makes his choice without considering the merits of the case. Though he does consider the matter, Chris decides what to do without forming any judgement about what he ought to do. 'I always wear clothes in public' is all that he thinks.

Habitual choice is not the only instance of choice without an ought-judgement. Confronted by a row of Mars Bars, I decide to take the one on the right-hand side. Here I plump for a particular Mars Bar without judging that I ought to take that particular bar. I may well judge that I ought to take a random Mars Bar, but there is no way of reasoning from that judgement to the choice of this particular bar. Yet I take this particular bar quite deliberately, i.e. because I choose to take. Here I may judge that my choice is at least permissible (i.e. is not such that I ought not to choose it), but Chris and Sarah do not even make that judgement.

How might Chris's habit of φ-ing enter into his thinking about whether to φ? No one would suppose that the *mere* fact that one is in the habit of φ-ing counts in favour of φ-ing, but might Chris judge that he has reason to do what he is in the habit of doing because he would feel uncomfortable doing anything else, because following habit saves time and other scarce cognitive resources? This suggestion likely misrepresents Chris's train of thought. Insofar as one thinks in this way and acts for these reasons, one is not acting *out of habit*. One who acts out of habit does not consider the pros and cons of acting out of habit, their habit of φ-ing is not treated by them as a consideration in favour of φ-ing which feeds into deliberation about whether to φ. Rather a habit bypasses or blocks such deliberation. To φ out of habit in a particular instance may or may not involve choosing to φ; either way, it involves no judgement that it would be good in this instance to φ out of habit.[12]

Until now I have been considering one form of rationalism according to which intentional action is action motivated by awareness of a reason. To see what other forms may be available we must distinguish *complying* with reason from *conforming* to reason (Raz 1999: 178). One who complies with a reason is motivated by their awareness of the reason with which they comply, but one can conform to a reason, in the sense of doing what it recommends, without complying with it and one's conformity can be non-accidental without being a case of compliance, without being a case of acting on the reason to which one conforms. (For example, one may habitually follow the advice of a wise parent and so conform to the reasons on which their advice is based without having any idea of what those reasons are.) Armed with this distinction, the rationalist may allow that acting out of habit is an intelligible case of intentional activity provided it involves non-accidental conformity with reason. Call this *Objective Rationalism*.

To see the point, return to Chris. There is little or nothing to be said in favour of Chris's keeping his trunks on, but suppose that by habitually remaining clothed in public Chris saves on the costs of deliberation about whether to

---

[12] The fact that one is in the habit of φ-ing does not imply that one always φs out of habit, i.e. without deliberating about the merits of φ-ing. Nor does it imply that it would always be intelligible to φ out of habit. Were the death penalty imposed on those who wore clothes on a nudist beach, doing so from habit would seem compulsive. I claim only that Chris can intelligibly choose to remain clothed without seeing anything desirable in so doing.

disrobe and is able to resist the temptation to disrobe in (other) situations where disrobing is a bad thing (James 1950: 121). Even if this beach is not a place in which Chris ought to remain clothed, by breaking the habit on this occasion he will weaken it (we may suppose), rendering it less likely that he will act out of habit on those occasions when it would be good so to do. Of course, Chris could not *comply* with such reasons to act out of habit (i.e. act because he thought those considerations counted in favour of his so acting) without ceasing to act out of habit, and the deliberation-saving or temptation-avoiding value of the habit would be lost if the maintenance of the habit became just one more factor in his deliberations. Nevertheless, by remaining clothed out of habit, Chris may *conform* to such reasons and thus vindicate his performance in the eyes of the Objective Rationalist. Perhaps acting on habit can be rationally intelligible, provided there is some reason to act out of habit, even if acting out of habit excludes acting *on* this reason.

This proposal raises two queries. First, it can't *suffice* for a piece of behaviour to constitute intelligible agency that the agent thereby non-accidentally conforms with a reason. Suppose our man's craving for sawdust is the product of some vitamin deficiency, a deficiency that the sawdust will somehow alleviate. That fact won't in itself render his action intelligible. An action may manifest a disposition to behave in beneficial ways without thereby making sense *qua* intentional action. Nor can it be *necessary* for a piece of behaviour to constitute intelligible agency that either it or the disposition it manifests reliably serves some good. What one might call *Subjective Rationalism* picks up on the fact that at least one way to render an action intelligible is to note that it appears to its agent to have something to be said for it and this appearance often renders the action intelligible even when it is illusory, even when there is in fact nothing to be said for it. If our man believes (perhaps wishfully) that eating sawdust will do him the world of good, this is usually enough to make sense of what he does. It is unclear how the Objective Rationalist can accommodate this fact given that no reason is conformed to in such a case.

We have yet to see how the objective and subjective aspects of practical intelligibility can fit together in a way consistent with the rationalist idea that practical intelligibility is, at bottom, a matter of pursuing the good. Now, rationalists have faced up to this issue in the course of explaining the formation of intentions and policies. Often people do things which they see no point in doing, simply because they are disposed to stick to their decisions. Such actions seem perfectly intelligible and their intelligibility depends on the fact that being resolute is a beneficial disposition. But it also depends on the fact that the agent retains some sensitivity to the reasons that led them to take those decisions in the first place. As we shall see, that prevents the rationalist from applying their account of action on policy to action on habit.

8.3 Habits and Policies

The Will, no less than the Intellect, requires a memory. We can't always be starting from scratch in the practical any more than in the theoretical realm. It must be possible to settle in advance what is to happen, to motivate future action. Thus it must be possible to store our choices so their influence persists beyond the moment at which they are made. And for this, it is not enough that we remember that we have chosen. The choice itself must persist in some form. That can happen in at least two ways.

First, the choice might lead to the formation of a future-directed intention, a decision to act at some future point or to adopt a general policy of so acting. Here, the choice persists in that the intention persists; we remain decided on a course of action until the moment of execution arrives, at which point the decision makes sense of its execution. Second, the choice might be part of a pattern of similar choices that together constitute a habit of choice. None of these choices need be future directed because repeated choice can make sense of future choices without being directed towards the future, without constituting a decision about the future or the adoption of a general policy.

In this section, I'll compare habits with policies. A policy is an intention to perform or refrain from a certain type of action in certain circumstances, e.g. to run every lunchtime or eat only twice a day. In recent years, philosophers working within a rationalist framework have formulated detailed and plausible accounts of how intentions, resolutions, and policies both motivate and rationalize human behaviour. These accounts are inspired by the idea that the function of policy is to preserve the motivational and justificational force of the reasons that led one to adopt the policy in the first place. I shall argue that habits make sense of action in a rather different way.

The similarities between habits and policies are undeniable. For one thing, habits have generality: I may be in the habit of going for a daily walk. For another, both habits (at least those that interest me) and policies stem from choice. I adopt the policy of going for a run every lunchtime by choosing to go for a run every lunchtime and I get into the habit of going for a daily walk by choosing to go for a walk on a certain number of days. Finally, we may suppose that these originating choices are all rationally intelligible, are all based on some desirable feature of the chosen thing. Still, both the thing chosen and the way that reasons support the choice differ markedly in the case of habit.

A policy of running every lunchtime is adopted when I choose to engage in that pattern of behaviour for reasons that make the whole pattern look good. I might adopt this policy because of the health benefits of regular exercise, or because I generally need a break in the middle of the day. By contrast, there need be no constant factor behind the various choices that established my daily walk. I choose to walk on Monday morning because the sun is shining and I need some exercise, on Tuesday morning to distract me from work and because I need some exercise, on Wednesday morning to get away from a family row and because the sun is shining, etc. And by Friday I am in the habit of taking a daily walk.

Recent writing on the psychological function of policies (and of future-directed intentions) has focused on two points, both of which are analogues of points I made earlier in connection with habit.[13] First, by adopting a policy of running I can avoid the costs of deliberating each morning about whether to run, of weighing up the pros and cons of running in order to arrive at a judgement about whether to run on that particular day. These costs include the time and energy consumed by any deliberation, but they also include the costs of any errors I'm likely to commit when forced to deliberate in unfavourable circumstances. If I can decide in advance then I can deliberate when I'm calmer, more focused, less tired than perhaps I would be at the time of action. Second, my policy of running may ward off the temptation not to run. When I resolve to do something, I frequently anticipate that I'll be less inclined to do it when the time comes. Lunch looks more inviting as midday approaches.[14] Knowing this, I've resolved to run rather than eat, and such resolutions frequently enable people to resist the temptations they are directed against.

Bratman and Holton suggest that a policy performs these functions principally by preventing reconsideration of the decision to implement the policy (Bratman 1987: Chapter 5; Holton 2009: 121–5). Were I to reconsider my decision to run each morning I would incur the costs of deliberation, and if I reconsider this decision anytime near lunch, my appetite for food will be significantly greater than my appetite for exercise, though the reverse may be true earlier on. And here's the thing: *were* I to consider whether to run today, it might be sensible for me to decide not to run (it's now raining, I've already incurred the costs of deliberation, and since I've being running so religiously, whether I go today will make little difference to anything). Nevertheless, it remains rational for me not

---

[13] (Bratman 1987: 2–3) emphasizes the first point (Holton 2009: 9–12) and (Raz 1999: 71–2) the second. Bratman and Holton see social coordination as a further function of policy, but I have my doubts about this.

[14] Lunch's 'looking more inviting' may involve my overestimating its value or else my failing to be motivated by an accurate estimate of its value (or both).

to reconsider. On the present view, running today may be rational because non-reconsideration of my decision to run is rational, even though, were I to reconsider, I would rationally decide not to run.

Bratman (1987: 66) speaks of (rational) habits of non-reconsideration and Holton (2009: 141) of tendencies not to reconsider. Neither thinks that the mere fact that I have resolved to run every lunchtime makes my running this lunchtime at all desirable. Should I get myself to run on a rainy day by rehearsing my policy, I am not getting myself to run under the guise of the good. The rain prompts me to consider what to do, but I can decide to stick to my policy simply by reminding myself of my policy and without considering whether I *ought* to stick to it, without considering its merits (Holton 2009: 123). Still, running as a matter of policy (unlike, say, running because of an hypnotic suggestion) is a paradigm case of intentional activity, activity that is under my control (Pink 1996: 93–9; Holton 2009: 147). Furthermore I here *choose* to act on policy, another instance of choice without normative judgement. Of course, I *could* make such a judgement and act on the basis of it, contemplating the very considerations outlined above, considerations which count in favour of sticking to one's resolutions, the costs involved, and so forth, but such a procedure is self-defeating since it incurs the costs of deliberation and makes one vulnerable to temptation by reopening the issue of what one ought to do. The special benefits of resolute action are won only if one is not motivated by the prospect of those benefits. Here we have a form of Objective Rationalism.

It would be foolish to suppose that one should never revise one's policies, or ask oneself whether they should be applied in this instance (Holton 2009: 75). When a tropical storm is in progress, one must reconsider whether to run, but (living in a rainy climate as you do) a summer shower shouldn't lead you to contemplate abandoning your daily run even though the prospect of getting wet is a genuine inconvenience. This is not the kind of reason you should even consider acting on, though regret at the rain and hope that it will stop are perfectly in order. Your policy has an exclusion zone around it, one that rules out consideration of discomfort but not of threats to your health. Policies exclude a certain range of reasons from our deliberations and should block deliberation altogether in those many instances in which the only reasons recommending breach of policy fall within the excluded range.[15]

---

[15] In some cases, policy is only part of the explanation of why we act as we do. Perhaps the stifling atmosphere in the house helps to get me out of it; my running policy alone is not enough. But my running policy is still crucial because it blocks deliberation about whether to run given that it is raining. In this mixed case I run because I think that I ought to run in order to get myself out of the house, a judgement which is not the result of an open-minded consideration of the pros and cons.

I'll say that policy implementation involves habits of exclusion. Often this exclusion (though intentional) will not involve any choice, will not require me to think about it, but sometimes I do *choose* to exclude the rain from my deliberations and choose to do so from habit.[16] True, if I need to *deliberate* about whether to exclude the rain from my considerations, I'll lose much of the benefit of so doing, but that shows only that my choice of exclusion need not be a product of deliberation about whether to exclude. Though choosing involves thinking, one can think about what to do without incurring the costs of deliberation that it is the function of policy to avoid. For example, I might ensure that I stick with my policy and choose to run precisely by *reminding myself that I have decided to run*.[17]

The model of policy rationality just sketched covers the two aspects of rational intelligibility I identified in Section 8.2. The subjective aspect is present in the idea that the original choice of policy must be intelligible in virtue of the policy's apparent benefits, benefits that need not be real for the adoption of the policy to be intelligible. The objective aspect is present in the idea that one can intelligibly stick to a policy without being guided either by an awareness of the reasons which led one to adopt the policy (or by any other reasons), provided that by sticking to one's policy one conforms with certain reasons. Those reasons are the very ones I outlined when describing the psychological function of policies. They determine what constitute good 'habits of non-reconsideration'.

More constraints are needed to arrive at an adequate model of policy implementation. A rational agent *would not implement a policy if they judged that the reasons for which they adopted the policy no longer applied*.[18] One need not recall these reasons to intelligibly implement the policy, and indeed, part of the point of settling on a policy is so you no longer need clutter your memory with the reasons that led you to adopt it. But where it is (in one way or another) evident to you that these reasons no longer apply, one must reconsider the policy.[19] Should one

---

Rather, it is the product of a policy that constrains without completely blocking my practical deliberations.

[16] Holton maintains that habit excludes choice (Holton 2009: 69).

[17] As (Soteriou 2013: 291) notes, remembering to do something that you earlier decided to do involves more than merely remembering that you decided to do it.

[18] True, one might be able think of new reasons for the policy (e.g. the fact that everyone now expects you to carry out the policy and will suffer if you don't). I would say that re-adopting the policy on those grounds would involve a new decision, a decision to adopt a different policy with the same content, rather than persistence of the old policy. Alternatively, one might add the clause 'unless they knew of other reasons for maintaining the policy' to the italicized phrase.

[19] (Bratman 1987: 65 and Holton 2009: 160) both endorse this principle, though Raz appears to reject it (Raz 1999: 197).

refuse to reconsider it, carrying on simply as a matter of policy is no longer even intelligible: the policy is now operating more like an hypnotic suggestion. I happen to recall that my policy of going for a run every morning is based on the notion that this will add five years to my life span and then I learn that running is more likely to cause a seizure. I have now lost my original reason to run and thereby acquired a decisive reason to reopen the issue of whether I should run. My running resolution no longer makes sense of my running. Where I don't realize that the original reasons for the policy no longer apply, it may still be rational to implement it without deliberation; to that extent, policies are a source of rational intelligibility. But where I know that the original reasons have gone, sticking with the policy makes no sense.

The need for this constraint suggests a further point: in characterizing the way that policies make sense of action, it isn't enough to allude merely to the instrumental benefits of being disposed to adhere to one's policies (saving on the costs of deliberation and so forth). For example, were you able to adopt the intention of drinking a mild toxin when someone offers you a large reward for adopting such an intention, you would acquire a disposition that is highly beneficial, namely, the disposition to drink the toxin when the time comes (Kavka 1983). But since the reward is for forming the intention and not for executing it, the benefits of that disposition will make little sense of your manifesting it by drinking the toxin precisely because you judge that there is no good in actually drinking. In general, it makes no sense to φ just because you have a policy of φ-ing where you also judge that there is nothing to be said for φ-ing.[20]

Can we tell a similar story about the intelligibility of habitual action? As already noted, there need be no reason or set of reasons for which I adopted the habit of a daily walk: I might well have acquired the habit of walking each morning by walking for a different reason on each of a sufficiently long series of mornings. Perhaps these reasons are not even consistent: I went for a walk on Day One to please my parents, on Day Two to defy them.[21] So the ability of this habit to make sense of the fact that I am walking today is not contingent on

---

[20] Holton (2009: 162–5) maintains that it is rational not to reconsider your resolution to drink the toxin even once you have got the money at least in cases where having a habit of not reconsidering such resolutions would produce good effects. In Section 8.4, I argue that attributing instrumental value to a habit is not enough to ensure that manifesting the habit makes sense in cases where it is clear that there is nothing to be said for acting on habit.

[21] In the case of policy, one might suppose that the psychological function of blocking deliberation as to whether to run this morning could be served by a belief that one ought to run every morning, a belief that one brings to mind in order to get oneself to run. This proposal may be resisted on the grounds that mere beliefs lack the motivational efficacy of intentions. Be that as it may, the idea can't be applied to habits since no such belief need have been formed.

whether the reasons leading me to walk on Day One or on Day Two still apply. Once I am in the habit of walking I may happen to know that none of those reasons apply today. Nevertheless, if it ever made sense for me to walk purely as a matter of habit then it may well make sense for me to walk today also, and that opens up the possibility that it might make sense for me to walk today even if I judge that there is nothing at all to be said in favour of walking. If habit alone can make sense of action then habit is a *source* of practical intelligibility, it creates lines of intelligible activity in a way that policy never could. The repetition of choice can render further choice intelligible on a basis quite different to that on which the initial choice was made.[22]

8.4 Habits and Virtues

For the rationalist, facts about goodness or value make sense of choice by making the chosen act desirable in some respect. I shall argue that facts about goodness or value can make sense of choice in another way. Sarah and Chris think 'I'm no liar' and 'I don't go naked in public', respectively. These thoughts concern character traits and represent the act in question as a manifestation of those traits. On a given occasion, Sarah and Chris may choose to act as they do without entertaining any such thoughts, but their aptness indicates something important: we should look for the values that make sense of these actions in the value of the traits they manifest rather than in the value of their manifestations.

Let's call any character trait that is valuable for its own sake a *virtue*. There is no restriction to traits conceived of as having 'moral' value. Sarah might think she is under an obligation to speak truthfully and so be blameworthy if she lies: her habit may present her with a moral demand. Alternatively, Sarah might regard truthfulness as a personal ideal, feeling only shame or regret when she falls short. Either way, truthfulness is in her eyes a virtue, a character trait valuable for its own sake.

It may be that some virtues are not habits: perhaps certain people are innately kind or generous. Kindness or generosity pose no problems for the rationalist, since the desirability of helping someone across a road can make sense of so doing regardless of any previous pattern of choice. I am interested in those virtues

---

[22] The line between policy and habit is frequently blurred by the fact that if I've implemented my policy of running on a sufficient number of occasions, I've probably acquired the habit of running and so, if I carry on running, that action may now be intelligible as a matter of habit. But this will not be so where, having had little chance to implement my policy, I have acquired no habit that might make sense of my run. And the underlying contrast remains even where both policy and habit are getting me to run.

that must take the form of habits because they can motivate action regardless of the desirability of the act in question. Such, I would argue, are Hume's 'artificial' virtues: respect for property, the keeping of promises, obedience to a legitimate authority, and so forth (Hume 1978: Book 3, Part 2).[23] Sarah's truthfulness is in this sense an artificial virtue, which is why she can tell the truth even when there is nothing to be said for it.[24]

People choose to tell the truth for all sorts of reasons: because it is extremely useful to be regarded as a trustworthy informant, because they are worried about inflicting harm on others by misleading them, because they get more pleasure out of describing than inventing, because they want to state their view and get it off their chest, because they can't be bothered to make something up. Suppose Sarah acquires the habit of truthfulness by being truthful for different reasons on different occasions. Then she finds herself in a situation in which none of these reasons apply. Can she intelligibly tell the truth even on this occasion?

The rationalist may suppose that if Sarah chooses to tell the truth, she must have adopted a policy of truthfulness for some of the reasons just cited and that her truthfulness on this occasion is a form of resolute behaviour. But intelligible policy implementation requires the absence of a certain judgement, namely, the judgement that the reasons for which one settled on the policy no longer apply and where it is clear to Sarah that there is nothing to be said for being truthful on this occasion, it must be equally clear that her original reasons, whatever they were, have lost their traction. There is no similar limitation on the intelligible manifestation of a habit. The reasons for which Sarah acquired the habit of truthfulness need not constitute a case for being truthful applicable whenever that habit is manifested. What enables the intelligible manifestation of a habit is the absence of a rather different judgement, namely, the judgement that truthfulness has no value.

For habitual agency to be intentional it must be under the control of a value judgement of some sort. I propose that there are at least two ways in which an action can be intentional. First, in virtue of being sensitive to your views about

---

[23] Here are two models of virtue. On the *resolution* model, one acquires the virtue of truthfulness by adopting (for the right reasons) a policy of telling the truth (Kant 1996: 258). On the habit model, one can acquire the virtue of truthfulness by first telling the truth for all sorts of reasons, e.g. love of praise or fear of punishment (Aquinas 2010 Part I–II, Question 92, Article 2). Once one has acquired the habit/virtue and acts out of that virtue then one tells the truth 'for its own sake', provided one is sensitive to whether truthfulness is a virtue.

[24] Can Sarah be intentionally truthful though she herself has neither acquired the habit of truthfulness nor sees any reason to be truthful on this occasion? I think she can, namely, by choosing to imitate the truthful behaviour of those around her (Owens 2012: 157–9). More generally, the habits of others can make sense of what we do, but this is a theme for another occasion.

whether there is anything desirable about performing the action. Second, in virtue of being sensitive to your views about whether there is anything intrinsically desirable about the habit that the action manifests. We should not require a virtuous agent to judge the habit they manifest to be a virtue, either now or at any point in the past; virtue need not involve the thought of itself. Indeed, if Sarah speaks truthfully today only because she has today considered whether truthfulness is a good habit, Sarah is not now being truthful from habit.[25] What being (intentionally) truthful from habit requires is only the absence of a negative appraisal. And if truthfulness can be valuable for its own sake then one can judge that there is nothing desirable about being truthful (on this occasion) without also judging that truthfulness is no virtue, without judging that truthfulness (on this occasion) would not manifest an intrinsically desirable habit. Therefore, Sarah can intentionally tell the author the truth about their book from habit.

One of the attractions of rationalism was its ability to explain why it matters to us whether we act intentionally. This advantage is inherited by my proposal. It often matters to us whether we could control what we are doing by taking a view of the merits of the habits we manifest in so acting. Nevertheless, such control isn't sufficient to ensure that one's behaviour is intentional (and so a candidate for virtue). Perhaps I can stop biting my nails should I become convinced that the sight of my biting my nails disgusts you, but it does not follow that I am biting my nails intentionally, for I never intentionally bit my nails. Motivation by an artificial virtue requires more than the absence of the judgement that one's habit is no virtue: the virtue must have been inculcated through repeated choice.

My proposal raises two questions. First, how can a habit be good except in virtue of the desirability of the actions to which it gives rise? Second, granted that a habit can be good for its own sake, how can your attitude to the value of the habit make sense of an action that manifests the habit when the value of the habit is no guide to the value of the action decided upon? As to the second question, the rationalist must answer that a habit's being valuable for its own sake isn't directly relevant to the intelligibility of the actions that manifest that habit. No rational agent could get themselves to φ simply by reflecting that the habit of φ-ing is a good thing. To make that argument, they'd need the further idea that there is something desirable about manifesting the habit of φ-ing on this occasion.[26]

---

[25] Similarly, if I ran this morning, only once I had reconsidered whether my running resolution was a good thing, today's run was not a manifestation of resolve.

[26] In this connection, see Thompson's discussion of 'transfer principles' (Thompson 2008: Chapter 10).

Suppose I am deliberating about whether to tell the truth, that is, I am trying to decide whether to tell the truth by arriving at a judgement about whether I ought to tell the truth. How does it help me to know that my habit of truthfulness is good for its own sake? That would help me if the question were whether to reinforce that habit or else to do something that might weaken it. For example, suppose I thought that being untruthful on this occasion would weaken my valuable habit of truthfulness. Then the value of this habit should register in my deliberations about whether to manifest it on this occasion. But if nothing like this is true, how can reflection on the desirability of the habit move me to manifest it? Here, no course of practical reasoning could get me to φ.

This is a problem only so long as we assume that intentional habitual agency must be agency we could have arrived at by practical deliberation. But why assume that? As already noted, to act out of habit is not to invoke one's habit as a consideration in one's deliberation about what to do (or indeed in one's deliberations about whether to deliberate). It is to allow one's habit of φ-ing to pre-empt such deliberations. And this is something one does intentionally, provided one wouldn't allow one's habit to pre-empt deliberation if one judged that one's habit of φ-ing were no virtue.[27] After the fact, Sarah might reflect on her tendency to tell the truth (without deliberation) even where this will do no good, but so long as she believes truthfulness itself to be valuable, such reflection need not disturb her.

Here, it is crucial that Sarah regard the habit she manifests as being valuable *for its own sake*. It wouldn't help her to know that being in the habit of speaking truthfully has many good effects. Suppose the value of the habit of φ-ing is purely instrumental: it derives from the value of its effects, behavioural and otherwise.[28] It is hard to see how a belief in that sort of value could render intelligible the manifestation of the habit in a case in which it is known that this manifestation will have no such desirable effects. But if the value of the habit resides in the habit rather than in the value of its manifestation, Sarah's approval of her habit provides reflective reassurance.

When confronted with the author, Sarah *chooses* to be truthful. Since she does so out of habit, she does not deliberate. So what goes through her mind here? On many occasions, the answer is nothing—she is intentionally truthful without choosing to be truthful—but on this occasion she is likely to feel the need for

---

[27] Though one regards smoking as a 'bad habit', one can still smoke intentionally, provided one thinks there is something to be said for smoking.

[28] I say 'otherwise' because having a certain motivational psychology might, for instance, enhance our capacity to take pleasure in things (Adams 1976: 470–2).

more. Sarah might feel obliged to be truthful. On the other hand, she might feel that were she untruthful, she'd be letting herself down, be vulnerable to her own and other people's contempt rather than their indignation. Calling an obligation or a personal ideal to mind can be a good way of getting yourself to do something it is hard to do (just like rehearsing a policy) but this need not involve treating the obligation, the ideal, or the policy as a consideration that counts in favour of truthfulness.[29] Rather, in cases of habitual agency (obligation included), a block on deliberation comes to your attention, often with the result that the block is reinforced.

Let's turn now to our first question: how can a habit be valuable for its own sake? No one will deny that a habit can be desirable because it is a cause of actions (or omissions) desirable for their own sake, yet many habits are thought to possess a value of a different kind, a value not derived from the value of the actions they motivate. That's how people like Sarah think about truthfulness, and that's why it makes sense for Sarah to be truthful even when she sees nothing desirable in being truthful. Chris may feel that in keeping his clothes on he is subscribing to a worthwhile custom of public dress, a custom flouted by the behaviour of those on the beach. Chris need not imagine that the existence of this valuable custom is affected one way or the other by whether he adheres to it on this occasion. Nevertheless, Chris thinks, his habit of remaining clothed in public is a virtue, is valuable for its own sake (though perhaps only because many others share this habit). In Chris's eyes, wearing clothes makes sense because *we* don't go naked in public. One need not endorse his way of thinking to agree that it renders Chris's behaviour intelligible.

I've said that habits are like resolutions in that they shape our deliberation by excluding a range of otherwise relevant considerations. The same is true of habits that constitute virtues.[30] To be truthful is not just to speak the truth more or less reliably; it also involves thinking in a certain way about whether to speak the truth. For example, a truthful person will not seriously consider telling a lie because it would improve their prospects of promotion.[31] And to exclude isn't to judge (say) that the claims of ambition are too weak to be worth considering once they are up against the demands of truthfulness. One who makes such

---

[29] For more on obligation as a block on deliberation, see (Owens 2012: Chapter 3).

[30] (Raz 1999: 198–9) floats the idea that deliberative exclusion may have non-instrumental value. Perhaps this can be true of the habits of exclusion involved in both policy implementation and habitual agency. Still, a difference remains: if you do somehow realize that there is no reason to implement your policy then it makes no sense to implement it.

[31] And Chris isn't a conventional dresser if he seriously contemplates indulging in the pleasure of exhibitionism.

judgements might still feel tempted to lie in order to further their career, might feel inclined to act on reasons of ambition. Of course exclusion has limits. Sometimes the consequences of being frank may be so grave that a truthful person *will* deliberate about whether to speak frankly in the light of them—lying to Kant's murderer and so forth—but much that would otherwise be relevant must be excluded.

Some rationalists argue that, for the virtuous person, certain otherwise relevant considerations will count for nothing, will be deprived of all force in the face of a 'moral' demand. To borrow an example from Scanlon, even a minimally decent person will not consider whether to hide their elderly relative's medicine in order to hasten an inheritance (Scanlon 1998: 156–7). That claim is perfectly consistent with rationalism provided we suppose that hastening the inheritance *is* no reason to precipitate our relative's death (though it remains a perfectly good reason for badgering the probate office once the relative has died a natural death). And that is precisely Scanlon's view: not only do we lack any reason to precipitate our relative's death, we lack any reason to even hope that he dies prematurely or to enjoy it when he does, and so forth. As a reason for hastening my relative's death, my need for money lacks all normative force. Can this line of thought enable the rationalist to accommodate the exclusionary character of virtue? I express no view on Scanlon's example, but his point will not generalize to artificial virtues like truthfulness.

The habits of exclusion characteristic of the truthful person are specifically deliberative: they exclude certain otherwise perfectly genuine reasons from the context of practical deliberation alone. In the emotional sphere these reasons are unimpeded by virtue. Sarah would be no less truthful were she to *regret* the fact that she can't advance her career by telling her boss what he wants to hear. Here, she may think, she is sacrificing a genuine good for the sake of telling the truth, and regret is perfectly in order, provided she feels no temptation to lie for this reason.[32] And Chris would be a no less conventional dresser for wishing that he could sunbathe naked on a deserted beach. For both parties, the excluded reason retains its normative force. In this respect, the habits of exclusion involved in artificial virtues are similar to those involved in being resolute: the rain makes the fact that one must run this morning regrettable. What the resolute person does not do is to reopen the issue of whether they ought to run that morning in the light of the fact that it is raining.

---

[32] This shows that we can't explain the phenomenon of exclusion by saying that the 'excluded' reason is 'not worth worrying about'.

I conclude that habit can make sense of both action and deliberative exclusion even in cases where you judge that there is nothing desirable about manifesting the habit. This is because the habit might be a virtue, valuable for its own sake. The value of such a virtue is not just a reflection of the value of its effects, and so its ability to make sense of both action and deliberative exclusion is not confined to cases where these constitute valuable effects. Provided honesty is the sort of thing that might be valuable for its own sake and I don't believe otherwise, my honesty can make sense of my speaking truthfully. And it can make sense of my speaking truthfully even though there is no way of reasoning from the value of the habit to the value of the act.[33]

---

[33] Many thanks to Jonathan Adler, Michael Bratman, John Broome, Stephen Butterfill, Julia Driver, Kati Farkas, John Gibbons, Alex Gregory, Adrian Haddock, Ulrike Heuer, Jennifer Hornsby, Agnieska Jaworska, Julia Markovits, Mike Martin, Simon Robertson, Nishi Shah, Peter Sullivan, Joseph Raz, Sharon Street, Matthew Silverstein, Victor Tadros, David Velleman, Jonathan Way, Gary Watson, Ralph Wedgwood, and Fiona Woollard for discussion and to audiences at the Central European University, University of California at Riverside, University of Southern California, Hebrew University of Jerusalem, and the universities of Stirling, Southampton, Leeds, Kent, London, and Warwick.

PART IV
Testimony

9

Testimony and Assertion

A number of writers have recently questioned the idea that an assertion can transmit knowledge only by serving as *evidence* for the truth of the proposition asserted. Instead, they maintain that successful testimony does its work by getting the audience to believe what the speaker asserts whilst putting the responsibility of justifying that belief onto the speaker.[1] Like many fruitful ideas, this line of thought has been developed in rather different ways by different authors. In this chapter, I shan't attempt to defend non-evidentialist views of testimony against their opponents. Rather, I shall compare two different forms of non-evidentialism, with a view to discovering the best version of this approach to testimony.

I am concerned with a distinctive way in which language users transmit information: they assert things. To accept testimony is take someone else's word for it. Thus, any epistemology of testimony presupposes some account of assertion and of the role that it plays in testimony. According to the *Assurance* model, we can learn that p when someone *tells us* that p; telling someone that p involves asserting that p with a view to providing them with an assurance that p is true. Assurance theorists maintain that the audience is usually entitled to accept these assurances, thereby acquiring a belief which it is up to the speaker to justify. When all goes well, the audience thereby learns that p.

According to the *belief expression* model of testimony, we can learn that p when we hear someone assert that p. On this view, to sincerely assert that p is to express (in a distinctive way) your belief in p, where *expressing* a belief differs both from indicating to others that you have it and from giving them an assurance that it is true. When such an expression of belief has an audience, and that audience believes what the speaker says, that audience may acquire a belief with the same justificational status. And when the belief expressed

---

[1] For example, see (Brandom 1983), (Ross 1986), (McDowell 1998: 438), (Burge 2013: 405), (Owens 2000: Chapter 12), and (Moran 2005b).

constitutes knowledge, they may thereby learn what the speaker knows. I shall begin by developing the notion of assertion implicit in the belief expression model.

9.1 Expressing and Indicating Belief

I start from the hypothesis that to sincerely assert that p is one way of expressing belief in p. Many writers would endorse this general idea, but there are various ways of understanding the notion of expression. In this section, I shall develop my own model of expression by contrasting *expressing* one's belief with *indicating* that one has this belief. I use 'indication' here to mean 'provide evidence for' as in 'the wet sidewalk indicates that it has rained'. I shall then characterize sincere assertion as an expression of belief.

Some philosophers influenced by Grice have treated belief expression as a matter of deliberately indicating one's state of mind to an audience (hoping then to explain assertion in terms of belief expression so understood).[2] For them, to express belief in p is to intentionally indicate to a given audience that one believes that p. I shall develop my own notion of expression by contrasting it with this notion, but my aim here is not to refute indication models of belief expression. Rather, I want to raise some difficulties for them, difficulties which suggest that an alternative notion of expression may be required.

One can express a belief to one's audience without aiming to convince them that it is so or even that one believes it to be so. For example, you can sensibly make assertions which you are quite confident will not affect your audience's beliefs, either because they have the relevant beliefs already or because they won't trust you on this matter, or are insufficiently interested in it (Grice 1989: 106–12; Williams 2002: 71–2; Watson 2004b: 63 and 70–1). If your audience doubts your sincerity, they may not even accept that you believe what you are saying. In these circumstances, it would be foolish to aim at affecting their beliefs, but a good many reasons for expressing your belief remain: to register your disagreement, to show you know the answer, or just to let off steam.

Given this, our Griceans allow that one can intentionally indicate that one believes that p without intending thereby to inform one's audience either of p or of one's belief in it. 'Indicating' belief in p here is a matter of furnishing your audience with evidence that you believe it, something you could do for many reasons. They also acknowledge that there are lots of ways of deliberately indicating to an audience that one believes that p other than by expressing a

---

[2] For one recent example of this approach, see (Davis 2003: Chapter 7).

belief in p to that audience. For example, one can leave evidence of one's belief in p where you know they will find it. To deal with this some have stipulated that when expressing a belief to an audience, one's intention to indicate this belief must be overt.

But even with these qualifications in place, problems remain, for I can with perfect frankness intentionally indicate to my audience that I believe that p—namely by asserting that I believe that p—without thereby expressing a belief in p. Suppose my analyst convinces me that I hate my brother because I believe he drove my father to an early grave. I don't feel inclined to avow or internally assent to the proposition that he drove my father to an early grave, but my analyst persuades me that this is the best explanation for the fraternal resentment which I do feel.[3] A third party now asks me whether I believe that my brother drove my father to an early grave. I answer as follows: 'my analyst has convinced me that I do believe this'. I am thereby intentionally indicating that I have this belief, an indication which is perfectly sincere. But even if the analyst is correct, I am not expressing the belief that my brother drove my father to an early grave.[4] Expressing a belief in p and indicating that one believes that p are two quite different things even in a case like this where both deeds are performed overtly by using language in the standard way.

One might attempt to avoid these difficulties by observing that I do not take myself to *know* that my brother drove my father to an early grave. Perhaps an expression of belief must be an indication that one knows the proposition believed. But once it is allowed that being disposed to assert p is not decisive evidence of belief in p, the problem re-emerges. Consider someone whose behaviour makes it clear that he believes that university degrees from different institutions are of unequal value but who is quite convinced that he believes, in fact knows, the opposite (Peacocke 1998: 90). In this case, when faced with a direct question, he will reply that all university degrees are of equal value and will think himself sincere in saying this. Here, he presents himself as expressing what he believes. But the rest of us can marshal evidence of his behaviour, both verbal and non-verbal, which shows that he does not believe this and so is not perfectly sincere in what he says. Yet he would have been perfectly sincere had he been

---

[3] Some writers, e.g. (Shoemaker 2003: 392–5), argue that a person can't believe that they believe something which they are not inclined to assert. For a persuasive response to Shoemaker, see (Moran 2003: 406–8).

[4] Were I to assert that my brother drove my father to an early grave, this assertion would not be sincere because it would not be connected to my belief in such a way as to constitute an expression of that belief.

telling us what he *takes* himself to both believe and know. Hence, these are different actions with different sincerity conditions.[5]

I doubt that either assertion or belief expression can be explained in terms of belief indication, but I shan't pursue that question any further here.[6] In this section and the next I develop an alternative notion of expressive action.

One can express a belief in action by making an assertion or one can do it by behaving in a way which constitutes a natural sign of belief (sounds, gestures, etc.). One thing these actions have in common is that they are directly motivated by the belief rather than by the belief that one has it (a higher-order belief which may be true or false). To put it another way, expressing a belief in action is one way of *acting on* that belief and one can't act on a belief which one does not have. So, as I use the term, an expression of belief may be poor or inadequate, but it can't be insincere: you can't express beliefs you don't have.

There is a broad sense of 'expression' on which you give expression to a belief whenever you act on it. In this sense, when you act on the belief that Red Rum is likely to win by laying your bets at the race course, your bet expresses your belief. But I shall be employing 'expression' in a much narrower sense to denote actions intended to express—i.e. to display or manifest—a belief and to achieve any further objectives they may have by means of that expression. Clearly, you often act on a belief without aiming to express it in that sense.

On a widely held view of intentional action, if such expressive action is to be a form of intentional action then there must some apparent good, some desirable objective which the agent is seeking to promote by expressing his belief. And this might tempt us to look for a wider goal which all belief expressers share (communicating information, giving an assurance, etc.) and to suppose that what makes their behaviour an expression of belief is the fact that it has that goal. But if there is a goal which all believers have in common, why can't it be the goal of expressing their belief? Doesn't it make perfect sense that one who believes something should wish to assert it, whether or not they have any further purpose in mind?[7] When you express your belief, you act on the desire to express it, a

---

[5] (Moran 2005a: 356-7) maintains that his assertion would be sincere. I agree that it is not a lie, for the speaker is not intending to misrepresent either the facts or the beliefs he holds. But it is hard to maintain that it is fully sincere either. As Moran notes (2005a: 346-7), lying is not the only form of insincerity.

[6] For a critique of Gricean accounts of assertion along different but related lines, see (Pagin 2004: 842-4).

[7] Though she rejects the view that all intentional action must be aimed at some apparently desirable objective (Hursthouse 1991: 61) implies that action intended to express anger must be thought to serve some further end (such as informing others of one's anger, relieving one's anger, etc.).

desire you have simply in virtue of believing it (as you are inclined to act on the assumption that it is true simply in virtue of believing it). This action may serve various goals and may be performed for that reason also, but it counts as an expressive action only if the expression itself is amongst these goals and not just an undesired means to some desirable end.

Consider the expression of mental states other than belief. Expressing one's anger in action involves performing some action directly motivated by anger. Those who smash the china don't generally do so because they believe they are angry and desire to inform their audience of this fact, nor because they anticipate enjoying the pleasures of release. Perhaps they don't intend to express their anger at all (only to smash the china). But where they do intend to express their anger, it is not required that there be any further purpose which expressing their anger is thought to serve: what is required is that they feel like displaying their anger, a feeling they have simply in virtue of being angry. Of course, when and how you express your anger will be influenced by things other than the anger itself (e.g. by your belief that this vase is owned by the object of your wrath and your aversion to attacking him directly), but it is one's anger and not one's belief that one is angry which gets expressed here. Similarly, how you express a belief—the words and occasions you choose—will be influenced by all sorts of things other than the belief, but what gets expressed is the thing you aim to express, namely, the belief itself.

The fact that sincere assertion is intelligible simply as an expression of belief gives it a spontaneity lacking in insincere assertion (Reid 1997: 193–4). As Williams says, 'sincerity at the most basic level is simply openness, a lack of inhibition. Insincerity requires me to adjust the content of what I say' (Williams 2002: 75).[8] Such adjustment makes sense only when it appears to serve some further purpose. But, as Williams also notes, we should not conclude that sincere assertion is any less voluntary or under our control than insincere assertion. Sincere assertion isn't like giggling, something we can (often) suppress but never initiate. Rather, we initiate an assertion in order to express our belief.

So why does a sincere person decide, on occasion, not to express their belief but rather to indicate it? Again it helps to think about states other than belief. I can let someone know that I am angry by having my secretary cancel an appointment with him. I mean him to infer that he is the object of my wrath from the cancellation (and perhaps also that I have this very intention). But I here let him know that I am angry without *expressing* my anger, at least in one good sense

---

[8] One may get into the habit of misrepresenting one's age and so lie readily, but this habit was not formed spontaneously.

of that term. Calmly cancelling the appointment may communicate the fact that I am angry, but it does not display or manifest my anger to him (or anyone else).

Why might I choose to signal my anger without expressing it? There are many possibilities (caution, a sense of one's own dignity, etc.) but we should focus on one in particular: displaying the force of my anger might provoke certain emotional reactions which I don't wish to provoke, at least in that fashion. Even if I want him to feel shameful or apprehensive and others to feel indignant on my behalf, I may prefer these emotions to be engendered by reflection on the information that I am angry rather than by a display of my fury. The expression of emotion influences the emotions of others in a more direct way.

We can draw a similar distinction with regard to beliefs. I may let a colleague know that I think them dishonest (and do so quite overtly) by closely scrutinizing their expenses claims, asking other people to handle the petty cash, etc. But to do this is not to express the force of my conviction. Others may infer my doubts and come to share these doubts themselves, and I may intend this to happen. But when I *assert* that our colleague is dishonest with a view to ensuring that they believe this on my say so, I am employing a rather different mechanism for influencing their beliefs. I mean them to acquire this belief, not by reflecting on the information that I myself believe it (and intend to inform them of this, etc.) but rather by 'catching' the belief from me, together with its judgemental force. And I needn't be present for this to happen: letters and books are filled with sentences which seek to convince their readers in just this way.

To sum up, the expression of a belief is directly motivated by the belief expressed and directly motivates the adoption of that belief by others. I hope I have said enough to distinguish my notion of expression from belief indication. I shall now say more about assertion.

9.2 Assertion as Expression

So far, we have it that to sincerely assert that p is at least to intend to express the belief that p. One thing which seems to distinguish assertion from other ways of expressing belief is that the assertor makes use of language. This raises certain questions: how does the public meaning of the words used in making the assertion relate to the content of the belief expressed? How much of what is communicated by the speaker to his hearers is part of what he literally asserts and how much is something else (e.g. an implication or a presupposition of what is said)? These are issues which confront any model of assertion. Putting such shared difficulties to one side, I shall address a concern which bears particularly on my own view: how is the belief expression model to accommodate insincere assertion, given that expression can't be insincere?

Williams also sets out to explain assertion in terms of belief expression. Williams agrees that someone 'can express his belief that p only if he has that belief, that is to say, if he is sincere' (Williams 2002: 73) but he rightly allows that an insincere assertion is a genuine assertion. A liar does not merely pretend to make assertions—he is no actor. Still, what the liar is doing may be parasitic on what the sincere assertor is doing. To capture this idea, Williams proposes a disjunctive theory of assertion: 'A asserts that p where A utters a sentence S which means that p, in doing which either he expresses his belief that p, or he intends the person addressed to take it that he believes that p' (Williams 2002: 74).[9] Williams comments that:

> sincere assertions do not necessarily have the aim of informing the hearer; but insincere assertions do have the aim of misinforming the hearer. In the primary case, they aim to misinform the hearer about the state of things, the truth of what the speaker asserts. Derivatively, they may aim to misinform the hearer merely about the speaker's beliefs; the speaker may know that the hearer will not believe what he falsely asserts but he wants her to believe that he himself believes it.   (Williams 2002: 73–4)

I think this formulation is along the right lines, but Williams appears to assume that insincere assertions are intended to mislead. This isn't so.

Recall our man who asserts that all university degrees are of equal value. His assertion is not sincere, yet he means to mislead us neither about the facts nor about his own beliefs. His aim is simply to express what he believes on the point. And even those who are intentionally insincere in what they say need not be aiming to mislead anyone about what they actually believe (Moran 2005a: 346). One might be speaking insincerely in obedience to an order, to avoid the embarrassment of an open admission of what everyone already knows, or for many other reasons without any expectation of being taken to be sincere.[10] The real asymmetry here is the one noted earlier: sincere assertions can be made simply to express the relevant belief, but you must have some further motive for deciding to *present* yourself as expressing a belief, i.e. for making an insincere assertion.

To accommodate these points, we should amend Williams's second clause. Let us say that whilst a sincere assertor is expressing the belief that p (and doing so

---

[9] As already indicated, I shall not pursue issues raised by the phrase 'a sentence which means that p'.
[10] Thanks to Seana Shiffrin for discussion of this point. (Williams 2002: 96–7) also adopts the widespread view that lying must involve the intent to deceive, at least about the speaker's own state of mind. I have my doubts about this but shall not pursue them here.

intentionally), one whose assertion is insincere merely intends to express their belief in p (when the insincerity is unintentional), or intends to present themselves as expressing belief in p (when the insincerity is intentional). 'Present themselves' here should not be taken to imply the intention to deceive, but nor should it be confused with mere pretence: as already noted, insincere assertions differ from the mock assertions made by actors or game players. As Williams remarks, 'formulations of this kind take for granted the notion of "an expression of belief" and return us to acknowledging the fact that this idea has to be understood first, and that insincerity is parasitic on it' (Williams 2002: 75).

I should highlight an implication of this expressive model of assertion which will matter to the epistemology of testimony. An intentionally insincere assertion is reasonable if it is reasonable to present oneself as expressing the belief in question. By contrast, an expression of belief is reasonable only if it is reasonable to actually express the belief in question, and this depends, in part, on the standing of the state of mind expressed. It cannot be reasonable to express an unreasonable belief. This is an instance of the general truth that it is unreasonable to *act on* unreasonable belief. No such thing is true of actions intended to indicate to others that you have the relevant belief. It may be perfectly rational for me to indicate that I doubt my colleague's honesty whether or not these doubts are themselves reasonable (and whether or not I actually feel them).

This normative fact has an important psychological consequence: I can't express a belief that I think to be unreasonable at will. As already urged, it makes perfect sense for someone to set out to express a conviction without their having any further objective in mind. But this claim needs to be qualified. This makes perfect sense only when the attitude in question strikes its possessor as a reasonable one. If the attitude seems unreasonable, if it makes no sense to he who has it, then it also makes no sense for him to express it simply for the sake of expressing it. Of course, he might wish to express it with a view to the relief this will bring or to communicate a message to others. But an action directly motivated by the desire for relief or the desire to communicate the attitude rather than by that attitude itself is not an expression of that attitude.

Clearly, there are circumstances in which it makes sense for me to get myself to express a belief (or to allow myself to express it) even if I think that belief to be unreasonable. But here I do need to *get* myself or *allow* myself to express this belief. For example, my psychoanalyst might need me to express an obviously unreasonable conviction as part of the treatment. Were he asking me to (sincerely) indicate that I had the belief or to make an insincere assertion of it, that would be easy. But such an utterance would not have the required therapeutic effect. Here, I might know some way of *getting* myself to express the belief, to sincerely assert what I now think I have no reason to believe, perhaps by bringing certain past incidents to mind, etc. On the other hand, if I know no such way, I might wait until these past incidents (or some other trigger) come to mind spontaneously and then *allow* myself to express the conviction I feel. In these cases it is reasonable for me to get or allow myself to express a groundless conviction, but this is not something I can do at will.[11]

These points will be crucial to the epistemology of testimony, but before exploring the epistemological implications of this expressive model of assertion, let's consider an alternative which points us in a rather different direction.

9.3 Assertion as Assurance

Assertions contribute in various ways to the transmission of knowledge. An assertion *can* serve as evidence, e.g. where the speaker infers the truth of the proposition from the fact that it is asserted together with other background knowledge about the speaker. Assertions can also be made in the course of an argument for a proposition, as when a mathematician takes us through a proof. But I am interested in a third sort of case where the audience simply accepts what the speaker says, cases in which they believe or trust the speaker (Moran 2005a: 347).[12]

Ross argues that a proper account of such cases cannot treat the speaker's assertion as evidence for the proposition asserted:

The main problem with the idea that the hearer views the speaker's words as evidence arises from the fact that, unlike the examples of natural signs which spring most readily to mind, saying something is a deliberate act under the speaker's conscious control and the hearer is aware that this is the case. The problem is not that of whether the hearer can in these circumstances see the speaker's words as *good* evidence; it is a question of whether the notion of evidence is appropriate here at all. There is, of course, nothing odd about the idea of deliberately presenting an audience with evidence in order to get them to draw a desired conclusion, as when a photograph is produced in court. But in such a case, what is presented is, or is presented as being, evidence independently of the fact of the speaker having chosen to present it. If a speaker's words are evidence of anything, they have that status only because he has chosen to use them. Speaking is not like allowing someone to see that you are blushing. (Ross 1986: 72)

---

[11] Both of these things may be impossible, in which case it will be impossible for me to sincerely assert something that I believe and know I believe.
[12] I may learn that p from someone who says to me that p but who does not present themselves as expressing the belief that p, provided they represent themselves as repeating what someone else has asserted to them. This is a case of 'proxy assertion', of expressing someone else's belief.

What alternative does Ross have in mind here? What sort of reason for belief *is* constituted by the fact that the speaker has chosen to present it as such? A little later on, Ross suggests that 'The speaker, in taking responsibility for the truth of what he is saying, is offering his hearer not evidence but a *guarantee* that it is true, and in believing what he is told the hearer accepts the guarantee' (Ross 1986: 79–80).

Fried expresses a similar idea:

> To make an assertion is to give an assurance that the statement is true. The analogy to promising is very close. An assertion may be seen as a kind of very general promise; it is a promise or assurance that the statement is true. It is offered not as evidence of the speaker's state of mind but as a deliberate act on the speaker's part on which the hearer is intended to rely. (Fried 1978: 56–7)

In testimony, the speaker gives the hearer his word that p; he promises that p is true.[13] Without this guarantee, the hearer would not be entitled to believe that p unless he had evidence which established the truth of p. The effect of the guarantee is to shift the responsibility for having established p's truth onto the speaker: the hearer is entitled to believe that p without himself establishing p's truth because, in accepting the speaker's guarantee, he has transferred this responsibility to the speaker.

The assurance theorist may allow that certain assertions are not intended to offer anyone a guarantee of their own truth (e.g. those made when expounding a proof from premises taken to be self-evident). But, he will say, for assertions to facilitate the acquisition of testimonial knowledge, the speaker must intend to provide his audience with such a guarantee. Indeed, this intention must lie behind any assertion which poses as a source of testimony, whether or not it is sincere, just as the intention to undertake an obligation must lie behind every genuine promise whether or not the promise is sincere (i.e. whether or not the promisor intends to perform). There is no disjunction.

I agree with the assurance theorist that the effect of testimony is to transfer certain responsibilities involved in having a belief from hearer to speaker. But it is a mistake to take promising as our model here.[14] The promisor intends to take on the responsibility of making a certain proposition true, a duty that is owed to the

---

[13] (Searle 1969: 66) tells us that an assertion of p 'counts as an undertaking to the effect that p represents an actual state of affairs'. See also (Van Fraassen 1984: 252–5) and (Brandom 1983). (Harman 1986: 50–1) compares claims to knowledge with promises or guarantees but does not discuss assertion. For an alternative critique of such views, see (Pagin 2004: 838–42).

[14] Here, I focus on those differences between promising and testifying which bear on the epistemology of testimony. For discussion of how the moral obligations generated by testimony differ from those generated by a promise, see (Owens 2012: Chapter 9).

promisee. By contrast, the kind of epistemic responsibilities at stake in testimony are not duties *owed to* anyone; testimony can be presented quite unintentionally to an audience who thereby learn that it is true because they are entitled to depend on the speaker for justification.[15]

Developing these points, let's start from the fact that some assertors have no audience in mind when they make their assertions. Think of a secret diary containing one's most intimate thoughts. It is not just that the author of this diary has no intention of communicating these thoughts to others by writing them down; he has every intention of not communicating them and is careful to keep his diary secret. Such a diary may be filled with assertions, but assertions which lack an intended audience and are not meant to assure anyone of anything.[16]

As Moran observes, a speaker can't make a promise to someone inadvertently (Moran 2005a: 360). Eavesdropping is not a way of garnering promises. Moran then reads this feature of promise into assertion, telling us that the special epistemic value of an assertion for an audience depends on the fact that an assertor is openly engaged in the act of providing this audience with a reason to believe what he says, thereby presenting himself as accountable for the audience's believing what he says (Moran 2005a: 355–6). But can't an audience learn from someone's assertions by trusting them even where these assertions were not addressed to that audience?[17]

Suppose that, unbeknownst to the speaker, I read his secret diary (or bug his private monologues). Here the diarist may have specifically intended to keep his diary away from me. Still, can't I learn from the author's diary in just the way I learn from his conversation, or his published works? True the diarist may not have told *me* anything, but his diary has, and to believe his diary is to believe him, to take his word for it. Yet nothing I read in the diary could constitute a promise made to me. In determining whether we should trust the diary, it *might* be important to know whether the diary was intended for an audience or not and

---

[15] (Moran 2005b: 24) presses the analogy with promise even further by maintaining that assertions must be actively accepted or refused. See also (Ross 1986: 80). In my view, what makes the speaker responsible for his audience's belief is the fact that he has convinced them of its truth and I doubt that becoming convinced of something is an activity.

[16] In these cases, is the speaker giving *himself* an assurance of the truth of what he says (Van Fraassen 1984: 254)? Is the intended audience of his own words? (Grice 1989: 112–13) mentions this possibility when considering an analogous objection to his theory of utterance meaning. (Moran 2005b: 21) rules this out, maintaining that one cannot give oneself an assurance. And even if one could (by means of some sort of vow) the diarist may not be making any vow in that he may have no intention of reading his own diary.

[17] A related point: one can understand many assertions (i.e. those without indexicals) without knowing the identity of either speaker or audience, but one can't understand any promise, order, etc., without knowing from whom it came and to whom it was given (Pagin 2004: 835–6).

which audience it was intended for. But the discovery that a public document was meant to be private will often leave the basis of our trust in it undisturbed. Though this diarist didn't intend to put himself under an obligation to us, we can learn from what he says, just as we could had he been speaking directly to us.

Another feature of valid promises is that they are made voluntarily. An involuntary promise does not commit the promisor to perform. The relevant notion of voluntariness cries out for further elucidation, but we can distinguish two elements. Firstly, a promise must be made intentionally; the promisor must be aware that he is making a promise as well as of the audience to whom he is addressing it. Secondly, this promise mustn't be made under duress or induced by trickery or deception. The act of asserting that p is indeed intentional under that description. But must a genuine assertion be freely made as valid promises are?

I doubt that the epistemic significance of an assertion depends on whether it was made voluntarily as the moral significance of a promise does. It is unfair to expect those who promised under duress or because of deception to fulfil their promises. Doubtless, the same considerations help to determine whether we are held to account for our assertions. If I give away my confederates' hiding place to the police but do so under pressure, or because of some wily trick, this may well affect my confederates' attitude to what I have done (just as the fact that our diarist intended to keep his diary secret will affect whether he is held responsible for the consequences of its publication). But it need not affect the epistemic significance of what I say. The police may learn of the hiding place by trusting me in just the same way as they could had I freely revealed it. Whether others may take my word for it does not turn on whether my words were uttered voluntarily.

To sum up, the assurance theorist and I agree that there is a range of examples in which people learn things by believing what other people tell them without treating what they hear as evidence for what they are being told. I have made my case against the assurance theorist by highlighting examples which are on the face of it part of this range but to which the assurance theory does not apply. This is a sound *prima facie* objection but my point won't be clinched until I provide an alternative non-evidential model of testimony which covers *both* the examples the assurance theorist takes as paradigmatic *and* those he can't deal with. In the face of a more comprehensive and successful theory, the assurance theorist can't happily set aside my counterexamples as cases requiring a different treatment.[18]

---

[18] (Williams 2002: 82) observes that assertion is not simply a means of expressing a pre-existing belief. Rather, we often decide what to believe about a given matter by working out what we are prepared to say about it. That seems right, but, as Williams notes, it does not tell against the belief expression model. Nor does it tell in favour of the assurance model. Our diarist could be engaged in working out what to think about a certain matter by trying to commit himself on paper.

9.4 Testimony

Learning that p by trusting someone's assertion that p is not a matter of learning that p from the fact that they believe p (however known). So much is common ground between myself and the assurance theorist. It is also common ground that the speaker *does* something which the hearer picks up on. I may learn what someone believes from a brain scan, but inferring that he is right from the scan is not an instance of learning by trusting him. For the assurance theorist, the act of telling effects a transfer of epistemic responsibility from hearer to speaker because it offers the hearer a guarantee of the belief's truth. Leaving promising behind, I shall develop a partial analogy between testimony and memory.

Memory is what I shall call a *rationality-preserving mechanism for belief*.[19] Suppose I prove a certain mathematical theorem and later recall the theorem without recalling the proof. If all has gone well, I now have the very same belief in the theorem that I had before, a belief which is justified by the proof which I can't now recall. Here, memory does not provide some new basis, some new evidence for the belief which replaces the proof; it is a means of conserving the justificational status of the belief without conserving the evidence which originally supported it. Where I overlooked some fairly obvious fallacy in the proof, memory will preserve my belief in the theorem as an unreasonable belief.

Testimony does not literally preserve belief, rather, it creates a new belief in another. But, I shall argue, it often creates a belief which matches its original in content and inherits its justificational status. So it too is a rationality-preserving mechanism for belief. Suppose Jones has proved another theorem and tells me of it without showing me his proof. If all goes well, I can acquire Jones's belief in the theorem (i.e. a belief based on the very grounds on which Jones's belief is based) even though I have never gone through the proof which convinced Jones of its truth. Obviously there are circumstances in which I ought not to credit Jones's word, as there are circumstances in which I should not rely on my own memory. But, in the absence of such grounds for doubt, I can tap into Jones's sources of justification as I tap into those of my earlier self. The testimonial mechanism must be working properly for this transmission to take place successfully—there must be no miscommunication, deception, etc.—but it is equally true that the subject's memory must be working properly for it to preserve rational belief. In neither case is the proper working of the mechanism part of the justification for the inherited belief.

---

[19] I borrow this notion of a rationality-preserving mechanism from Pink's discussion of intention. See (Pink 1996: 93–9).

I have defended the view that memory is a rationality-preserving mechanism elsewhere.[20] In particular, I have argued that it is not at all obvious how else memory could facilitate the justification of belief, for memory beliefs cannot (in general) be justified by reference to the fact that they are remembered. Here, I want to suggest that, since testimony is a rationality-preserving mechanism, it can effect a transfer of responsibility for belief from hearer to speaker without the speaker's needing to offer the hearer a guarantee of the belief's truth.

It is significant that whilst speaker and hearer are different people, memory is an intrapersonal affair. This fact generates various disanalogies between testimony and memory. Firstly, memory involves only the belief already acquired, usually stripped of the material which was originally used to support it. By contrast, testimony requires an action—assertion—intended to express the belief in question, an action which creates a belief in the hearer distinct from the belief the speaker expresses. Furthermore, the notion of sincerity has a clear point of application in the case of testimony—namely to the act of assertion—but no obvious point of application in memory. Can one acknowledge these disanalogies whilst holding onto the idea that testimony, like memory, is a rationality-preserving mechanism?

I'll first ask why the testifier must express his belief at all and then consider why he must intend to express his belief, before moving onto the issue of sincerity. Since memory is an intrapersonal affair there is no need for the person who remembers to be made aware of the fact that he has the belief remembered. All memory need do is to preserve the belief in question. A normal person will know that he has this belief, but it is not by knowing this fact that he remembers the thing believed. Since testimony is an interpersonal affair, the recipient does need to be made aware of the belief by the believer. But 'being made aware of the belief' here can't just be a matter of acquiring the knowledge that the speaker has it. Testimony no more involves an inference from the fact of belief than memory does. Rather, the belief must be *expressed* to the hearer. Only in this way can the force of the speaker's conviction—and not mere knowledge of his belief—be transmitted to the hearer.

But why must the speaker *intend* to express his belief? Why isn't it enough that he express his belief and that this expression induce a similar belief in another? Wouldn't this be a rationality-preserving mechanism for belief? After all, memory preserves the rationality of belief regardless of the subject's intentions. I will now argue that testimony is rationality preserving only because assertion is intentional.

---

[20] See Part III of (Owens 2000). Much of what I say there about memory and testimony was inspired by reading (Burge 2013: Essay 10), though the view I arrived at may not be the same as his.

Remembering that p involves a prior belief in p, and such conviction requires at least the appearance of evidential support. One can't simply decide to install a belief in one's memory. And it is because our memory is constrained in this way that memory is a rationality-preserving mechanism. When it works normally, memory fixes belief in place by tapping into the force of the reasons, good or bad, which convinced us of it in the first place. Contrast someone who wishes to retain a belief and visits the hypnotist to ensure that it sticks. Here, the justificational status of the initial belief is not inherited by a hypnotically induced belief unless the efficacy of the hypnosis depends on the apparent rationality of the initial belief (Owens 2000: 154–5).

To make testimony a rationality-preserving mechanism, we need to ensure that the rationality of the belief which the hearer ends up with reflects the rationality of the quite distinct belief that the speaker expresses. Clearly this link won't be established unless the speaker believes what he says. But more is required than mere sincerity. Suppose a speaker finds himself expressing or lets himself express a belief which he thinks to be irrational. Whether or not the speaker is right about this belief's irrationality,[21] a hearer cannot acquire a rational belief by crediting this expression of it. You can't come to know something by taking the word of a speaker who thinks there are no adequate grounds for believing what he says (though you may infer its truth from the fact that he believes it), any more than you can by taking the word of a speaker who thinks that there are adequate grounds for believing what he says but doesn't himself believe it (though you may infer its truth from the fact that he thinks he ought to believe it).

If testimony is to preserve the rationality of the belief expressed, the expression of belief involved must be constrained by the speaker's view of the rationality of the state expressed. But, as we saw earlier, it is so constrained precisely when he speaks with the intention of expressing his belief. A speaker can no more easily get himself to sincerely assert something for which he now thinks there is very little evidence (i.e. to express a belief that seems unreasonable) than he can install in memory a proposition which strikes him as dubious. True, one *finds* oneself expressing (or *allows* oneself to express) all sorts of beliefs (and emotions) one regards as unreasonable. But apparent irrationality is a block to acting with the intention of expressing the state in question. That is why an expression of belief must be intentional to be part of a rationality-preserving mechanism.

---

[21] The mere fact that you think a certain belief of yours to be irrational does not make it irrational for you to believe it (Owens 2000: 108).

If I am right, a sincere assertion reflects the rationality (good or bad) of the belief it expresses and it transmits a belief with those epistemic credentials to an audience who are convinced by it. Trusting an expression of belief by accepting what a speaker says involves entering a state of mind which gets its rationality from the rationality of the belief expressed. This state's rationality depends on the speaker's justification for the belief she expresses, not his justification for the action of expressing it. And to hear a speaker as making a sincere assertion, as expressing a belief, is *ceteris paribus* to feel able to tap into *that* justification (whether or not her assertion was directed at you) by accepting what she says. The assertion may be irrelevant, impolite, imprudent, and unreasonable in all sorts of other ways but if it is well founded, we can learn that it is true by trusting the speaker.

Only an action expressive of belief could pull this trick off. Should someone merely indicate that they believe that p, that indication may be taken as evidence for the truth of p. But her audience won't feel able to learn that p simply by trusting the speaker, by sharing the speaker's conviction because they know that the speaker could be perfectly entitled to indicate that they have that belief (perhaps sincerely) without having any title to the belief itself. If we are to believe what the speaker indicates that she believes, either the speaker must justify this belief to us, or we must supply some justification of our own (which may or may not involve the fact that she believes it). The same applies to the action of offering a guarantee of p's truth: it could be reasonable for someone to guarantee p's truth, though they had no reason to believe p. Neither act can be part of a rationality-preserving mechanism for belief.

I have suggested that testimony is, like memory, a mechanism for preserving the rationality of belief. Yet whilst there is no such thing as insincere recollection, insincere assertion is all too common. And the points just made about sincere assertion do not apply to assertion as such. The rationality of an insincere assertion does not depend on the rationality of some expressed belief and so there is no psychological obstacle to insincerely asserting something for which you think you have no evidence. All this must be admitted, but does it follow that memory and testimony require different epistemologies?

I maintain that 'insincere assertion' is not an *epistemologically* significant category. The significant category is a broader one, that of 'illusory transfers of epistemic responsibility' of which memory and testimony furnish us with parallel instances. Illusory transfers are cases in which the receiver of the belief is entitled to depend on the source of the belief for its justification, but the source of the belief is not in fact responsible for the epistemic status of the belief. (Such illusory transfers are to be distinguished from cases in which the transfer was successful and the groundlessness of the receiver's belief can be traced to the irrationality of the source's belief.)[22]

One way in which illusory transfer happens in testimony is when the audience mishears the speaker, perhaps through no fault of their own. Here, the audience may be entitled to depend on the speaker for justification of their belief in p but the speaker is not irrational if they possess no such justification. Illusory transfers happen in memory when the content of a perfectly justified memory is corrupted by the preservation mechanism. Here, my later self may be entitled to depend on my earlier self for justification of this belief even though the fact that I lacked such a justification does not show up any flaw in my earlier beliefs. Insincere assertion also falls into the category of illusory transfers of epistemic responsibility: the hearer may be entitled to depend on the speaker for justification, but the speaker is not, so far as their beliefs go, unreasonable if they can't provide it (Owens 2000: 171–2).

The assurance theorist will agree that in cases of misunderstanding there is an illusory transfer of responsibility. But, for him, what is crucial in effecting a genuine transfer is the intentions expressed by the parties to the conversation. In his eyes, the convincing liar should be grouped with the sincere assertor and not with the speaker who is misunderstood because both the convincing liar and the sincere assertor express the intention to guarantee the truth of the relevant belief and they thereby accept responsibility for this belief. Someone whose assertion is misunderstood expresses no such intention and so fails to take on any responsibility.

On my belief-expression model of assertion, the situation is more complex. From the speaker's perspective, sincere assertion is like misunderstood assertion in that both are genuine expressions of belief. But from the hearer's perspective, assertions misunderstood are more like lies (and other insincere assertions) in that they appear to do what sincere assertion actually does, namely, transfer responsibility for the belief (apparently) expressed. They merely appear to do this because the speaker does not actually give expression to the belief which the hearer picks up. On my account, what is crucial to the transfer of responsibility is not what intention the speaker expresses but rather what belief he (intentionally) expresses. Since both the insincere and the misunderstood fail to give expression to the belief that their hearer acquires, they can't transmit it to the hearer (as opposed to inducing it in him) and so can't assume a believer's responsibility for it.

---

[22] For discussion of what should be said about the rationality of the recipient in such cases, see (Owens 2000: 138–9).

When considering the ethical relations between speaker and hearer, it may indeed be inappropriate to classify insincere assertion with genuine misunderstanding. For example, by asserting something he knows to be false, the liar makes himself responsible for the audience's acquisition of a false belief and/or other consequences which may ensue. And this usually differentiates him from the person who is misunderstood. But the liar's responsibility here is a moral responsibility for the foreseeable consequences of his actions, not a believer's responsibility for what is believed.

9.5 Conclusion

For the evidentialist about testimony, the act of assertion is a fallible indicator of the speaker's belief. Would we could know of this belief directly without the mediation of this act. The assurance theorist responds that the act of assertion provides the hearer with something which he could never get simply from knowledge of the speaker's beliefs. But the assurance theorist mischaracterizes this something as a guarantee or promise, tracing the special epistemic significance of assertion to the addressive relation it establishes with the hearer. I have proposed that the act of assertion expresses belief and thereby enables its audience to acquire not knowledge of the speaker's belief but a belief with the same content and epistemic credentials, and thus knowledge, of the fact testified to.[23]

---

[23] Many thanks to Paul Faulkner, Robert Hopkins, Jennifer Saul, Andy McGonigal, Peter Pagin, Seana Shiffrin, Fabian Freyenhagen, Michael Martin, Christopher Hookway, Richard Moran, Duncan Prichard, and Michael Brady for comments. My work on this chapter was supported by the Arts and Humanities Research Council.

10

Human Testimony

Learning from other human beings cannot be equated with learning from things. The clouds indicate rain and thereby give us a basis for believing that it will rain, but the statements of others are not *mere* indications of the truth of what they say. Human beings have reasons for what they think and their assertions are (standardly) expressions of what they think. This gives these assertions an epistemological significance different from either the rain clouds in the sky or the fuel gauge in my car. We learn from the utterances of others in a distinctive fashion, and this is so because our fellows have reasons for their attitudes and actions. But is it *purely* because they are rational creatures that we can learn from our fellows in the ways that we do? Human beings have an emotional psychology that other rational creatures might not share. As I shall argue, such creatures would be unable to learn from one another as we do.

An assertion is expressive of belief. This fact alone has been thought to ground a *prima facie* entitlement to believe what you hear to be asserted. In taking advantage of this entitlement one need not be deploying some background belief about the reliability of such assertions. Nor need one have moralistic thoughts about trust, obligation, truthfulness, and so forth. One need only accept what one hears in order to benefit from the knowledge of others. I agree that human beings acquire knowledge from each other in something like this fashion and furthermore that this is a fundamental way in which we learn from one another. However, I doubt that this entitlement to believe what another speaker tells us rests purely on our being addressed by a fellow person, by a rational believer. Rather, it depends on distinctive features of human psychology, on what Reid called the instincts of veracity and credulity, our tendency to express our own beliefs and our tendency to adopt the beliefs others express to us.

Our topic here is the epistemology of testimony, and testimony involves the transmission of knowledge, but my main focus will be on the transmission of justification, of an entitlement to believe. Given that, as I assume here, knowledge involves justification, the difference often does not matter, but where the distinction needs to be made, it is the issue of transmission of justification or entitlement on which we shall focus. (The relationship between justification and entitlement will be addressed later.) The distinctive and puzzling feature of testimony is that my belief in p can be justified by what justifies someone else's belief in it, even where I have no idea why they believe that p. Accepting testimony that p also involves thinking that one can learn that p (i.e. acquire knowledge of p) from the speaker, but whether one actually comes to know the proposition depends on all sorts of other factors not specific to the epistemology of testimony. Thus, the question of the transmission of knowledge is, from this point of view, a secondary issue.

I'll begin with Burge's attempt to ground the authority of testimony in our nature as rational persons. In the second and third sections I'll formulate and defend an 'inheritance' model of testimony partly inspired by Reid, a model which places the emphasis on our emotional psychology.[1] In the final section, I turn to consider the recent wave of assurance theories and the difficulties they face in basing an epistemology of testimony on the ethics of assertion. I conclude that we don't learn from the speech of others *qua* conscientious agents or fellow reasoners but under a more specific guise.

10.1 The Rational Entitlement Model of Testimony

Let's start with the following fact: people tend to believe what they hear from other people. Human life would be impossible in anything like its present form were this not so. One might ask by what right people believe what others say, but we should first ask by what mechanism people believe it. Then we can assess whether the mechanism is one on which they ought to be relying. One possible mechanism here is inductive inference. In the past, clouds have been followed by rain and the statements of John about Jane have turned out to be accurate. So, you infer, this cloud is a good indication of rain, and John's statement is a good guide to how it is with Jane. The statements of others are often used as the basis for such inferences, but a fair number of writers now agree that this cannot be the only way in which we learn from them.

On this point, Burge can stand in for many:

When we ask someone on the street the time or the direction of some landmark or when we ask someone to do a simple sum, we rely on the answer. We make use of a presumption of credibility when we read books, signs or newspapers or talk to strangers on unloaded topics. We need not engage in reasoning about the person's qualifications to be rational in accepting what he or she says, in the absence of grounds for doubt.   (Burge 2013: 238)

---

[1] I borrow the 'inheritance' label from (McMyler 2011: Chapter 3).

So what mechanism of belief transmission is at work here? In this section and the next, I'll contrast the *Inheritance* model of testimony with the *Rational Entitlement* model.

In defending what I'll call the Rational Entitlement model, Burge enunciates the *Acceptance Principle*: 'A person is entitled to accept as true something that is presented as true and is intelligible to him, unless there are stronger reasons not to do so' (Burge 2013: 237). The Acceptance Principle contains two elements. First, if you understand some event (e.g. a speech act) as presenting p as true, you are entitled to presume that you have understood correctly. Second, if p is presented to you as true, you are entitled to presume that it is true.

The Acceptance Principle is not a principle of reasoning: you don't come to believe what you are told by using the Acceptance Principle as the basis for a (non-inductive) inference. Rather, 'We are entitled to acquire information according to the principle—without using it as a justification—accepting the information instinctively' (ibid.).

Burge then grounds the Acceptance Principle in a more general claim:

A person is *a priori* entitled to accept a proposition that is presented as true and that is intelligible to him, unless there are stronger reasons not to do so because it is *prima facie* preserved (received) from a rational source, or resource for reason; reliance on rational sources—or resources for reason—is, others things being equal, necessary to the function of reason. (Burge 2013: 238)

Burge compares reliance on the word of others with the faith we all place in the deliverances of what he calls 'preservative memory'. Such memory preserves the beliefs we have acquired in the past, usually without preserving the grounds on which we acquired them:

A person clearly *can* be entitled to believe a theorem she believes because of preservative memory even if she cannot remember the proof she gave long ago, and even if she cannot remember that she gave a proof. Most of what one is entitled to believe from past reading, past interlocution, past reasoning or past empirical learning derives from sources and warrants that one has forgotten. (Burge 2013: 300–1; see also 303–4)

Since preservative memory is a 'resource for reason', it falls under Burge's more general claim, and so we are entitled to rely on it in much the same way and on much the same grounds as we are entitled to rely on testimony.

In any testimonial mechanism there are two crucial elements: the speaker's statement and the hearer's reaction. How are these to be understood on the Rational Entitlement model? What it is for the speaker to present something as true (in the context of testimony) and what it is for their audience to accept what is said?

Let's start with a speaker's 'presenting a proposition as true' to their audience. Burge clearly intends us to think of the speaker as asserting that p: the comprehension presupposed by testimony is comprehension of statements, not of general behaviour. In the course of summarizing his view, he says that 'the intelligibility of an assertion is *a priori* related to the assertion's having an origin in a being with reason' (Burge 2013: 229). I agree with Burge that assertion is the crucial notion here: for the audience to learn that p by taking the speaker's word for it, the speaker must assert that p. But it is worth asking exactly why it is assertion on which we should focus, for there are other ways in which a being with reason might 'present p as true'.

You can present p as true by saying 'I suspect that p', 'I'd guess that p', 'I fear that p', or 'I hope that p'. All of these statements will have to be withdrawn (just like an assertion) if p turns out to be false (Chapter 2: Section 2.2 and Chapter 4: Section 4.2), but none involves asserting that p, in that none implies any belief in p (i.e. any claim to know that p). And, except in special circumstances, the audience would not be inclined to base a belief on these utterances, though they might come to share the speaker's hopes, suspicions, and so forth.

To assert that p is to present p as true in a special belief-involving way. For the audience to accept the speaker's (sincere) assertion that p, the audience must come to believe what the speaker believes on this matter and must base their belief on the speaker's belief.[2] But we are not yet done, for you can get someone to believe that p by letting them know that you believe it without actually asserting that p and so without their being in a position to base their belief on yours in the relevant way. For example, suppose a colleague is going around the room asking to borrow a valuable tool. By declining their request in my presence you can (deliberately and openly) communicate to me that they shouldn't be trusted with the tool, something I come to believe by interpreting your behaviour in just the way you intend. Here, you communicate the fact that they are untrustworthy and that is the basis on which I believe that they are not to be trusted, but you do not assert this and so I cannot take your word for it. In this case I come to believe that p because you present yourself as believing that p with a view to getting me to believe that p, but I don't come to believe it in the way relevant to testimony.[3]

---

[2] (Lackey 2008: 47–59) maintains that a good source of testimony need not believe what they are saying. Some of the examples she offers in support of this claim can be dealt with by carefully identifying the source of the testimony (Burge 2013: 254–64). Others depend on Lackey's operating with an insufficiently discriminating notion of testimony (McMyler 2011: 80–7).

[3] Your behaviour does, in Grice's terms, (non-naturally) mean that p since you intend that my recognition of your intention to get me to believe that p be my reason for coming to believe that p (Grice 1989: 213–23). But there is no assertion of p. Indeed you may engage in this performance precisely to communicate that p without asserting it, so as to preclude my taking your word for it.

The point will be missed if we equate 'taking someone's word for it' with 'trusting them by accepting what they are trying to communicate'.[4] There are various ways of communicating information without offering testimony on the point. A disguised St Athanasius famously told his pursuers who asked him where Athanasius was that he had seen him in a different place only a few minutes earlier. Here Athanasius did not assert his own absence but he did communicate this information to his pursuers and thereby misled them. Clearly, he felt entitled to mislead them in this way though not by asserting 'Athanasius is not here' and thereby offering them his word on the point.[5]

For the purposes of the Acceptance Principle, why does it matter whether the speaker asserts that p, given that they can present p as true in all these other ways? For example, why aren't I *prima facie* entitled to believe that our colleague is not to be trusted simply because you (a rational source) let me know that you regard them as untrustworthy? Indeed, why should it matter exactly how I learn that you believe it: your belief in p presents p as true, I have no reason to doubt it (we may suppose), so can't I learn that p from you when you make me aware of your belief in it? Perhaps I can, but, if so, I'm not learning from you in the special way that concerns us here, namely, by relying on your testimony.[6]

Consider memory once more. When I claim to know the date of my birth, I do not base my claim to knowledge on facts about what I already believe. It is not merely that I don't infer the truth of my belief from the fact of my belief in it. I don't make any movement of thought at all, whether by inference or by instinct. I simply continue to believe what I believed all along with the aid of (preservative memory). As Burge puts it: 'Purely preservative memory introduces no subject matter, constitutes no element in justification, and adds no force to a justification or entitlement. It simply maintains in justificational space a cognitive content together with its judgemental force' (Burge 2013: 235). Modeling testimony on preservative memory, one might propose that when you accept someone's assertion that p, you actually inherit their (token) belief in p, but it is enough

---

[4] (McMyler 2011: 107-9 and 2013: 1070-3) argues that testimony involves the open communication of information. McMyler also wants to explain reliance on testimony in terms of the prior idea of 'trusting a person'. I would argue that the order of explanation runs in the opposite direction, that the nature of testimony (or assertion) must be grasped before we can explain trust in an assertion (Owens 2017).

[5] Burge denies that the Acceptance Principle applies to such conversational implicatures (Burge 2013: 248 n.21).

[6] Perhaps one can learn from others by attributing beliefs to them and charitably presuming that those beliefs are true (unless one has grounds for doubt), but to do so is not to learn from them by taking their word for it (Moran 2005b: 3-4). Even though you base your belief on theirs, their assertion plays no essential role, for you could have done the same having learnt of their thoughts on the matter from a third party.

for my purposes if the audience simply base their belief in p on the speaker's belief in p in a way that enables the hearer's belief to inherit the speaker's justification for it. The crux of the analogy between memory and testimony is that both are mechanisms for the inheritance of justification, and we can leave it open whether the beliefs at each end of the process are the very same belief. So how does assertion, and assertion alone, ensure transmission of justificational status from a belief in the mind of the speaker to one in the mind of the hearer?

In Section 10.2 I'll suggest that assertion can do this because assertion involves the intentional *expression* of belief, but now I'll broach our second issue: why do we accept what people assert? Burge maintains that we are entitled to accept an assertion simply in virtue of the apparent rationality of our informant: 'The minimum source of warrant for receiving communication is more general than [the] human social context. The source lies in something universal to intelligible, propositional presentations-as-true (centrally assertions)' (Burge 2013: 268). But Burge also says that such acceptance involves instinctual movements of thought rather than reasoning. Why should we expect the required instinct to be a feature of all rational creatures?

Again, the analogy with memory is supposed to be doing some work here. Burge maintains that reliance on preservative memory is 'necessary to the function of reason'. This reliance has two aspects. First, we presume correct understanding of the contents of our memory, as of our own thought in general. Burge acknowledges that this understanding can be at least partially erroneous: we may lack a firm grasp of the concepts required to formulate even our own thoughts, but, Burge says, reasoning would be impossible unless we were a priori entitled to presume an adequate grasp of the contents of our own thoughts (Burge 2013: 352). That seems plausible enough, but does the very possibility of reasoning also require that we be entitled to rely on our retained (and *prima facie* comprehended) beliefs without being in a position to recall the grounds on which we acquired those beliefs?

Any reasoner with a limited capacity for conscious attention must be entitled to believe the many propositions of which their past reasoning has convinced them, even though they are incapable of simultaneously attending to the grounds for them all. For example, as Descartes observes, I must be entitled to complete a six-step proof without being able to hold all six steps simultaneously before the mind (Descartes 1985: 15). Were this not so, all but the simplest reasoning would be impossible. Here I can still respond to a demand for justification provided I can recall the earlier steps of the proof from working memory. Our question is this: does the very possibility of conscious reasoning also require that we are entitled to believe what we find in memory, even though we have quite forgotten the grounds for our belief? To put it another way, does rationality presuppose the 'instinct' of our continuing to believe what we already do (call it the *preservative instinct*) even when we can't recall why we believe it however hard we try? Is preservative memory so understood an indispensable resource of reason?[7]

Pursuing the analogy with testimony, a similar question may be asked of what I'll call the instinct of *credulity*, of our willingness to accept what others tell us. Once more, two entitlements are in play. First, an entitlement to presume understanding of what other people say, at least where that understanding presents itself as immediate (we are being addressed in our native language, no metaphor, implicature, etc. (Burge 2013: 355–6)). Second, an entitlement to believe what others say without requiring knowledge of their grounds. Are these entitlements really essential to the functioning of Reason as such?

Speaking of testimony, Burge concedes that the answer may well be 'No':

Relying on others is perhaps not metaphysically necessary for any possible rational being. But it is cognitively fundamental to beings like us. Though ontogenetically later than perception and memory, reliance on others for learning language and acquiring beliefs is deeply engrained in our evolutionary history.... Most of the information that we have, and many of the methods that we have for evaluating it, depend on interlocution. If we did not acquire a massive number of beliefs from others, our cognitive lives would be little different from the animals. (Burge 2013: 235–6, see also 267)

And he goes on:

I think that I need not show that other rational beings are necessary to the function of one's reason in order to have these entitlements. One has a general entitlement to rely on the rationality of rational beings.... So I think that to maintain that one is *a priori* entitled to rely upon rational interlocutors, I need not show that a solitary reasoner is impossible.
(Burge 2013: 238)

My own suspicion is that the same applies to preservative memory. We can perhaps conceive of a rational being with a working memory capacious enough to facilitate a fair amount of reasoning and thus enjoy a tolerably rich mental life without needing to rely on beliefs whose basis it has forgotten. But human beings are not like that. Our mental lives would be impossible unless memory could preserve justification simply by preserving the justified belief. The preservative

---

[7] Barnett maintains that the central cases of preservative memory are 'cases in which you retain both a belief and the evidence that it is based on over a relatively short period of time' (Barnett 2015: 369). On this view, the function of memory is purely to deal with limitations on cognitive attention, e.g. on our capacity to simultaneously review all the premises in a proof or all of our evidence for a proposition (ibid.: 369–88). In my view, the ability of memory to preserve justification even when you have forgotten your original grounds is an equally central function of memory. This is the crux of the analogy with testimony where you rarely know exactly what your informant knows.

instinct and the instinct of credulity both make possible not the life of the mind but the life of the human species.[8] Thus, the Burgean entitlements to rely on both memory and testimony are not entitlements we have simply in virtue of being rational thinkers.

10.2 The Inheritance Model of Testimony

In the course of presenting his rational entitlement model, Burge quotes with approval the following passage from Reid's *Inquiry*:

> The wise and beneficent Author of nature, who intended that we should be social creatures, and that we should receive the greatest and most important part of our knowledge by the information of others, hath, for these purposes implanted in our natures two principles that tally one with each other. The first of these principles is a propensity to speak the truth...the second is a disposition to confide in the veracity of others, and to believe what they tell us   (Burge 2013: 237/Reid 1997: 193–4).

Call these dispositions the *instinct of veracity* and the *instinct of credulity* (Reid 1997: 194). I would argue that, when implanting these principles in us, the 'Author of Nature' did more than give us the capacity for rational thought.

Reid compares articulate speech to the 'natural language of human features and gestures': 'It is by one particular principle of our constitution that certain features express anger; and by another particular principle that certain features express benevolence' (Reid 1997: 191; see also Reid 2010: 332–3). There are two elements in play here. First, there is the idea that one who feels anger or benevolence is instinctively inclined to express that emotion in a characteristic way. Second, there is the idea that such expression has a certain impact on their audience. That impact is in part a matter of the audience's becoming aware of the speaker's feelings, but it usually goes much further. Reid describes an 'intercourse of human minds, by which their thoughts and sentiments are exchanged and their souls mingle together as it were, [which] is common to the whole species from infancy' (Reid 2010: 332–3). Witnessing (or reading) an expression of emotion standardly changes your own emotional state, often ensuring that you come to share either the same emotion or some reciprocal attitude ('souls mingle'), though how exactly it affects you depends on all sorts of factors (e.g. on whether or not you happen to be the object of the anger).

How do these observations about the expression of emotion bear on testimony? Testimony involves assertion and assertion involves the expression of

---

[8] Here, I am modifying the view expressed in (Owens 2000: 167).

belief, and so it is natural to compare the latter with the expression of emotion. The transmission of belief by testimony depends on our shared human emotional psychology and, in particular, on two underlying instincts. First, our need to express what we believe. Part of being convinced of p is wanting to express that conviction should the question arise as to whether p: hence the principle of veracity. Second, our tendency to react to other people's expressions of belief in a specific way, namely, by coming to share the conviction in question. We are standardly convinced by other people's assertions: hence the principle of credulity.

There are some important differences between the process by which testimony transmits belief and that by which the expression of emotion transmits the emotion expressed. First, our native tongue differs from Reid's natural language of gesture in the conventional nature of the connection between sound and sentiment, but, as both Burge and Reid urge, the fact that our native language needs to be learnt does not imply that, once acquired, our comprehension of it involves any inference.[9] Secondly, and more importantly, one who asserts that p expresses their belief in p with the intention of so doing and, as we'll see later (Section 10.3), this fact is essential to testimony's ability to preserve the rationality of the belief transmitted. When you accept someone's testimony, you are deferring to your interlocutor's assertion *qua* assertion, i.e. to their intentional expression of belief. Someone who believes what I say in the way relevant to testimony must think of themselves as believing it because I asserted it, because I intentionally expressed that belief. By contrast, an expression of anger need not be intentional and need not be taken to be intentional in order to have the relevant emotional impact. Still, the transmission of belief via testimony depends on the above aspects of our emotional psychology. I'll now explore the two instincts in more detail.

10.2.1 Veracity

This is what Reid tells us about veracity:

Truth is always uppermost and is the natural issue of the mind. It requires no art or training, no inducement or temptation, but only that we yield to a natural impulse. Lying, on the contrary, is doing violence to our natures; and is never practiced, even by the worst men, without some temptation. Speaking truth is like using our natural food, which we would do from appetite though it answered no end but lying is like taking physic, which is nauseous to the taste, and which no man takes but for some end which he cannot otherwise attain. (Reid 1997: 193)

---

[9] Both Burge and Reid compare linguistic comprehension with perception, see (Burge 2013: 354–5) and (Reid 1997: 190–2).

When the question arises as to whether p, we tend to feel some desire to express our view as to whether p simply for the sake of expressing our view, as we tend to feel some desire to express our anger once its object becomes salient. This is because, for creatures like us with beliefs and emotions, there is something good or desirable about expressing those beliefs and emotions (Chapter 9: Section 9.1). Consequently, it makes sense to express one's convictions (where relevant) even when there is no further reason to do so. Of course, there are many situations in which (all things considered) it would not be sensible to express one's view about p, even though the subject has come up. Indeed, it is often perfectly reasonable to lie on the matter. But a speaker sees some point in telling the truth and they'll do so absent other considerations.

What is expression? I shall limit myself to expanding on the contrast, made in the last section, between expression and communication. One can let someone know that one is angry by doing something that it would make sense for you to do only if you were angry and one can do that thing for that very reason whilst at the same time refraining from any expression of anger (Chapter 9: Section 9.1). Similarly, I can let someone know that I believe X is untrustworthy by behaving in a way that makes sense only given that I don't trust them (e.g. decline to lend him the tool) and can do that thing for that very reason whilst declining to express the belief that they are untrustworthy.[10] Here, I am inviting my audience to share my belief without imposing it on them. To express my views is to communicate them in charged fashion, one that brings into play the mechanism of credulity: assertion demands conviction from its audience. People frequently wish to communicate the fact that they believe something with a view to getting their audience to share that belief but without exercising that sort of influence.[11] They rely on non-linguistic behaviour or conversational implicature.[12]

Now compare all this with what Burge has to say on the matter. Burge faces the following question: how can the presumed *theoretical* rationality of the source (its rationality *qua* thinker) ground a further presumption that it would be practically rational for the speaker to be truthful? He answers as follows.

---

[10] It is because assertion is a form of expression that assertion is not a 'social act' in the sense of an act that consists in the communication of its own social significance (Pagin 2004). I cannot express either anger or belief simply by saying 'I hereby express my anger' or 'I hereby express my belief'. Promising and other performatives are quite different in this respect. (Reid 2010: 330–1) treats both assertion and promise as being equally 'social operations', and this may be the source of the difficulties in his later views: see note 27.

[11] There are other reasons for communicating without asserting. For example, communication may be deniable in a way that assertions are not.

[12] What is expressed by an assertion may be taken to include the obvious presuppositions and conventional implicatures of what is asserted.

One of reason's primary functions is that of presenting truth, independently of special personal interests. Lying is sometimes rational in the sense that it is in the liar's best interests. But lying occasions a disunity among functions of reason. It conflicts with reason's transpersonal function of presenting the truth, independently of special personal interests.   (Burge 2013: 242–3)

Burge and Reid agree that, when the subject comes up, we always have an (in itself sufficient) reason to tell the truth as we see it, and that failing to do so makes sense only when some other interest is in play, but there are significant differences between them. For Burge, Reason's alethic function doesn't just give us *a* reason to be truthful, a reason which might be overridden by other reasons, as our aversion to the taste of the medicine is overridden by our need for a cure. For Burge, lying always involves an element of irrationality: 'Generic rationality has practical and impersonally theoretical dimensions. I think that, *prima facie*, when a speaker fails to tell the truth because of special interests, the speaker crosses rationality in one significant dimension, the latter one' (Burge 2013: 271 nn.15 and 18). Why so? For Burge, the reason we always have to be truthful is not merely an aspect of the psychology of human conviction but derives from the speaker's very rationality or personhood and this, in Burge's eyes, gives that reason an indefeasible status. We cannot weigh it against other reasons (reasons which are not intrinsic to our personhood) without compromising our rationality.

Burge supposes that 'one has a general entitlement to rely on the rationality of rational beings' because one is entitled to presume that a rational being will tell the truth simply in virtue of their rationality. By contrast, on my Reidian hypothesis, the desirability of telling the truth may be weighed against other relevant considerations without calling the speaker's rationality into question. Thus, it can be perfectly rational for a speaker to lie. Is this a problem? For Burge we are able to presume that our informant is being sincere simply because they are rational and he doubts we would be entitled to this presumption unless lying were, in some degree, irrational *tout court*. I disagree. Suppose our informant is a certain sort of rational creature, a creature with an interest in being truthful unless it has some reason to be otherwise. Given this alone, we can presume on its truthfulness unless there are grounds to suspect the presence of an ulterior motive.[13]

10.2.2 Credulity

This takes us to the principle of credulity. Reid says:

It is evident that in the matter of testimony the balance of human judgment is by nature inclined to the side of belief, and turns to that side of itself, when there is nothing put into

---

[13] This response to the problem of rational lying is different from that offered in (Owens 2000: 171–2).

the opposite scale. If it was not so, no proposition that is uttered in discourse would be believed until it was examined and tried by reason; and most men would be unable to find reasons for believing the thousandt part of what is told to them. Such distrust and incredulity would deprive us of the greatest benefits of society and place us in a worse condition than that of the savages. (Reid 1997: 194; see also Reid 2010: 334)

Again, Burge puts Reid's points in a more rationalistic key: 'Neutrality, as well as doubt, is I think a rationally unnatural towards an interlocutor's presentation of something as true' (Burge 2013: 242). But is it the mere fact that speaker and hearer are both rational creatures that renders this attitude unnatural? Or is it, as Reid perhaps implies, more a matter of how human animals relate to each other? It is hard to imagine intelligent creatures of any sort living together without some form of communication, without some way of letting each other know what they believe about the world. Nevertheless, there might be communities of rational beings with no interest in expressing their convictions through assertion, and who are not moved by each other's assertions as we are.

To illustrate these points, let's consider a view of testimony that is opposed to both Burge's and my own, according to which testimonial knowledge involves not inheriting your informant's belief but rather making an inference from the fact that they believe it together with the background information that you have on them. In the course of objecting to the idea that we are entitled to believe what we are told without any further grounds (at least in the absence of countervailing evidence), several recent authors ask us to imagine that we are presented with intelligible words or speech but outside the normal human context (e.g. utterances by aliens or announcements emanating from clouds and machines of mysterious origin).[14] Here, they say, we can no longer deploy the mass of background information about the reliability of various informants that our experience of human social life gives us. So, these authors conclude, we should adopt a non-committal attitude to what is (apparently) asserted. The wealth of experience that entitles us to trust perfect strangers in the matter of directions (etc.) has no application.

For these authors, the speaker's humanity matters in so far as it furnishes us with some positive evidence of their testimony's reliability, but our shared humanity might matter in a rather different way: it may function as a trigger to the comprehension of speech and in particular to appreciation of the *force* of a speech act. Describing our interactions with our least experienced interlocutors, namely our children, Reid tell us that:

It is not the words of the testifier but his belief that produces [this] belief in a child: For children soon learn to distinguish what is said in jest, from what is said in good earnest.

[14] See, for example (Lackey 2008: 168–75).

What appears to them to be said in jest produces no belief. They glory in showing that they are not to be imposed on. When the signs of belief in the speaker are ambiguous, it is pleasant to observe with what sagacity they pry into his features, to discern whether he really believes what he says, or only counterfeits belief. As soon as this point is determined, their belief is regulated by his. If he be doubtful, they are doubtful, if he be assured, they are assured. (Reid 2010: 87)

When adults are confronted by unusual or bizarre sources of testimony they face a similar situation. Having settled what is being said, they must still determine whether or not these things are being asserted, imagined, suspected, etc.

Such a source of testimony is described by Hume's Cleanthes. Suppose that in parallel to the natural human language of emotion:

there is a natural, universal, invariable language, common to every individual of the human race; and that books are natural productions, which perpetuate themselves in the same manner with animals and vegetables by descent and propagation... Suppose therefore that you enter into your library thus peopled by natural volumes, containing the most refined reason and most exquisite beauty: Could you possibly open one of them and doubt that its original cause bore the strongest analogy to mind and intelligence? When it reasons and discourses; when it expostulates, argues, and enforces its views and topics; when it applies sometimes to the pure intellect, sometimes to the affections; when it collects, disposes and adorns every consideration suited to the subject: could you persist in asserting that all this, at the bottom, had really no meaning and that the first formation of this volume in the loins of its original parent proceeded not from thought and design?
(Hume 1948: 27)[15]

Here we are dealing with statements produced by means of a mechanism unsuited (in our experience) to the purpose. Still, there may be enough to persuade us that the volume contains assertions, expressions of belief: the 'appeals to pure intellect' but also 'expostulations', appeals to the 'affections', and so forth. These words have a certain hold over us and signal that the text is a piece of testimony, a candidate for being taken on trust.

It may be objected that, for all we know, Hume's vegetable books could be novels or careful records of someone's dreams and yet have the same persuasive quality. Are we entitled to presume otherwise any more than to presume that a page found at random on the internet contains assertions rather than an artfully constructed story? This challenge gets its force by tapping into the experience we actually have of the internet, physical libraries, and so forth. Knowing the variety of books that are published, I know I must check which section of the library I am in before deciding how to take its contents—similarly for the internet—but to

---

[15] Cleanthes's point may not be endorsed by Hume, but there is no rebuttal.

insist on my adopting a non-committal attitude to the apparent force of *any* intelligible statement until I am independently confident of the mechanism that produced it would be like insisting that I remain agnostic about the contents of preservative memory because they might be the products of my own imagination (Burge 2013: 265–8). In the absence of any indication to the contrary we seem entitled to accept the appearance that Hume's vegetable books are indeed filled with assertions.

Once this is all conceded, it may still be wondered whether our entitlement to believe what is said in the absence of any other evidence on the matter can do much epistemological work. Are we ever really in the position of knowing nothing relevant to the credibility of an assertion? For instance, shouldn't our background knowledge of organic life lead us to doubt the credibility of Hume's books? The answer is not obvious, but the question seems a good one, and if some such question can be posed whenever the *prima facie* entitlement might come into play, what is the theoretical significance of this entitlement?

It is widely believed that we are *prima facie* entitled to rely on the deliverances of our senses: I'm entitled to believe that p on the basis of my experience as of p, provided I have no grounds for doubting the veridicality of that experience. Such an entitlement matters because it is very hard to see how one might otherwise ground reliance on sensory experience without courting circularity. In particular, those background beliefs that throw doubt on (or else support) the veridicality of a particular experience have their origin in some form of sensory experience. So the whole process of accepting or rejecting the deliverances of our senses can be rationally reconstructed only given a *prima facie* entitlement to rely on the senses.

The reasoning just rehearsed would stand even if the *prima facie* entitlement to rely on the deliverances of our senses were never the only consideration relevant to whether we ought to believe them on this occasion. The point generalizes. True, the idea of a *prima facie* entitlement to credit the assertions of others is less widely accepted (in part because it is less obvious that a rational reconstruction of our reliance on testimony is impossible without invoking reliance on testimony[16]), but it remains the case that even if there were no single instance in which our *prima facie* entitlement to rely on testimony were the only relevant consideration, such an entitlement might still be an indispensable element in any rational reconstruction of our epistemological position. Hence the theoretical significance of the entitlement is secure (Burge 2013: 264–72).

---

[16] For discussion of this see (Coady 1992: Chapter 4) and (Lackey 2008: Chapter 6).

10.3 Objections and Clarifications

The inheritance model outlined in Section 10.2 has encountered various lines of criticism and the present section is devoted to rebutting them. In Section 10.4 I consider the assurance model of testimony and argue for the superiority of the inheritance model, but here I'll be contrasting the inheritance model with a different competitor, one with which it is perhaps more easily confused, namely, a purely externalist or reliabilist model of testimony.

Some have argued that it is simply inappropriate to speak of the transmission or inheritance of justification. A *justification* for a belief is something to which the believer has access, yet the whole point of testimony is to enable us to benefit from the evidence available to others but not to ourselves. This way of thinking leaves the epistemologist of testimony with just two options: either they find some other form of justification which is available to the hearer and which justifies their reliance on the speaker (viz. evidence of their reliability) or else they maintain that testimony can work, can be a source of knowledge without the transmission of justification.

To certain authors, the inheritance model seems to be taking the latter route (Barnett 2015: 356–69) and my emphasis here on the role of shared emotional psychology might encourage that interpretation. If human beings are, in general, reliable on the subjects they choose to make assertions about then the instincts of veracity and credulity described in Section 10.2 together produce a generally secure conduit of information. Furthermore, if we agree with the externalist that one can know things without having any justification for believing them providing one's knowledge is the product of a reliable process of belief acquisition, then testimony, so understood, may transmit knowledge. But, says the objector, we should not pretend that testimony also transmits justification.

One might respond to this worry by drawing a distinction between justification and entitlement. Burge tells us that although both justification and entitlement 'have positive force in rationally supporting a propositional attitude or cognitive practice, and in constituting an epistemic right to it, entitlements are epistemic rights or warrants that need not be understood by or even accessible to the subject' (Burge 2013: 230). As already noted, I agree with Burge that an entitlement to rely on testimony (or memory) is not a principle of inference that the subject employs in reasoning from the fact that they hear (or recall) that p to the conclusion that p. Nevertheless, being so entitled involves more than having one's belief caused by a reliable mechanism. According to the inheritance model, the mechanism in play in both testimony and memory transmits knowledge precisely by transmitting the belief *together with its justificational status* from speaker to hearer. Hence, knowledge derived from both testimony and memory is rationally supported. How so?

Memory works by preserving a belief, and to remember that p is to be aware that you already believe it, that this belief was installed in memory. Furthermore, you can't install beliefs in memory unless you already believe them and you can't believe them at will: only beliefs with some appearance of rational support may be installed in memory. Thus, the mechanism by which belief is installed in memory is rationality preserving in that it is sensitive to whatever justificational status the belief already possesses. And, in relying on this mechanism, the remembering subject defers to their earlier self for the justification of this belief.

As I argue elsewhere, these features of preservative memory are replicated in the case of testimony Chapter 9: Section 9.4. Because the expression of belief in assertion is intentional it is rational to express a belief only if the belief expressed is itself rational, and so the mechanism by which belief is transmitted in testimony is, in the same way, sensitive to the justificational status of the belief.[17] And the subject who bases a belief on testimony is aware of their reliance on this mechanism and defers to their informant for the justification of this belief. So the case for regarding testimony as rationality preserving is much the same as that for memory.

This entitlement to defer to another for one's justification is what distinguishes the inheritance model from a brute externalism about memory or testimony. I reject the idea that a belief may constitute knowledge without any justification—there must be justification for this belief in the system and no believer will feel entitled to their belief unless they suppose this to be so—but, if preservative memory is a possibility, you must also be able to benefit from a justification that is unavailable to you, namely, by passing the buck of justification to someone to whom the justification is or was available. This opens up the following possibility: two people may be equally entitled to transfer the responsibility of justifying a given belief onto their earlier selves (or onto another informant), but whilst the first ends up with a justified belief, the second inherits an unjustified belief.[18]

On the inheritance model there are two questions one can ask about a belief preserved in memory or testimony (Owens 2000: 138–42, 157–8, and 170). First: does the belief transmitted by memory or testimony remain rational throughout the process of transmission? My answer is that it does, provided the belief was both rational when formed and has been reliably transmitted by the mechanism. I now have a rational belief in Theorem T because I once proved the theorem for

---

[17] This is consistent with the possibility of rational lying since liars merely purport to express their beliefs.

[18] (Barnett 2015: 358–63) regards this implication as a problem.

myself and have successfully preserved the belief (though not the proof) in memory. And you rationally believe Theorem T because you once took my word for it, the testimonial mechanism worked well (no misunderstandings, etc.) and you thereby inherited a rational belief from me.

But there is the further issue of whether it is reasonable for the believer to acquire the belief from testimony or else to maintain the belief in memory. The rationality of the maintenance/acquisition of a given belief is governed by the *prima facie* entitlement to presume on the reliability of the relevant transmission mechanism, an entitlement that is defeated under certain conditions. The integrity or defeat of this entitlement is independent of the justificational status of the belief transmitted. Thus, it may be irrational to acquire or maintain a rational belief and rational to acquire or maintain an irrational belief. Acknowledging this complexity is the key to avoiding some potential difficulties for the inheritance model.

To see how these two aspects of the rationality of belief interact, suppose that when I told you about Theorem T, I had some reason to doubt my memory on this point. Or suppose that you had some independent reason to doubt my assertions about T. These reasons for doubt were good ones in the sense that they deprived me (or you) of the entitlement to presume on the reliability of memory/testimony and should have blocked the transmission of the relevant belief, though they didn't due to our inattentiveness, wishfulness, or whatever. But the reasons for doubt were also misleading in that both my memory and my testimony were, in fact, perfectly reliable on the point. What should we say here?

Both my belief and yours are perfectly rational beliefs. After all, my belief in T was soundly based, was successfully transmitted to you, and nothing has subsequently emerged to undermine the cogency of the proof. What did emerge was misleading evidence which ought to have raised doubts but did not. This shows that one or other of us was not entirely reasonable in believing T. One of us irrationally adopted or irrationally preserved a perfectly rational belief but without affecting the rationality of the belief preserved. If, for example, it was me who ignored the misleading evidence about my memory, then I cannot benefit from the justification available to my earlier self since I am no longer entitled to defer to my earlier self. But, if the misleading evidence about my memory is unavailable to you, this leaves the status of your belief in T unaffected in both dimensions. You are entitled to defer to my earlier self for the justification of the belief you inherit from me, a justification which is successfully transmitted to you. Neither you nor your belief are impugned by my irresponsibility.[19]

---

[19] Is one of these two aspects of the rationality of belief more fundamental than the other? I doubt that there is any clear answer to this. It might be thought that believer rationality is more

With the distinction between two aspects of the rationality of belief in hand we can respond to a couple of worries about the inheritance model. One worry concerns how, in a case of testimony, your belief in theorem T could be justified on the very same basis as my belief in that theorem. After all, you base your belief on your experience of my saying that T is true and such an experience played no role in my acquisition of that belief.[20] Here, we must separate the grounds that determine the rationality of the belief transmitted (namely, the proof) from the grounds on which you acquired that belief. The latter may involve sense experience and so your entitlement to form the belief on the basis of my testimony may be partly empirical. Nevertheless, the rationality of the transmitted belief depends on the cogency of the proof alone.

Another worry applies equally to memory and testimony.[21] On the inheritance model, the justificational force of the grounds on which a certain belief was acquired is preserved in both testimony and memory, and so, provided these mechanisms reliably transmit the relevant belief, the rationality of that belief should not vary across time or between persons. Now consider the defeaters relevant to one's entitlement to rely on either memory or testimony. These clearly can vary over time and from person to person quite independently both of the grounds on which the belief was originally acquired and of the reliability of the transmission mechanism. For example, whether it is reasonable for me to retain a certain belief in memory can vary over time, depending on whether certain (misleading) defeaters have appeared, even though the rationality of the retained belief remains unchanged. And it can be reasonable for the speaker to believe that p but not the hearer or vice versa because different defeaters

---

fundamental than belief rationality, since the rationality of a belief depends on the rationality of its formation (or initial acquisition). On the other hand, belief rationality might be thought more fundamental than believer rationality on the grounds that one can't reasonably acquire, preserve, or inherit a belief that one thinks it would be irrational to believe. I also leave open the issue as to which of these two notions is involved in the attribution of knowledge. Does knowledge require belief rationality, believer rationality, or both? For example, does a rational belief, successfully preserved in memory in the face of good though misleading grounds for doubt constitute knowledge? As already noted, the inheritance model is primarily a model of the transmission of justification rather than of knowledge.

[20] In earlier work, I responded to this worry by maintaining that sensory experience of testimony was 'no part of my reason for believing the proposition in question' but was simply a stage in the psychological mechanism by which the belief was transmitted (Owens 2000: 169–70). In saying this, I was inspired by Burge's claim that testimonial entitlement is non-empirical. Burge has recently retracted this claim (Burge 2013: 273–84) and, I now think, an advocate of the inheritance model need place no reliance on it. It is enough to distinguish the (always partly empirical) nature of the entitlement to accept someone's testimony from the (perhaps non-empirical) nature of the justification whose force is thereby transmitted.

[21] This is raised as an objection to the inheritance model in (Lackey 2008: 59–71 and 251–63).

are available to each of them, even though, were the belief to be transmitted regardless, it would be as rational in the one mind as in the other. Apparent variations in the rationality of the transmitted belief disappear once we distinguish the rationality of the belief transmitted from the rationality of its transmission and thus pose no problem for the inheritance model.[22]

10.4 Assertion and Assurance

Until now, we have been focused on assertion, defending the notion that testimony is a distinctive epistemic resource, one that we tap by crediting the assertions of others and so inheriting their beliefs. There is a rarer phenomenon, perhaps better deserving the title of 'testimony'. Especially when our assertions may otherwise be doubted, we sometimes offer our audience an additional assurance or a guarantee of the truth of what we are saying. This assurance acquires a legal form in the act of swearing to what you say in court, but it is familiar from daily life. People guarantee that their assertions are correct and they are often believed on the basis of that extra assurance. On what I'll call the *assurance theory* (or *model*) of testimony, the acquisition of testimonial knowledge involves such guarantees.[23]

How are assertion and assurance related? Perhaps the former is necessary for the latter in that we can only give someone an assurance that p is true by asserting that p (albeit in a special context or with a special emphasis).[24] However this may be, I want first to argue that assertion and assurance are distinct speech acts and then to criticize what I'll call the pure assurance theory of testimony, namely, the view that *all* testimony is assurance, that whenever an audience 'takes the speaker's word for it' they must be treating their assertions as assurances.

---

[22] Graham describes cases in which the hearer comes to know that p by taking the speaker's word for it that p even though the speaker does not themselves know that p because they cannot rule out some relevant alternative to p. Here the speaker *is* justified in believing something of the form 'p v q' and, by taking their word for it, the hearer inherits their justification for that proposition. Given that the hearer already knows q to be false, they are, furthermore, entitled to believe that p on the basis of the inherited belief that p v q (Graham 2000: 374).

[23] Several authors have suggested that an assertion always involves a promise that what is asserted is true: (Ross 1930: 21), (Searle 1969: 66), and (Fried 1978: 57). (Ross 1986: 79–80) and (Carson 2006: 292) develop this idea in more detail. The assurance theorist need not endorse such a general claim about assertion.

[24] Can one assure A that p or offer A a guarantee of p's truth without asserting that p? This possibility is invoked as an argument against assurance theories of assertion by Pagin (2004: 838–42). For a response to Pagin, see (MacFarlane 2011: 90–5). At least one assurance theorist is ready to embrace the possibility that you might sincerely assure someone of p without yourself believing that p (Hinchman 2014: 9).

10.4.1 Assertion without Assurance

Any model of testimony provides an account of how the speaker offers testimony and of how the hearer is meant to react to it. On the pure assurance model, that will be a matter of first explaining what is involved in offering someone an assurance and then explaining what is involved in trusting (or accepting) that assurance. For the assurance theory, guaranteeing p's truth involves more than (intentionally) expressing one's belief in p, and trusting that guarantee involves more than (knowingly) inheriting the belief expressed. So much is clear, but it is less clear what more is involved. Some guidance is provided by the parallel that assurance theorists often draw between testimony and promise. There are various accounts of what is involved in making a promise and of how promises affect the normative situation. On the whole, assurance theorists of testimony do not discuss these matters in any detail, nor do they commit themselves to any particular account of promissory obligation. In the interests of accurate exposition, I shall try to avoid controversial claims about the nature of promissory obligation.

It is generally agreed that the promisor does something which (usually) makes it the case that they would be wronging the promisee should they fail to fulfil their promise. Views differ over what that something is. On the *performative* model of promise, the promisor communicates the intention of hereby making it the case that they would be wronging the promisee by not fulfilling their promise (Owens 2012: Chapter 8).[25] On the *reliance* model of promise, the promisor communicates the intention of doing what they are promising to do and invites the promisee to rely on their executing this intention.[26] We will assume for the sake of argument that each of these acts may, in the right circumstances, oblige the speaker to follow through and so each may count as a promise. Our question is this: does the transmission of knowledge by testimony require the speaker to perform an act of *either* sort?

When introducing his principle of veracity, Reid emphasizes the instinctual nature of the desire to tell the truth. He then considers the objection:

---

[25] One can treat testimonial assertion as a performative without assimilating it to a promise. For example, one might regard it as a verdictive rather than a commissive, to use Austin's helpful classification (Austin 1961: Lecture 12). See also McMyler's assimilation of testimony to command (McMyler 2011), but, amongst those who wish to treat testimonial assertion as a performative, the promissory analogy is the most prevalent.

[26] For an application of the performative model of promise to assertion, see (MacFarlane 2011: 90–5). For an application of something more like the reliance model to testimony see (Pink 2009: 394 and 409–10). I am drastically simplifying the logical geography of the promising literature. For a full discussion, see (Owens 2012: Parts 2 and 3).

That men be influenced by moral or political considerations to speak truth and therefore that their doing so is no proof of such an original principle as we have mentioned; I answer, first that moral and political considerations can have no influence until we arrive at years of understanding and reflection; and it is certain from experience that children keep to truth invariably before they are capable of being influenced by such considerations. Secondly when we are influenced by moral and political considerations, we must be conscious of that influence and capable of perceiving it upon reflection. Now when I reflect upon my actions most attentively, I am not conscious that in speaking truth I am influenced on ordinary occasions by any motive moral or political. I find that truth is always at the door of my lips and goes forth spontaneously if not held back. It requires neither good nor bad intention to bring it forth but only that I be artless and undesigning.
(Reid 1997: 193)[27]

On the performative model of testimony, the speaker must intend to put themselves under an obligation to their audience. On the reliance model of testimony, the speaker must intend to induce reliance in their audience. Reid's observations suggest that both are wrong: the analogy between testimony and promise underplays the sheer spontaneity of truthful assertion, a spontaneity that is largely unhindered in children and remains the default posture in adult life. When making an assertion, the speaker need only intend to express their view.

Though people are generally obliged to be truthful, it is unusual for people to tell the truth as they see it because they feel obliged to tell the truth: veracity is instinctual. Given a suitable audience and a topic of mutual interest, the speaker feels some inclination to hold forth simply in order to say what they think on the matter. Even when they don't expect to be believed or else are 'preaching to the choir' (and so there is no chance of misleading anyone) they may still wish to state their view. And since it is their beliefs they are expressing, they are *ipso facto* trying to be accurate about how things are. A desire to express what you think involves a desire to be both sincere in speech and accurate in what you say. There are cases in which we are tempted to exaggerate, mislead, or represent mere opinions as considered judgements, and the motive of duty may be needed to stop us, but these are exceptional.

---

[27] This quotation comes from Reid's *Inquiry*. In his later *Essay*, Reid treats 'the communication of knowledge of facts by testimony' and 'entering into engagements by promise' as on a par (Reid 2010: 333). Reid does still say that 'the things essential to human society, I mean good faith on the one part and trust on the other, are formed by nature in the minds of children, before they are capable of knowing their utility or being influenced by considerations of duty or interest' (Reid 2010: 335), but he goes on to maintain that promising (at least) involves the 'will to be bound' (Reid 2010: 336). If so, it is hard to see how a child could understand promising well enough to either make or trust a promise without deploying the idea of obligation (Reid 2010: 340). This apparent inconsistency can be resolved by abandoning the parallel between testimony and promise.

In this respect, promises are rather different. Promises are frequently given and accepted where (a) the audience has an interest in the promisor's performance, and (b) the audience can't assume that the promisor has sufficient motive to perform independently of a binding promise. Doing what you promised to do simply (or largely) because you promised to do it is quite normal, and in trusting a promise, the promisee often relies on such conscientiousness, on the promisor's desire not to abuse the promisee's trust.[28] If I am right, sincerity in speech need not present itself to the speaker as something they owe to their audience and we need not assume that it does so present itself whenever we trust what they tell us.[29] The normal motive for truth-telling is a simple desire to express your view. Even when dealing with a person of dubious character, we are prepared to trust what they tell us on all sorts of matters (directions, etc.) because we assume that they want to tell us what they know, that they want to be open with us. Perhaps conscientiousness would not prevent them from lying (or bullshitting) about other topics—they might never feel remotely inclined to tell the truth because of some obligation to tell the truth—but this does not make us distrust what they tell us about where the station is, and so forth.

10.4.2 Testimony without Assurance

Some recent defenders of the assurance model have adopted what I've called the pure assurance theory of testimony. They argue that, unless an assertion constitutes an assurance, we can learn from it only by treating it as a form of inductive evidence. In such cases, they maintain, we cannot 'take the speaker's word for it', since the speaker is not offering us any guarantee of the truth of what they say. Instead the audience must decide whether the speaker's expression of belief in p constitutes a sufficiently reliable indicator of the truth of p. In the rest of this section I'll consider purported examples of assertion without assurance and ask how we can learn from them. We shall find either that these examples do not involve the expression of belief and therefore are not really assertions or else that the audience can in fact 'take the speaker's word for it' (in line with the inheritance theory) despite the absence of assurance. Therefore, the pure assurance theory should be rejected.

Moran describes a student in a history class reciting what he has been taught in an oral examination (Moran 2005a: 330). Moran says that the student is making

---

[28] I say 'frequently' and 'often' because I think that the promisee has an interest in binding the promisor (an 'authority interest') that is not just an interest in securing performance. See (Owens 2012: Chapter 6). If so, this only reinforces the contrast with assertion.

[29] This is consistent with the claim that believing an assertion counts as trusting the assertion only when the speaker is in fact obliged to be truthful.

assertions here even though the examination is not an inquiry into the student's own convictions but merely a test of his ability to recall the contents of the class. I would argue that the student is not making assertions *in his own voice* because the student does not represent himself as personally believing what he is saying (any more than a spokesman who reads a statement on behalf of a client). That is why his audience can't acquire knowledge by believing what *he* says, by treating what he says as things he asserts. Perhaps the student is speaking for someone else (e.g. the teacher or the author of the class text), in which case it is possible to take *their* word for it by accepting what the student says provided one trusts the person (or institution) whose mouthpiece he is.

In other instances cited by Moran, the speaker is indeed expressing their own convictions but makes it clear that they do not wish the audience to trust their assertions but rather to arrive at the relevant belief in some other way ((Moran 2005a: 328–9) and (Moran 2005b: 8)). Moran says of these cases also that the audience cannot acquire knowledge by trusting the speaker. I think Moran is wrong about that. I agree that, when a teacher runs through a mathematical proof on the board, the class are meant to believe the conclusion because they grasp the proof, not because they take the teacher's word for it.[30] Nevertheless, so long as the teacher represents themselves as expressing their own belief, the audience are in a position to take the demonstrator's word for it, even though they are not being invited to do so. And if they do trust the speaker, they can thereby acquire knowledge of the theorem without having grasped the proof (though this would deprive the whole exercise of its educational value).[31] Trust in an assertion does not require an invitation to trust, it only requires that the speech act is presented as an expression of belief, i.e. is an assertion.

The same applies to cases in which the speaker is explicitly withholding the element of guarantee from their assertion. Hinchman asks us to consider the statement: 'The Liar Paradox was discussed much earlier in history but don't take my word for it, consult Diogenes Laertius' (Hinchman 2005: 571). Here the words 'The Liar Paradox was discussed much earlier in history' may still possess assertoric force, and so long as this is so, you can take the speaker's word for it, their invitation to do otherwise notwithstanding. A speaker can't reserve the right

---

[30] (Moran 2005a: 344–5) takes the line that in such a case the audience is not being *told* anything, whilst (Hinchman 2005: 571) concedes that they are.

[31] Suppose the proof is invalid and that the speaker is lying when they utter 'therefore'. The speaker couldn't excuse themselves simply by observing that their manifest intention was that the audience inspect the proof and make up their own mind rather than take the speaker's word for it. So long as the speaker asserts that p, the audience can take their word for it that p, and if the speaker untruthfully asserts that p, that alone puts them in the wrong.

to be insincere or inaccurate in what they genuinely assert, though they may suggest that you learn (or confirm) the truth in other ways. As Hinchman himself observes, the effect of adding 'but don't take my word for it' is quite different from the effect of adding 'but perhaps I'm confusing the Liar with one of the Heraclitean Paradoxes'. The effect of the latter is to *retract* the expression of belief and thereby pre-empt anyone's taking your word on the point.[32]

I'll wrap up this section by introducing a further instance of testimony without assurance, namely, where you are the recipient of an assertion that was not meant for you. A guarantee is like a promise in that it must be directed towards a specific audience, an audience that is wronged when the assurance goes unfulfilled. By failing to perform, a promisor thereby wrongs the promisee. The promisor does not in the same way wrong those who merely overhear their promise (whom they did not intend to address) since the promisor did not promise *them* anything. At least the promisor does not wrong them simply in virtue of having breached a promise. The promisor might owe some duty of care to those who foreseeably learn of their statement, but, unlike a promissory obligation, such a duty could usually be discharged with a timely warning of non-performance.

An assurance theorist who models testimony on promise must predict a corresponding asymmetry when it comes to testimonial assurance: those addressed by the speaker can benefit from the assurance in a way that those who merely overhear cannot. Supporters of the pure assurance theory of testimony must conclude that (unlike those to whom the testimony is addressed) overhearers cannot acquire knowledge by testimony.[33] By contrast, opponents of the pure assurance theory may allow addressees and overhearers to learn from the speaker's statement in much the same fashion: testimonial knowledge is a public good from which overhearers cannot be excluded (Fricker 2006: 598). On the latter view, if the

---

[32] This raises the issue of how we are to understand the retraction of an assertion (Moran 2005b: 21, 27). Macfarlane contends that a performative account of assertion like the assurance theory has an advantage on this point in that, whilst assurances may be retracted, it is unclear how we should understand the retraction of an act of expression (Macfarlane 2011: 84, 91). I see no great difference between assurance and expression on this point: if there is a puzzle here, it applies equally to both. An offer can be retracted before it is accepted and an expression of belief can turn doubtful before completed; the tricky case is where an assertion has been made and is later withdrawn. Whatever is going on here, the assurance theory is not well placed to explain it. You can't deprive either your earlier promises or your previous assertions of their normative significance simply by retracting them and so you can't evade responsibility for another's earlier trust simply by repudiating those promises or assertions. At best you can pre-empt continued or new instances of unfounded trust and limit the damage done by another's earlier reliance on your word.

[33] (Hinchman 2005: 569), (Faulkner 2007: 542, 554–6), (McMyler 2011: 66, 101–12), and (McMyler 2013).

intended audience has a special claim on the speaker, this is a matter of mores or morals, and of no direct concern to the epistemologist of testimony.[34]

Opponents of the pure assurance theory are right to insist that all who hear an assertion can learn from it, and, I would argue, the inheritance model described in earlier sections provides the correct account of how this knowledge is made available. Anyone who witnesses an intentional expression of belief can inherit the belief expressed (together with its justificational status) and thereby come to know what the speaker knows, whether or not they are part of the intended audience. Assurance theorists may still be right that speakers sometimes go beyond the expression of belief by offering their intended audience an assurance of the truth of what is asserted. It might even be that such directed guarantees change the epistemological as well as the moral situation, though I leave that issue open.[35] In the remainder of this section I make the case against the pure assurance theory.

It is generally agreed that all who hear a given assertion can, by treating the assertion as inductive evidence for the proposition asserted, learn that the asserted proposition is true. The present dispute concerns how its assertion might give hearers knowledge of the asserted proposition in another way. Our answer to the question about overhearers will be influenced by our views on that dispute but there are certain pre-theoretical markers of the reception of testimony and we may usefully ask whether the overhearers bear them. For example, can overhearers *trust* the speaker, can they *believe* the speaker, or *take their word for it* even though this word was not addressed to them? I'm happy to apply these idioms to both intended and unintended members of the audience; indeed, I feel no awkwardness about employing them in a case where the statement in question was made with the intention of addressing no one at all: the intentional expression of belief does not require the intention to address some audience. For example one may trust a secret diary, believe the writer, take their word for it, and so forth, even though (as one knows) the writer was quite determined to have the diary destroyed before anyone could see it (Chapter 9: Section 9.3).

Proponents of the pure assurance theory have responded that, for it to be a source of testimonial knowledge, an assertion must have an intended audience,

---

[34] (Fricker 2006: 597–9) and (Lackey 2008: 27–36, 230–40).

[35] We might be able to use inductive evidence about the reliability of people's assurances in order to glean information from them (Fricker 2006: 600–3), though Moran argues that the attitude of regarding people's assurances as an indication of what is likely to be so is parasitic on a more basic attitude, that of trusting the assurance, of regarding an assurance as a reason to believe it will be fulfilled simply because it is binding on the speaker (Moran 2005b: 23).

though the audience intended could be the writer's own future self or some vaguely conceived future person.[36] But need a reader satisfy themselves that the writer did not plan to destroy the work as soon as it was written before they can trust it? And even where there is an intended audience, the assurance model will not apply unless the reader of the diary is part of the audience that the writer meant to address. Yet it seems I can trust the diary, take the writer's word for it about where they were on the day of the murder, believe them on this point even though I know the writer specifically intended that I not see their diary.[37]

Pure assurance theorists have drawn our attention to various other differences between the intended and the unintended audience. Where real, the relevance of these differences to the epistemology of testimony remains unclear.[38] For example, if you rip open my secret diary and are seriously misled by what it says, it would be a bit rich for you to blame me, to complain to me, to demand that I justify what I say in the diary, and so forth. (Not so if I voluntarily showed you the thing.) But these differences seem rooted in norms of privacy and in thoughts about how our responsibility for undesirable consequences depends on our ability to control them, rather than in the workings of testimony (Nickel 2012: 309–15).

To sum up, the accounts of testimony here considered vary in how they understand the epistemological significance of the act of testifying to the truth of a proposition. Some treat a speaker's testimony just as a more or less reliable indication of how things are with both the speaker and the world. Some treat the act of testifying as a form of communication, as a way of openly letting your audience know what you believe about a certain matter. Some treat the act of

---

[36] McMyler (2011: 105–6), (McMyler 2013: 1076–7), Hinchman (2005: 556 n.13), and (Hinchman 2014: 14 n.37).

[37] (Fricker 2006: 597) maintains that a statement 'must have an intended audience. Without this there is no distinction between asserting that p...and merely voicing a thought of or wish that p'. See also (Moran 2005b: 22). Yet we make that distinction all the time when reading books and it is unclear why the discovery that a diary was meant to be secret would make this task any more difficult.

[38] Moran maintains that the intended audience has a special status in that they (and not the overhearers) have a 'right of complaint' when the assurance turns out to be unfounded (Moran 2005b: 22). This is so in some cases but not in others, and who has the right of complaint depends on ethical rather than epistemological factors (Lackey 2008: 236). Moran admits that one who overhears an assurance can nevertheless 'avail themselves' of the assurance and thereby access the special way of learning from another that such an assurance provides. So it turns out that overhearers don't need the 'right of complaint' in order to be able to take the speaker's word for it. McMyler rejects Moran's concession (McMyler 2011: 103 n.19).

testifying as an act which operates on the ethical situation and changes what the speaker owes the hearer. My own suggestion is that the special significance of the act of testifying depends rather on its being an expressive action and that progress in the epistemology of testimony awaits a deeper understanding of that notion.[39]

---

[39] Thanks to John Macfarlane, Peter Graham, Nishi Shah, Conor McHugh, Collin O'Neil, Matthew Parrott, and Ben McMyler for comments on earlier drafts.

Bibliography

Adams, R. (1976) 'Motive Utilitarianism', *Journal of Philosophy* 73: 467–81.
Adler, J. (2002) *Belief's Own Ethics* (Cambridge: MIT Press).
Aquinas, T. (2010) *Summa Theologiae*, trans. Fathers of the English Dominican Province (Claremont: Coyote Canyon Press).
Arpaly, N. (2003) *Unprincipled Virtue* (Oxford: Oxford University Press).
Austin, J.L. (1961) *How To Do Things With Words* (Oxford: Oxford University Press).
Barnett, D. (2015) 'Is Memory Testimony From One's Former Self?', *Philosophical Review* 124: 353–92.
Bergson, H. (1991) *Matter and Memory* (New York: Zone Books).
Boghossian, P. (2014) 'What is Inference?', *Philosophical Studies* 169: 1–18.
Boyle, M. (2011) '"Making Up Your Mind" and the Activity of Reason', *Philosopher's Imprint* 11: 1–24.
Brandom, R. (1983) 'Asserting', *Nous* 17: 637–50.
Bratman, M. (1987) *Intentions, Plans and Practical Reason* (Cambridge: Harvard University Press).
Bratman, M. (1999) *Faces of Intention* (Cambridge: Cambridge University Press).
Broome, J. (2001) 'Normative Practical Reasoning', *Proceedings of the Aristotelian Society Supplementary Volume* 75: 175–93.
Broughton, J. (2002) *Descartes's Method of Doubt* (Princeton: Princeton University Press).
Brown, J. (2008) 'Subject-Sensitive Invariantism and the Knowledge Norm for Practical Reasoning', *Nous* 42: 167–98.
Burge, T. (2013) *Cognition Through Understanding* (Oxford: Oxford University Press).
Burnyeat, M. (1982) 'Idealism and Greek Philosophy: What Descartes Saw and Berkeley Missed' in *Idealism Past and Present*, Ed. G. Vesey (Cambridge: Cambridge University Press).
Burnyeat, M. (1997) 'The sceptic in his place and time' in *The Original Sceptics*, Eds M. Burnyeat and M. Frede (Indianapolis: Hackett).
Carroll, L. (1895) 'What the Tortoise Said to Achilles', *Mind* 4: 278–80.
Carson, T. (2006) 'The Definition of Lying', *Nous* 40: 284–306.
Coady, C. (1992) *Testimony* (Oxford: Oxford University Press).
Cohen, J. (1974) 'Guessing', *Proceedings of the Aristotelian Society* 74: 189–210.
Craig, E. (1990) *Knowledge and the State of Nature* (Oxford: Oxford University Press).
Curley, E. (1978) *Descartes Against the Sceptics* (Cambridge: Harvard University Press).
Curley, E. (1993) 'Certainty: psychological, moral and metaphysical' in *Essays on the Philosophy of Science of Rene Descartes*, Ed. S. Voss (Oxford: Oxford University Press).
Davidson, D. (1980) *Essays on Actions and Events* (Oxford: Oxford University Press).
Davis, W. (2003) *Meaning, Expression and Thought* (Cambridge: Cambridge University Press).

Descartes, R. (1984) *The Philosophical Writings of Descartes Volume II* (trans.) J. Cottingham, R. Stoothoff, and D. Murdoch (Cambridge: Cambridge University Press).
Descartes, R. (1985) *The Philosophical Writings of Descartes Volume I* (trans.) J. Cottingham, R. Stoothoff, and D. Murdoch (Cambridge: Cambridge University Press).
Descartes, R. (1991) *The Philosophical Writings of Descartes Volume III* (trans.) J. Cottingham, R. Stoothoff, D. Murdoch, and A. Kenny (Cambridge: Cambridge University Press).
Dretske, F. (1971) 'Reasons, Knowledge and Probability', *Philosophy of Science* 38: 216–20.
Empiricus, S. (1994) *Outlines of Scepticism* (Cambridge: Cambridge University Press).
Fantl, J. and M. McGrath (2002) 'Evidence, Pragmatics and Justification', *Philosophical Review* 111: 67–94.
Fantl, J. and M. McGrath (2007) 'On Pragmatic Encroachment in Epistemology', *Philosophy and Phenomenological Research* 75: 558–89.
Fantl, J. and M. McGrath (2009) *Knowledge in an Uncertain World* (Oxford: Oxford University Press).
Faulkner, P. (2007) 'What is Wrong With Lying?', *Philosophy and Phenomenological Research* 75: 535–57.
Finkelstein, D. (2003) *Expression and the Inner* (Cambridge: Harvard University Press).
Fogelin, R. (1993) 'Hume's Scepticism' in *Cambridge Companion to Hume*, Ed. D. Fate-Norton (Cambridge: Cambridge University Press).
Foley, R. (1993) *Working Without a Net* (Oxford: Oxford University Press).
Foley, R. (2001) 'The Foundational Role of Epistemology in General Theory of Rationality' in *Virtue Epistemology*, Eds Fairweather and Zagzebski (Oxford: Oxford University Press).
Foucault, M. (1998) *Aesthetics* (London: Penguin).
Frankfurt, H. (1970) *Demons, Dreamers and Madmen* (Indianapolis: Bobbs-Merrill).
Freud, S. (1961) *The Future of an Illusion* (London: Norton).
Fricker, E. (2006) 'Second-Hand Knowledge', *Philosophy and Phenomenological Research* 73: 592–618.
Fried, C. (1978) *Right and Wrong* (Cambridge: Harvard University Press).
Gilson, E. (1947) *Discours De La Methode: Text et Commentaire* (Paris: J. Vrin).
Goldman, A. (1980) 'The Internalist Conception of Justification' in *Midwest Studies in Philosophy V*, Eds P. French, T. Uehling, and H. Wettstein (Minneapolis: University of Minnesota).
Gordon, R. (1987) *The Structure of Emotion* (Cambridge: Cambridge University Press).
Graham, P. (2000) 'Conveying Information', *Synthese* 123: 365–92.
Greenspan P. (1988) *Emotions and Reasons* (New York: Routledge).
Grice, P. (1989) *Studies in the Way of Words* (Cambridge: Harvard University Press).
Grimm, S. (2015) 'Knowledge, Practical Interests and Rising Tides' in *Epistemic Evaluation*, Eds J. Greco and D. Henderson (Oxford: Oxford University Press).
Harman, G. (1980) 'Reasoning and Evidence One Does Not Possess' in *Midwest Studies in Philosophy*, Volume V, Eds P. French, T. Uehling, and H. Wettstein (Minneapolis: University of Minnesota Press).
Harman, G. (1986) *Change in View* (Cambridge: MIT Press).

Harman, G. (1999) *Reasoning, Meaning and Mind* (Oxford: Oxford University Press).
Hart, H. (2008) *Punishment and Responsibility*, Second Edition (Oxford: Oxford University Press).
Hawthorne, J. (2004) *Knowledge and Lotteries* (Oxford: Oxford University Press).
Hawthorne, J. and J. Stanley (2008) 'Knowledge and Action', *Journal of Philosophy* 105: 571–90.
Hayek, F. (1960) *The Constitution of Liberty* (London: Routledge).
Hieronymi, P. (2008) 'Responsibility for Believing', *Synthese* 161: 357–73.
Hieronymi, P. (2014) 'Reflection and Responsibility', *Philosophy and Public Affairs* 42: 3–41.
Hinchman, E. (2005) 'Telling as Inviting to Trust', *Philosophy and Phenomenological Research* 70: 562–87.
Hinchman, E. (2014) 'Assurance and Warrant', *Philosopher's Imprint* 14: 1–58.
Holton, R. (2009) *Willing, Wanting, Waiting* (Oxford: Oxford University Press).
Hookway, C. (1990) *Scepticism* (London: Routledge).
Humberstone, L. (1992) 'Direction of Fit', *Mind* 101: 59–83.
Hume, D. (1948) *Dialogues Concerning Natural Religion* (New York: Hafner).
Hume, D. (1975) *Enquiry Concerning Human Understanding*, Ed. L. Selby-Bigge (Oxford: Oxford University Press).
Hume, D. (1978) *Treatise of Human Nature*, Ed. L. Selby-Bigge (Oxford: Oxford University Press).
Hurley, S. (1993) *Natural Reasons* (Oxford: Oxford University Press).
Hursthouse, R. (1991) 'Arational Actions', *Journal of Philosophy* 88: 57–68.
James, W. (1950) *The Principles of Psychology*, Volume 1 (New York: Dover).
James, W. (1956) *The Will to Believe* (New York: Dover).
Kant, I. (1996) *Practical Philosophy* (Cambridge: Cambridge University Press).
Kaplan, M. (1981) 'A Bayesian Theory of Rational Acceptance', *Journal of Philosophy* 78: 305–30.
Kavka, G. (1983) 'The Toxin Puzzle', *Analysis* 43: 33–6.
Kolodny, N. (2005) 'Why Be Rational?', *Mind* 114: 509–63.
Korsgaard, C. (1996) *The Sources of Normativity* (Cambridge: Cambridge University Press).
Korsgaard, C. (2009) 'The Activity of Reason', *Proceedings and Addresses of the American Philosophical Association* 83: 23–43.
Lackey, J. (2008) *Learning from Words* (Oxford: Oxford University Press).
MacArthur, D. (2003) 'The Seriousness of Doubt in the First Meditation', *Canadian Journal of Philosophy* 33: 159–82.
MacFarlane, J. (2011) 'What is Assertion?' in *Assertion: New Philosophical Essays*, Eds J. Brown and H. Cappelen (Oxford: Oxford University Press).
Marshall, J. (1998) *Descartes's Moral Theory* (Ithaca: Cornell University Press).
McDowell, J. (1998) *Meaning, Knowledge and Reality* (Cambridge: Harvard University Press).
McHugh, C. (2011) 'Judging as a Non-Voluntary Action', *Philosophical Studies* 152: 245–69.
McIntyre, A. (2006) 'What is Wrong With Weakness of Will?', *The Journal of Philosophy* 103: 284–311.

McMyler, B. (2011) *Testimony, Trust and Authority* (Oxford: Oxford University Press).
McMyler, B. (2013) 'The Epistemic Significance of Address', *Synthese* 190: 1059–78.
Menn, S. (1998) *Augustine and Descartes* (Cambridge: Cambridge University Press).
Mill, J.S. (1961) *Essential Works* (New York: Bantam Books).
Miller, I. (2000) *The Mystery of Courage* (Cambridge: Harvard University Press).
Moran, R. (1997) 'Self-Knowledge: Discovery, Resolution and Undoing', *European Journal of Philosophy* 5: 141–61.
Moran, R. (2001) *Authority and Estrangement* (Princeton: Princeton University Press).
Moran, R. (2003) 'Responses to O'Brien and Shoemaker', *European Journal of Philosophy* 11: 391–401.
Moran, R. (2005a) 'Problems of Sincerity', *Proceedings of the Aristotelian Society* 105: 341–61.
Moran, R. (2005b) 'Getting Told, Being Believed', *Philosopher's Imprint* 5: 1–29.
Moran, R. (2012) 'Self-Knowledge, Transparency and the Forms of Activity' in *Introspection and Consciousness*, Eds D. Smithies and D. Stoljar (Oxford: Oxford University Press).
Nagel, T. (1970) *The Possibility of Altruism* (Princeton: Princeton University Press).
Nickel, P. (2012) 'Trust and Testimony', *Pacific Philosophical Quarterly* 93: 301–16.
Nozick, R. (1993) *The Nature of Rationality* (Princeton: Princeton University Press).
O'Shaughnessy, B. (1980) *The Will*, Volume 2 (Cambridge: Cambridge University Press).
Oakeshott, M. (1991) *Rationalism in Politics* (Indianapolis: Liberty Fund).
Owens, D. (2000) *Reason Without Freedom* (London: Routledge).
Owens, D. (2003) 'Knowing One's Own Mind', *Dialogue* 42: 791–8.
Owens, D. (2012) *Shaping the Normative Landscape* (Oxford: Oxford University Press).
Owens, D. (2017) 'Trusting a Promise' in *New Philosophical Perspectives on Trust*, Eds P. Faulkner and T. Simpson (Oxford: Oxford University Press).
Pagin, P. (2004) 'Is Assertion Social?', *Journal of Pragmatics* 36: 833–59.
Papineau, D. (1999) 'Normativity and Judgement', *Proceedings of the Aristotelian Society Supplementary* 73: 17–43.
Peacocke, C. (1996) 'Entitlement, Self-Knowledge and Conceptual Redeployment', *Proceedings of the Aristotelian Society* 96: 91–116.
Peacocke, C. (1998) 'Conscious Attitudes, Attention and Self-Knowledge' in *Knowing Our Own Minds*, Eds C. Wright, B. Smith, and C. MacDonald (Oxford: Oxford University Press).
Perry, J. (1979) 'The Problem of the Essential Indexical', *Nous* 13: 3–21.
Pettit, P. and M. Smith (1996) 'Freedom in Belief and Desire', *Journal of Philosophy* 93: 433–6.
Piller, C. (2009) 'Desiring the Truth and Nothing but the Truth', *Nous* 43: 193–213.
Pink, T. (1996) *The Psychology of Freedom* (Cambridge: Cambridge University Press).
Pink, T. (2009) 'Promising and Obligation', *Philosophical Perspectives* 23: 389–420.
Railton, P. (1994) 'Truth, Reason and the Regulation of Belief', *Philosophical Issues* 5: 71–93.
Railton, P. (1997) 'On the Hypothetical and non-Hypothetical in Reasoning About Belief and Action', *Ethics and Practical Reason*, Eds Cullity and Gaut (Oxford: Oxford University Press).
Raz, J. (1999) *Practical Reason and Norms*, Second Edition (Oxford: Oxford University Press).

Raz. J. (2011) *From Normativity to Responsibility* (Oxford: Oxford University Press).
Reid, T. (1997) *An Inquiry into the Human Mind*, Ed. D. Brookes (Edinburgh: Edinburgh University Press).
Reid, T. (2010) *Essays on the Active Powers of Man* (Edinburgh: Edinburgh University Press).
Ross, A. (1986) 'Why Do We Believe What We Are Told?', *Ratio* 28: 69–88.
Ross, D. (1930) *The Right and the Good* (Oxford: Oxford University Press).
Ross, J. and Schroeder, M. (2012) 'Belief, Credence and Pragmatic Encroachment', *Philosophy and Phenomenological Research* doi: 10.1111/j.1933-1592.2011.00552.x.
Ryle, G. (1949) *The Concept of Mind* (London: Hutchinson).
Scanlon, T. (1998) *What We Owe To Each Other* (Cambridge: Harvard University Press).
Scanlon, T. (2003) 'Metaphysics and Morals', *Proceedings and Addresses of the American Philosophical Association* 77: 7–22.
Scanlon, T. (2008) *Moral Dimensions: Permissibility, Meaning, Blame* (Cambridge: Harvard University Press).
Searle, J. (1969) *Speech Acts* (Cambridge: Cambridge University Press).
Shah, N. (2013) 'Why We Reason The Way We Do', *Philosophical Issues* 23: 311–25.
Shah, N. and D. Velleman (2005) 'Doxastic Deliberation', *The Philosophical Review* 114: 497–534.
Shoemaker, S. (1996) *The First-Person Perspective and Other Essays* (Cambridge: Cambridge University Press).
Shoemaker, S. (2003) 'Moran on Self-Knowledge', *European Journal of Philosophy* 11: 391–401.
Sosa, E. (2001) 'For the Love of Truth?' in *Virtue Epistemology*, Eds Fairweather and Zagzebski (Oxford: Oxford University Press).
Soteriou, M. (2013) *The Mind's Construction* (Oxford: Oxford University Press).
Stalnaker, R. (1984) *Inquiry* (Cambridge: MIT Press).
Strawson, G. (2003) 'Mental Ballistics or the Involuntariness of Spontaneity', *Proceedings of the Aristotelian Society* 103: 227–57.
Stroud, B. (1989) 'Understanding Human Knowledge in General' in *Knowledge and Scepticism*, Eds M. Clay and K. Lehrer (Boulder: Westview 1989).
Stroud, B. (1999) 'Hume's Scepticism' in *The Empiricists*, Ed. M. Atherton (Lanham, MD: Rowman and Littlefield).
Stroud, B. (2000) 'Practical Reasoning' in *Reasoning Practically*, Ed. Ullmann-Margalit (Oxford: Oxford University Press).
Thompson, M. (2008) *Life and Action* (Cambridge: Harvard University Press).
Unger, P. (1975) *Ignorance* (Oxford: Oxford University Press).
Van Fraasen, B. (1984) 'Belief and the Will', *Journal of Philosophy* 81: 235–56.
Velleman, D. (1989) *Practical Reflection* (Princeton: Princeton University Press).
Velleman, D. (1996) 'Self to Self', *Philosophical Review* 105: 39–76.
Velleman, D. (2000) *The Possibility of Practical Reason* (Oxford: Oxford University Press).
Walton, K. (1990) *Mimesis as Make-Believe* (Cambridge: Harvard University Press).
Watson, G. (2004a) *Agency and Answerability* (Oxford: Oxford University Press).
Watson, G. (2004b) 'Asserting and Promising', *Philosophical Studies* 117: 57–77.

Weber, M. (1947) *The Theory of Social and Economic Organization* (New York: Free Press).
Wedgwood, R. (2002) 'The Aim of Belief', *Philosophical Perspectives* 16: 267–97.
Williams, B. (1973) *Problems of the Self* (Cambridge: Cambridge University Press).
Williams, B. (1978) *Descartes: The Project of Pure Inquiry* (London: Penguin).
Williams, B. (1983) 'Descartes's Use of Scepticism' in *The Sceptical Tradition*, Ed. M. Burnyeat (Berkeley: University of California Press).
Williams, B. (1985) *Ethics and the Limits of Philosophy* (London: Fontana).
Williams, B. (2002) *Truth and Truthfulness* (Princeton: Princeton University Press).
Williams, M. (1986) 'The Metaphysics of Doubt' in *Essays on Descartes' Meditations*, Ed. R. Rorty (California: California University Press).
Williamson, T. (2000) *Knowledge and its Limits* (Oxford: Oxford University Press).
Wilson, M. (1978) *Descartes* (London: Routledge).
Wollheim, R. (1999) *On the Emotions* (New Haven: Yale University Press).
Wolterstorff, N. (1996) *John Locke and the Ethics of Belief* (Cambridge: Cambridge University Press).

Index

action
  and knowledge 94–8, 142–5, 146, 155–63
  control over 1–15, 18–20, 23, 31–4, 37, 43–4, 76, 79, 82–6, 126, 129, 155–68, 184–5
  deliberate 47, 70, 171
  free 151, 163–8
  intentional 169–78
  norms of 51, 60, 68
  responsibility for 27–30
Adams, R. 186 n.28
Adler J. 16 n.23, 101
akrasia
  emotional 17, 41
  epistemic 16–18, 37–50
  practical 6–9, 41–2, 43–4, 47, 49
Anscombe, G.E.M. 171 n.4
Aquinas, T. 2 n.1, 27 n.33, 184 n.23
Arpaly, N. 152
assertion 16, 38–9, 53, 58, 61, 64, 154, 193–210, 211–37
assurance 193, 201–4, 229–37
Austin, J.L. 230 n.25

Barnett, D. 217 n.7, 225–6
Bayesianism 15, 32, 88–9, 95, 98, 106–7
belief
  and action 21, 94–8, 155–7, 196
  and assertion 16, 38–9, 193–210, 211–37
  and certainty 4–5, 113–19, 124–31, 132–42
  and consistency 55, 77–9, 90, 92, 163
  and evidence 20–6, 38–9, 45–8, 53–63, 83–4, 88–93, 193, 224–9
  and judgement 9, 85, 151–5, 160–3, 166–7
  and knowledge 68, 92–109, 152–4
  and truth 51–68, 89–92, 152–4
  and the will 18, 30, 44–5, 126, 165, 182
  control over 2–4, 9, 17–19, 23–6, 37, 43–5, 48–50, 63–8, 69–86, 119–20, 122–31 134–42, 165–6
  expression of 38–9, 60, 193–201, 204, 206–10, 211, 216, 218–20, 222, 223, 226, 230–7
  knowledge of 17, 40–1, 195–6
  nature and function of 15–17, 31–4, 70–1, 88–9, 98–109, 158–63
  responsibility for 26–30, 79–82, 106, 126–31, 193, 202–10, 226–7
Bergson, H. 174 n.11
blame 26–30, 33, 183, 236

Boghossian, P. 1, 24 n.31
Bourdin, P. 137
Boyle, M. 2 n.2, 16 n.22, 17 n.25, 22 n.30
Braithwaite, R.B. 94
Brandom, R. 193 n.1, 202 n.13
Bratman, M. 70 n.1, 162 n.16, 179–81
Broome, J. 152–3
Broughton, J. 133
Brown, J. 96 n.21
Burge, T. 2 n.2, 11 n.14, 16 n.24, 76, 78–83, 86, 193 n.1, 206 n.20, 212–22, 224–5, 228 n.20
Burnyeat, M. 116, 133

Carroll, L. 25
Carson, T. 229 n.23
Coady, C. 224 n.16
Cohen, J. 60 n.13
conjecture 58, 92, 128, 134–6, 140, 142–8, *see also* guess
conviction, *see* belief
Craig, E. 21 n.29, 94
Curley, E. 119 n.5, 144

Davidson, D. 44 n.6, 171 n.4
Davis, W. 194 n.2
deliberation 11–12, 22, 24, 66, 69–86, 95, 101–2, 136–9, 152, 154–8, 160–2, 166–8, 171–3, 175–7, 179–82, 186–9
Descartes, R. 4–5, 69, 77, 79, 86, 113–21, 123–31, 132–48, 216
Dretske, F. 46

emotion
  and knowledge 98–103, 161
  and suspicion 92–3, 100, 107, 159
  control over 3–4, 6–15, 17
  expression of 197–8, 218–20
  function of 98–103
  knowledge of 41, 161
Empiricus, S. 142–3

Fantl, J. 21 n.28, 94, 98, 101 n.28, 158–9, 162
Faulkner, P. 234 n.33
Finkelstein, D. 6 n.6
first person 3–4, 6, 8, 17, 69–86, 137–9
Fogelin, R. 119 n.6
Foley, R. 51 n.2, 54 n.4, 55
Foucault, M. 137
Frankfurt, H. 118 n.4, 119 n.5, 133, 137

Freud, S. 27
Fricker, E. 234–6
Fried, C. 202, 229 n.23

Gassendi, P. 130
Gettier, E. 154 n.5
Gilson, E. 145
Goldman, A. 54 n.4
Gordon, R. 99 n.23, 100 n.25, 100 n.27, 158
Graham, P. 229 n.22
Greenspan, P. 41 n.4, 92 n.11, 153 n.2
Grice, P. 194, 203 n.16, 214 n.3
Grimm, S. 21 n.29
guess 32, 48–50, 57–68, 92, 144–7, 153–61, 214, *see also* conjecture

Harman, G. 46, 55, 70 n.1, 95 n.18, 202 n.13
Hart, H. 29 n.35
Hawthorne, J. 94, 97–8, 101 n.28, 158 n.10, 160
Hayek, F. 172 n.7
Hieronymi, P. 10 n.12, 13 n.18
Hinchman, E. 21, 229 n.24, 233–4, 236 n.36
Holton, R. 42 n.5, 155 n.7, 179–82
Hookway, C. 122
Humberstone, L. 57 n.9
Hume, D. 113, 117–26, 130, 171 n.4, 175, 184, 223–4
Hurley, S. 45
Hursthouse, R. 196 n.7
hypothesis, *see* supposition

intention
 and action 13–14, 42, 43–4, 76, 165, 169–71
 and akrasia 43–4
 and assertion 194–209, 216, 219, 226, 230–7
 and belief formation 44, 48, 52–3, 64
 and deliberation 70, 73–4, 76–86, 178–83
 and habit 178–83
 and practical judgement 155–7, 167–8
 and responsibility 28
 control over 2–3, 5–6, 10–11, 18–20, 23–4, 26, 31, 34, 77–86, 164–5
 function of 95–6, 151–2, 178–83

James, W. 66, 91 n.10, 94, 174 n.11, 177
judgement 3–6, 16–19, 26–7, 33, 38–42, 46–50, 85, 119–23, 126–8, 133–5, 140–2, 154, 170–1, 184, 185–6, 187–8
 and belief 9, 85, 160–3, 166–7
 and intention 155–7, 167–8
 force of 198, 215
 higher-order 7, 16, 19, 22, 37, 166–7
 practical 7–15, 18, 32, 42–5, 83–4, 129, 143, 151–68, 175–6, 179–80

Kant, I. 171 n.4, 184 n.23, 188
Kaplan, M. 62 n.17

Kavka, G. 76 n.10, 182
knowledge
 and action 94–8, 158–63
 and belief 68, 92–8, 152–4
 and certainty 113–31, 132–42
 and deliberation 73–4, 155–7
 and emotion 98–103, 161
 and guess or conjecture 59, 64–5, 142–5, 154, 157
 and practical judgement 154–7
 and responsibility 28, 30
 and testimony 21, 193–4, 201–10, 211–37
 function or value of 98–109, 158–63
Kolodny, N. 9 n.11, 13 n.16, 13 n.17
Korsgaard, C. 2 n.2, 11 n.14, 72 n.4, 84 n.13

Lackey, J. 214 n.2, 222 n.14, 224 n.16, 228 n.21, 235 n.34, 236 n.38
Lewis, C.I. 94

MacArthur, D. 133
McDowell, J. 193 n.1
MacFarlane, J. 229 n.24, 230 n.26, 234 n.32
McGrath, M. 21 n.28, 94, 98, 101 n.28, 158–9, 162
McHugh, C. 24
McIntyre, A. 9
McMyler, B. 212 n.1, 214 n.2, 215 n.4, 230 n.25, 234 n.33, 236 n.36, 236 n.38
Marshall, J. 145
memory 54, 97, 124, 159, 166, 178, 181, 205–10, 213, 215–18, 224, 225–8
Menn, S. 126 n.8
Mill, J.S. 174 n.11
Miller, I. 15 n.20
Moore, G.E. 17, 38–9
Moran, R. 2 n.2, 6 n.6, 10 n.12, 16 n.22, 17 n.25, 17 n.26, 22 n.30, 40, 42 n.5, 70, 73, 77–9, 81–2, 84 n.13, 193 n.1, 195 n.3, 196 n.5, 199, 201, 203, 215 n.6, 232–6

Nagel, T. 152
Nickel, P. 236
normative interests 33, 103–7
Nozick, R. 56 n.7, 61 n.15

O'Shaughnessy, B. 173
Oakeshott, M. 172 n.7

Pagin, P. 196 n.6, 202 n.13, 203 n.17, 220 n.10, 229 n.24
Papineau, D. 52 n.3
Peacocke, C. 70, 72 n.5, 154 n.6, 195
Peirce, C.S. 94
Perry, J. 75
Pettit, P. 38–42
Piller, C. 90 n.8

Pink, T. 11 n.13, 64 n.20, 180, 205 n.19, 230 n.26
policy, *see* intention
promise 28–9, 171, 175, 184, 202–4, 220, 230–2, 234

Railton, P. 52–3, 57 n.10, 58
Ramsey, F. 94
Raz, J. 9 n.11, 16 n.23, 16 n.24, 17 n.26, 25 n.32, 87 n.2, 90 n.7, 90 n.8, 93, 169–70, 173 n.10, 176, 179 n.13, 181 n.19, 187 n.30
Reid, T. 173 n.9, 174 n.11, 197, 211–12, 218–23, 230–1
reflective control 1–34, 50, 66–7, 69–86, 119–31, 136–42, 165–8, 186
resolution, *see* intention
Ross, A. 193 n.1, 201–3, 229 n.23
Ross, J. 89 n.6, 95 n.18, 97 n.22
Ross, W.D. 229 n.23
Ryle, F. 174 n.11

Scanlon, T. 12–13, 27–9, 46, 152, 188
Schroeder, M. 89 n.6, 95 n.18, 97 n.22
Searle, J. 202 n.13, 229 n.23
Shah, N. 17 n.25, 87 n.2, 89–90, 92 n.11, 152, 154 n.6
Shoemaker, S. 70, 74 n.6, 77–9, 195 n.3
Smith, M. 38–42
Sosa, E. 57 n.9
Soteriou, M. 2 n.2, 17 n.25, 22 n.30, 181 n.17

Stalnaker, R. 89, 94–5, 107
Stanley, J. 94, 98, 101 n.28
Strawson, G. 2 n.2
Stroud, B. 70, 73, 117 n.3, 119 n.6
supposition 58, 65–7, 92, 145–8
suspicion 17, 20, 22, 32, 92–102, 107–8, 153–8, 166–7, 214

Thompson, M. 185 n.26

Unger, P. 99

Van Fraassen, B. 202 n.13, 203 n.16
Velleman, D. 17 n.25, 44, 51–2, 54 n.5, 57–8, 64, 66 n.22, 67, 76 n.9, 89, 92 n.11, 94 n.17, 104 n.31, 153–4, 171 n.5, 174 n.11

Walton, K. 104 n.31
Watson, G. 9, 13 n.17, 29 n.35, 194
Weber, M. 169 n.1
Wedgwood, R. 56 n.7, 68 n.24
Williams, B. 15 n.20, 44, 47, 58 n.12, 63–4, 68 n.24, 74–6, 82, 85, 114, 117 n.3, 119 n.5, 125, 147, 194, 197, 199–200, 204 n.18
Williamson, T. 58 n.11, 61 n.16, 68 n.24, 157 n.8, 159 n.11
Wilson, M. 125, 133, 137
Wollheim, R. 100 n.25, 107 n.32
Wolterstorff, N. 133, 145, 147

Printed and bound by CPI Group (UK) Ltd, Croydon, CR0 4YY